OECD Public Governance Reviews

Public Procurement in Nuevo León, Mexico

PROMOTING EFFICIENCY THROUGH CENTRALISATION AND PROFESSIONALISATION

OECD
BETTER POLICIES FOR BETTER LIVES

This document, as well as any data and any map included herein, are without prejudice to the status of or sovereignty over any territory, to the delimitation of international frontiers and boundaries and to the name of any territory, city or area.

Please cite this publication as:
OECD (2018), *Public Procurement in Nuevo León, Mexico: Promoting Efficiency through Centralisation and Professionalisation*, OECD Public Governance Reviews, OECD Publishing, Paris.
http://dx.doi.org/10.1787/9789264288225-en

ISBN 978-92-64-23543-4 (print)
ISBN 978-92-64-28822-5 (PDF)

Series: OECD Public Governance Reviews
ISSN 2219-0406 (print)
ISSN 2219-0414 (online)

The statistical data for Israel are supplied by and under the responsibility of the relevant Israeli authorities. The use of such data by the OECD is without prejudice to the status of the Golan Heights, East Jerusalem and Israeli settlements in the West Bank under the terms of international law.

Photo credits: Cover © Barna Tanko/Shutterstock.com

Corrigenda to OECD publications may be found on line at: *www.oecd.org/about/publishing/corrigenda.htm*.

Foreword

The state of Nuevo León is one of the fastest-growing economies in Mexico. In 2015, Nuevo León had a growth rate of 4.3%, well above the national average of 2.5%. That year, Nuevo León also had the second-highest GDP per capita in the country. The state's primary engine of growth is the export-led manufacturing sector. It also relies heavily on construction, transport, financial services and insurance. However, many challenges lie ahead, including uncertainties about future access to major export markets and its effects on the state's economy and finances. It is in this context that the new administration will be implementing an ambitious reform plan to improve productivity and maintain this growth trajectory. Public procurement will play a key part in the success of those reforms; improving the competency of the workforce and introducing up-to-date methods will thus be crucial for the entire procurement cycle.

Trust in public institutions in Mexico is currently quite low by international comparison, with the level of perceived corruption much higher than the average among OECD countries. The business community of Nuevo León recognises corruption as a serious problem. Indeed, almost nine out of ten local companies (86.7%) stated in 2016 that acts of corruption by public servants were "frequent" or "very frequent", above the national average of 82.2%.

The new administration of Nuevo León, in place since October 2015, is seeking to address this issue and to ensure long-term growth through a variety of initiatives. These initiatives include investments in infrastructure – especially transport and energy – and boosting productivity and competitiveness through investment in research and development, as well as innovation. The administration is also determined to improve trust in government. To help it achieve that goal, the government commissioned the OECD to carry out two major peer reviews: an integrity review and a public procurement review. The public procurement review is the first of its kind at the subnational level.

This report presents the findings and policy recommendations of the public procurement review. The review addresses existing strategic and operational gaps, and reflects on how the state can establish a coherent and comprehensive public procurement system. Furthermore, the review suggests how Nuevo León can strengthen its governance model, based on the framework set by the 2015 OECD Recommendation on Public Procurement, by developing a culture of efficiency and competency among the key procurement stakeholders. To support the State Government of Nuevo León (SGNL) in achieving successful implementation, the review draws on the invaluable support and input of peer reviewers from Ireland and Colombia, as well as international good practices and lessons learned from across the OECD, including Australia, Canada, Korea and the United States. The review process has also included workshops on the key phases of the public procurement cycle, such as planning, market analysis, award criteria, payment systems and framework agreements.

This review recognises the progress made so far, such as the introduction of a central purchasing body for the centralised administration, which is a common practice in almost all OECD countries. As in many other Latin American countries, public procurement practices in Nuevo León have long focused on instilling a culture of procedural compliance among procurement officials and other stakeholders. There is an understanding within the SGNL that further centralisation of the purchasing system is needed, with a greater focus on aggregated procurement. However, the workforce culture needs to change if the new vision is to materialise. In order to achieve results in the future, the SGNL will need to continue on its current path for years to come. Sustaining the momentum is crucial; the state must galvanise and maintain strong political support for the reform of the procurement process. It must also ensure a clear understanding of the priorities and responsibilities of the public procurement system. If the administration can achieve these objectives, it will be able to modernise the state's procurement processes and create the conditions for long-term and inclusive growth.

Marcos Bonturi

Director, OECD Public Governance Directorate

Acknowledgements

Under the guidance of Janos Bertók, Head of the Public Sector Integrity Division at the OECD, this review was co-ordinated by Senior Policy Analyst Jacobo Pastor García Villarreal, with support from Paulo Magina, Head of the Procurement Unit. The authors of the different chapters include Pétur Berg Matthíasson, Lena Diesing, Jacobo Pastor Garcia Villarreal, Natalia Sandoval Peña, Minjoo Son and Jennifer Eddie. Fundación Idea provided input to the draft of the chapter on implementing robust post-award contract management in Nuevo León. Editorial assistance was provided by Meral Gedik, Thibaut Gigou, Juan Pablo Bolaños and Marissa Colón-Margolies. Edwina Collins, Pauline Alexandrov and Alpha Zambou provided administrative assistance. The OECD Mexico Centre, under the leadership of Roberto Martinez, and the staff in charge of publications, notably Alejandro Camacho, were instrumental in co-ordinating the editorial process for the Spanish publication.

The report benefited from the insights and comments from the staff of the Office of the Comptroller for Government Transparency of Nuevo León (Contraloría y Transparencia Gubernamental), especially Nora Elia Cantú Suárez, Comptroller for Government Transparency in Nuevo León; (Titular de la Contraloría y Transparencia Gubernamental del Estado de Nuevo León) Mariana Téllez Yáñez, Head of the Anticorruption Unit (Jefa de la Unidad Anticorrupción del Poder Ejecutivo); Roberto de la Peña Herrera, Director for Administration (Director Administrativo); Adriana Guadalupe Hernández Martínez. Director of the Legal Department (Directora Jurídica); Carlos Alberto Chavarría Muñoz, Director of Internal Control Bodies (Director de Órganos de Control Interno y Vigilancia); Esteban Ortega Arreola, Director for Control and Audit of Public Works (Director de Control y Auditoría de Obra Pública); Marybel Rivera Villa, Director of Control and Audit for the Central Administration (Directora de Control y Auditoría del Sector Central); Roberto Santos Zapata, Director of Control and Audit for the Paraestatal Sector (Director de Control y Auditoría del Sector Paraestatal); Héctor Horacio Garza Sánchez, Director for Government Transparency and Quality (Director de Transparencia Gubernamental y Calidad); Juan Gilberto Espinosa Mata, Financial Resources Analyst (Analista de Recursos Financieros); Abraham Lizardo Silva, Head of Information Audits (Jefe de Auditoría en Informática); Medardo de Jesús Herrera Moreno, Head of Audit for Public Works (Jefe de Auditoría de Obra Pública); Bernabé Luciano Cruz, Co-ordinator for Public Works (Coordinador de Obra Pública); Jaime Soria Liguez, Co-ordinator of Audit (Coordinador de Auditoría), Soichi Sakay Garza, Audit Co-ordinator (Coordinador de Auditorías) and Ramiro Garza Paz, Co-ordinator of CompraNET (Coordinador de CompraNET).

Additionally the report benefited from input from the Secretariat of Administration (Secretaría de Administración), especially Enrique Torres Elizondo, Secretary of Administration (Secretario de Administración); Hiram Menchaca Villarreal, Deputy Secretary of Administration; Gonzalo Padilla Orozco, General Director for Procurement and General Services (Director General de Adquisiciones y Servicios Generales); Elvia Ivette Ham Rivas, Technical Secretariat (Secretaria Técnica); Alma Delia Cavazos

García, Director of Public Tenders and President of the Procurement Committee (Directora de Concursos y Presidenta del Comité de Adquisiciones); Juan Enrique Villarreal Salazar, Director for Procurement (Director de Adquisiciones); Liliana Gómez de Ossio, Director for Human Resources (Directora de Recursos Humanos); Mitzy Anahí Macías Garza, Director for Government Systems (Directora de Sistemas Gubernamentales) and Alejandra Mariana Torres Garcia, Head of Administration (Jefa de Administración).

During the fact finding mission the OECD also met with Edna Sarabia, Head of the Unit for Administration and Finance Co-ordination (Titular de la Unidad de Enlace de Administración y Finanzas) at the Secretariat for Economy and Employment (Secretaría de Economía y Trabajo) and Adriana Quiroz Quiroz, Co-ordinator of Strategic Priorities and Management (Coordinadora de Prioridades Estratégicas y Gestión de Cumplimiento) at the Executive Agency for Co-ordination of the Public Administration of Nuevo León (Coordinación Ejecutiva de la Administración Pública del Estado de Nuevo León). The OECD expresses its gratitude to other institutions from the government of Nuevo León, which also participated in interviews during the fact-finding missions, particularly the Secretariat of Infrastructure (Secretaría de Infraestructura), namely Jesús Humberto Torres Padilla, Secretary of Infrastructure (Secretario de Infraestructura); Juan Guadalupe Uribe Longoria, Co-ordinator of the Public Works Committee (Coordinador del Comité de Obra Pública); and José Eleuterio García Velázquez, Secretariat of the Public Works Committee (Secretario del Comoté de Obra Pública); as well as the Secretariat of Finance and General Treasury (Secretaría de Finanzas y Tesorería General), namely Carlos Alberto Garza Ibarra, Secretary of Finance and General Treasury (Secretario de Finanzas y Tesorería General); Ramiro Adrián Bravo García, Deputy Secretary for Revenues (Subsecretario de Ingresos); Rosalva González Zúñiga, Director for Financial Management (Directora de Administración Financiera); and Carlos Comsille Villarreal, Director for Budget Control (Director de Presupuesto y Control Presupuestal). Likewise, the OECD thanks the Attorney General Office (Procuraduría General de Justicia); the Secretariat of Public Security (Secretaría de Seguridad Pública); the Secretariat of Social Development (Secretaría de Desarrollo Social); the Secretariat of Education (Secretaría de Educación); Health Services (Servicios de Salud); the Institute of Vehicle Control (Instituto de Control Vehicular); Metrorrey (Sistema de Transporte Colectivo Metrorrey); the Water and Drainage Services of Monterrey (Agua y Drenaje de Monterrey); the Municipality of Monterrey (Municipio de Monterrey); the Municipality of San Pedro Garza García (Municipio de San Pedro Garza García); the Municipality de Apodaca (Municipio de Apodaca); and the Municipality of Guadalupe (Municipio de Guadalupe).

Furthermore, the OECD expresses its appreciation to the non-governmental parties met during fact-finding missions to Monterrey, particularly the local chapter of the Chamber of the Construction Industry (Cámara Mexicana de la Industria de la Construcción, CMIC); the Association of Architects (Colegio de Arquitectos); the Association of Civil Engineers (Colegio de Ingenieros Civiles), Citizens against Corruption (Ciudadanos contra la Corrupción, A.C.), How is it going Nuevo León (Cómo vamos Nuevo León), Citizen Council of the Institutions of Nuevo León (Consejo Cívico de las Instituciones de Nuevo León), the local chapter of the Chamber of Commerce (Cámara Nacional de Comercio, CANACO), and Nuevo León's Chamber of the Transformation Industry (Cámara de la Industria de la Transformación de Nuevo León, CAINTRA).

Finally, this review benefited from the invaluable input provided by OECD peers: Nicolás Penagos, Deputy Director of Colombia Compra Eficiente (Colombia), and Ronan O'Reilly, Procurement Policy Adviser at the Department of Public Expenditure and

Reform, Office of Government Procurement (Ireland). These peers contributed significantly to the policy dialogue with their Nuevo León counterparts and enriched the Public Procurement Review with their views, experience and comments. Dag Strømsnes, Chief Procurement Officer in Norway at the Agency for Public Management and eGovernment (Difi), chaired the peer review discussions of the OECD Working Party of the Leading Practitioners on Public Procurement on 16 October 2017. The document was declassified by the Public Governance Committee on 15 December 2017. It was prepared for publication by the OECD Secretariat.

Table of contents

Tables

Figures

Boxes

Acronyms and abbreviations

APE	*Administración Pública del Estado de Nuevo León* The Public Administration of the State of Nuevo León
ASENL	*Auditoría Superior del Estado de Nuevo León* The Superior Audit Office of the State of Nuevo León
ASF	*Auditoría Superior de la Federación* The Superior Audit Office of the Federation
AUAPENL	*Acuerdo por el que se crea la Unidad Anticorruption del Poder Ejecutivo del Estado de Nuevo León* Agreement Establishing the Unit for Anticorruption of the Executive Power of Nuevo León
CA	Contracting Authorities
CFSMM	Certified Federal Specialist in Materiel Management
CFSP	Certified Federal Specialist in Procurement
CMO	Communities Management Office
COSO	Committee of Sponsoring Organizations of the Treadway Commission
CPC	Central Procurement Committee
CPEUM	*Constitución Política de los Estados Unidos Mexicanos* Mexico's Constitution
CTAINL	*Comisión de Transparencia y Acceso a la Información del Estado de Nuevo León* Transparency and Access to Information Commission of the State of Nuevo León
CTG	*Contraloría y Transparencia Gubernamental* Office of the Comptroller for Government Transparency

DGASG	*Dirección General de Adquisiciones y Servicios Generales* General Directorate for Acquisitions and General Services
DJEI	Department of Jobs, Enterprise and Innovation in Ireland
EU	European Union
GPS	Government Procurement Service
ICIFED	Institute for Education and Sports
INAI	*Instituto Nacional de Transparencia, Acceso a la Información y Protección de Datos* National Institute for Transparency, Access to Information and Protection of Data
INEGI	*Instituto Nacional de Estadística y Geografía* National Institute of Statistic and Geography (Instituto Nacional de Estadística y Geografía
INFRA	Secretariat of Infrastructure
KPI	Key Performance Indicators
LAACSENL	*Ley de Adquisiciones, Enajenaciones, Arredamientos y Prestaciones de Servicios para la Administración Pública del Estado de Nuevo León* Law for Acquisitions, Sales, Leasing and Delivery of Services for the Public Administration of the State of Nuevo León
LAASNL	*Ley de Adquisiciones, Arrendamientos y Contratación de Servicios del Estado de Nuevo León* Law for Acquisitions, Leasing, and Procurement of Services for the State of Nuevo León
LAASP	*Ley de Adquisiciones, Arrendamientos y Servicios del Sector Público* Law for Acquisitions, Leasing, and Services of the Public Sector
LIDACSP	*Ley para Incentivar la Denuncia de Actos de Corrupción de Servidores Públicos del Estado de Nuevo León* Law to Promote the Reporting of Corrupt Conduct of Public Officials of Nuevo León

LOPNL	*Ley de Obras Públicas para el Estado y Municipios de Nuevo León* Law of Public Works for the State and Municipalities of Nuevo León
LOAPENL	*Ley Orgánica de la Administración Pública para el Estado de Nuevo León* Organisational Law of the Public Administration of the State of Nuevo León
LOPSR	*Ley de Obras Públicas y Servicios Relacionados con las Mismas* Law for Public Works and Related Services
LRSPEMNL	*Ley de Responsabilidades de los Servidores Públicos del Estado y Municipios de Nuevo León* Law of Responsibilities of Public Officials of the State and Municipalities of Nuevo León
LRSPNLM	*Ley de Responsabilidades de los Servidores Públicos del Estado y Municipios de Nuevo León* Law of Responsibilities of Public Servants of the State and Municipalities of Nuevo León
MAPS	Methodology for Assessing Procurement Systems
MOU	Memoranda of Understanding
ÖBB Infra	*ÖBB Infrastruktur AG* Austrian State-Owned Railways Infrastructure Company
OGP	Office of Government Procurement
OP	Operation Department
OSCE	Government Procurement Supervising Agency
PAA	*Programas Anuales de Adquisiciones, Arrendamientos y Servicios* Annual Programmes for Procurement, Leasing and Services
PAACI	*Programa Anual de Auditoría y Control Interno* Annual Audit and Internal Control Program
PGJE	State Attorney General's Office

PMMRP	The Procurement Materiel Management and Real Property
PPSD	Public Procurement Supply Directorate
PWGSC	Public Works and Government Services Canada
REA	*Red Estatal de Autopistas* State Highway Network
REC	*Registro Estatal de Contratistas* State Registry of Contractors
RUPC	*Registro Único de Proveedores y Contratistas* Unique Registry of Suppliers and Contractors
RUSPEF	*Registro de Servidores Públicos que Intervienen en Procedimientos de Contrataciones Públicas, Licencias y Permisos con Recursos Federales* Registry of Public Officials who Intervene in Contracts to be Executed with Federal Funds
RWS	*Rijkswaterstaat* Department of Public Works of the Ministry of Infrastructure and the Environment
SA	*Secretaría de Administración* Secretariat of Administration
SECOP	*Sistema Electrónico de Compras Públicas* Electronic System for Public Procurement
SECOP	*Sistema Electrónico para la Contratación Pública* Electronic System for Public Hiring
SFP	*Secretaría de la Función Pública* Ministry of Public Administration
SGNL	State Government of Nuevo León
SIREGOB	*Sistema Integrador de Recursos Electrónicos Gubernamentables* Electronic Integrated Government Resources System
SMEs	*MIPYMES, micro, pequeñas y medianas empresas* Small and medium enterprises

SNA	National Anticorruption System
SOEs	State-owned enterprises
SSPE	State Ministry for Public Safety
TAS	Tender Advisory Service
UCC	*Unidad Centralizada de Compras* Central Purchasing Body
UGAP	*Union des Groupements d'Achats Publics* Association of Public Purchasing Groups
UNDP	United Nations Development Programme

Executive summary

This review of public procurement in Nuevo León is the first OECD Public Procurement Review conducted at the subnational level in any OECD country or non-member economy. This review thoroughly describes the role public procurement can play in enhancing good governance and public administration at the subnational level. This is important, because, on average, two-thirds of OECD spending related to public procurement occurs at this level.

Nuevo León is one of the most important federal states in Mexico. Highly industrialised, it is located in the northeast part of the country. The current administration of the State Government of Nuevo León (SGNL), elected for the 2015-2021 term, is reorganising the structure of the government. Importantly, the administration is working to centralise the procurement of goods and services under the Secretariat of Administration (*Secretaría de Administración*, SA). Changes to the procurement legislation in 2013 and the reorganisation of state secretariats in 2016 expanded the role of the central purchasing body in Nuevo León.

The administration could reap significant benefits by creating a strong procurement structure that would allow both for more consolidation and the uptake of framework agreements. This would significantly improve and simplify common purchases. In terms of further improving efficiency and effectiveness, the SGNL faces several challenges. First, it needs to establish an electronic procurement system. Second, it needs to determine how the SA will exercise its role and be empowered as a leading force within the public procurement system. The OECD policy recommendations underline the importance of the SGNL's ability to advance to the next stage, while proposing concrete avenues for implementation.

Key recommendations

Set a strategy and a business model for the procurement function.

Centralisation of procurement operations may lead to significant benefits, but if not properly managed, centralisation can also entail risks. Many central purchasing bodies lack the experience and knowledge necessary to ensure procurement operations. It would be wise for the SA to develop a strategy that includes a business model for the procurement function.

Work towards a more efficient and fair solicitation process.

Procurement procedures are highly control oriented. Introducing framework agreements would simplify and accelerate the solicitation process for smaller and common purchases. The SGNL should also focus on improving its market research, looking beyond quotes and historical prices. The emphasis should be more on value for money, not just on the lowest price. Broadening the award criteria by applying points and percentages for public tenders could be of value.

Implement strategic public procurement by linking it to high-level policy goals.

Pursuing complementary policy objectives through public procurement could offer substantial benefits for the SGNL. At the general policy level, the administration has taken some steps towards a sustainable plan for the future by developing strategies such as the State Development Plan. To date, the targets of these overarching strategies have yet to be translated into the area of public procurement. That could be done by including environmental, social or innovative considerations into the public procurement process.

Enhance procurement capabilities.

Professionalising the procurement workforce should be a priority. Currently, public procurers are selected, trained and promoted according to the general public service rules. Specific profiles, a dedicated career path and targeted training would help professionalise the procurement workforce. These steps would also help the administration take into account the specific challenges associated with managing public procurement processes.

Better utilise the electronic public procurement system as a communication tool with stakeholders.

The use of electronic mechanisms for public procurement in the SGNL has led to increased transparency of the processes. However, this practice has focused mainly on publishing and storing information on the public procurement processes. In line with the growing international recognition of the efficiency benefits of e-procurement systems, the SGNL should consider implementing an e-procurement solution that would cover the whole public procurement cycle, including e-bidding and e-invoicing.

Ensure integrity in public procurement processes.

Despite many efforts to provide an institutional, legal and regulatory framework to prevent corruption and properly manage conflict of interest in government activities, public trust in government institutions and activities in Nuevo León remains low, while public perception of corruption remains high. The SGNL could benefit from building a coherent and efficient institutional and normative public procurement framework, including dedicated and tailored measures against corruption.

Strengthen, standardise and integrate internal control and risk management activities.

The SGNL has internal control normative provisions in place, and has established an internal control framework. However, further efforts are needed to strengthen, standardise and integrate its internal control and risk management activities. These efforts will help ensure the integrity of procurement processes. Coupled with a culture of integrity and a supportive and balanced internal control environment, such measures would promote good governance.

Encourage participation in the dispute resolution system.

The dispute resolution system is fragmented and untested, which can reduce the public trust in the system. This is problematic, given that many actors involved in the procurement process have expressed their desire to raise the issue of non-conformity through the system. The way the current system functions adds to the risk of corruption.

SGNL needs to instil confidence in the system and ensure that those who do complain are not ostracized or retaliated against in future tendering opportunities.

Implement robust post-award contract management.

The SGNL has a rather elementary approach to contract management, whereby final users of goods and services certify that the delivered good meets the requirements established in their contracts. The SGNL should strengthen the framework for establishing relationships with suppliers, allowing for an appropriate follow-up of contracts. The management of contracts should not be a purely administrative activity, but a strategic task that allows the government to anticipate different types of situations and respond to them.

Chapter 1. The legal and institutional framework of the public procurement function in Nuevo León

This chapter describes the governance structure of the procurement function of the State Government of Nuevo León, which is currently undergoing a process of centralisation. The chapter analyses the potential benefits and risks of a centralised purchasing arrangement, as well as the role of a procurement strategy and business model in advancing value-for-money. In addition, this chapter discusses the regulatory framework applicable not only to the acquisition of goods and services, but also to the development of public works. Finally, the chapter describes the process of procurement planning followed by central ministries of the state government, and the extent to which public procurement processes are linked to budgeting and public financial management.

1.1. Procurement structure and governance

As of February 2017, the public administration of the state of Nuevo León (APE) included 329 administrative units of the centralised administration (i.e., ministries, deputy ministries and directorates). The parastatal sector comprised 71 entities, including decentralised public bodies, decentralised public bodies with citizen participation, enterprises with state participation and public funds (*fideicomisos públicos*).

The current administration, elected for the 2015-2021 term, is reorganising the structure of the government, according to an amendment to the Organisational Law of the Public Administration of the State of Nuevo León (Ley Orgánica de la Administración Pública para el Estado de Nuevo León, LOAPENL), passed in April 2016. This amendment establishes the separation of the Undersecretariat of Administration from the Secretariat of Finance and General Treasury (Secretaría de Finanzas y Tesorería General del Estado) to create a new Secretariat of Administration (Secretaría de Administración, SA). In principle, the SA will gradually absorb the administrative personnel, including procurement staff, from the central administration and parastatal entities. The State Attorney General's Office (PGJE), the State Secretariat of Public Security (SSPE), and the Office of the Comptroller for Government Transparency (Contraloría y Transparencia Gubernamental, CTG) are notable exceptions.[1] The SA is structured according to the organisational chart in Figure 1.1.

Figure 1.1. Organisational chart of the Secretariat of Administration

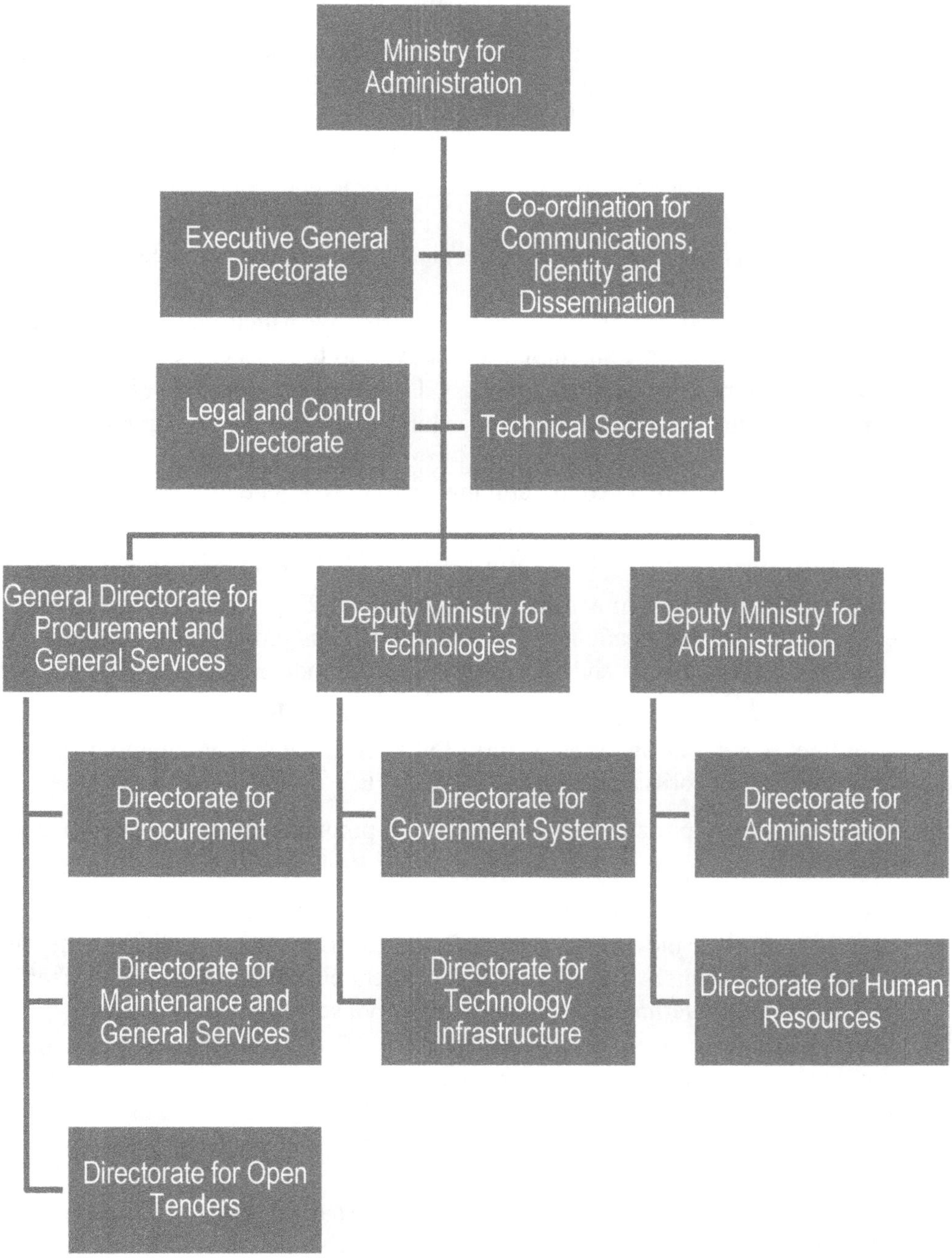

Source: (Secretariat of Administration, 2016[1]).

For all practical purposes, the SA represents the Central Purchasing Body (UCC) of the State Government of Nuevo León (SGNL). The SA has the following procurement-related powers (State Government of Nuevo León, 2017[2]):

- monitoring compliance with the laws and regulations applicable to material resources and services, and supervising and ensuring that ministries and entities comply with their powers related to these matters
- monitoring compliance with the normative framework applicable to procurement of goods and services of the state government, and presiding over the Procurement Committee
- assisting ministries and entities in the planning of the procurement of goods and services
- programming and formalising the contracts by which goods, services and information systems are purchased for the APE to fulfil its objectives
- managing the registry of suppliers of goods and services for the APE
- representing the state in the legal procedures related to the procurement of goods and services
- suing individuals involved in criminal activities affecting the procurement of goods and services of the state government.

As of September 2017, the SA managed the procurement of goods and services for 18 central administration bodies. In addition, as of this date, 27 parastatal entities signed an agreement with the SA that guaranteed its support for their procurement activities, once these entities made a requisition and allocated the corresponding budgets.

A similar process of centralisation is taking place for public works, only it is being managed by the Secretariat of Infrastructure (INFRA). INFRA is in charge of planning and building the public works administered by the APE.

Other ministries with important roles related to the procurement of goods and services include the following:

- Executive Co-ordinator of the APE: Suggests public policies and evaluates their results, proposes the organisation of the government, co-ordinates the fiscal programme, organises cabinet meetings, fosters citizen participation mechanisms and links state government institutions with civil society.
- Secretariat of Finance and General Treasury: Establishes financial and income administration policies to make revenue collection more efficient and optimise expenditures, following equity and transparency principles. For procurement purposes, it allocates the procurement budget and processes and makes payments to suppliers.
- Office of the Comptroller for Government Transparency (CTG): Plans, organises, and co-ordinates control systems, and fosters the modernisation of the APE. The CTG also supervises expenditures, and carries out inspections, reviews, audits, and surveillance actions. It co-ordinates attention to complaints, challenges, claims and suggestions, and applies sanctions. It provides the necessary support, so that any individual may have access to public information. The CTG supervises and ensures that the supply of public services follows principles of legality, efficiency, honesty, transparency and impartiality. Finally, the CTG fosters a culture of transparency and service quality, and upholds the ethical values that public servants should follow.

Figure 1.2. Institutional map of the procurement function in the state of Nuevo León

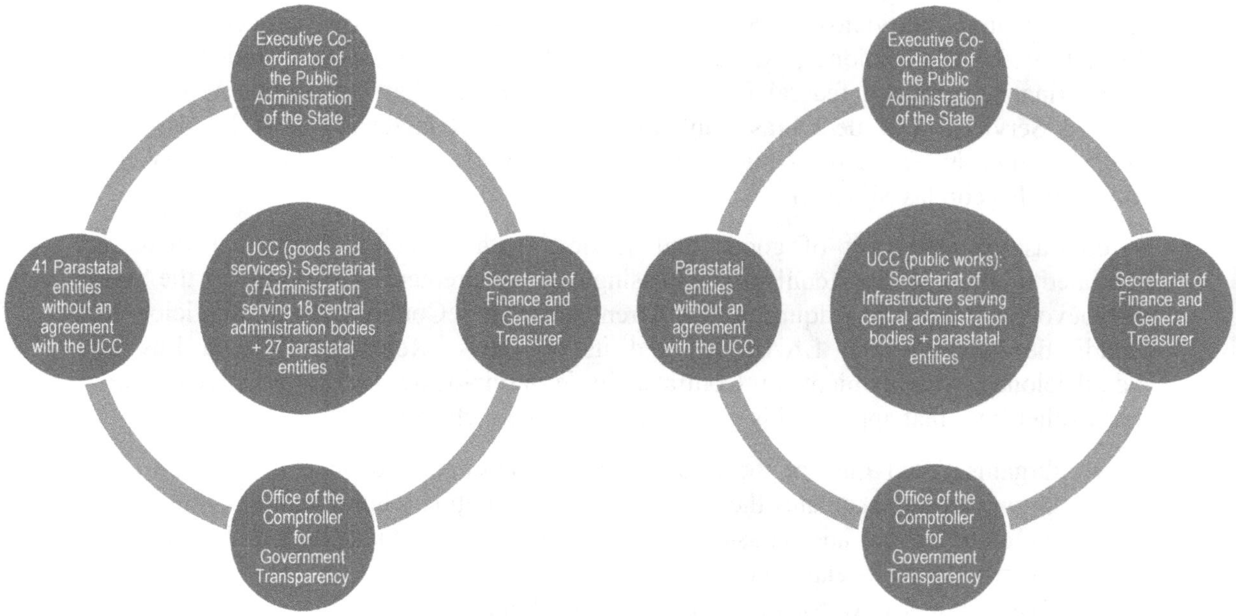

In addition to the set up described above, there are 51 municipalities in the state of Nuevo León, which make their own decisions concerning contracts for the purchase of goods and services. However, when such procurement activities involve federal or state transfers, the Superior Audit Office of the State of Nuevo León (Auditoría Superior del Estado de Nuevo León, ASENL) and other control entities from the federal level intervene to control and oversee the use of the resources.

1.2. The normative framework for procurement in Nuevo León

There are six basic procurement modalities in Nuevo León, each one subject to different rules and regulations. When federal resources are applied – no matter the amount of either goods and services or public works – the federal regulations prevail. When only state or municipal resources are applied, the state regulations are to be observed. Table 1.1 illustrates this classification.

Table 1.1. The six procurement modalities in Nuevo León

Origin of resources	Goods and services	Public works
Federal	Federal regulations	Federal regulations
State/municipal	State Regulations	State Regulations
Mixed (Federal & State/municipal)	Federal regulations	Federal regulations

Article 134 of Mexico's Constitution (Constitución Política de los Estados Unidos Mexicanos, CPEUM), establishes the principle that the procurement of goods and services should be carried out through public tenders in order to achieve the best terms with regards to price, quantity, financing arrangements and convenience. The principles set out in the CPEUM are then detailed in a set of normative instruments, applicable for procurement financed through federal or state funding.

Procurement of goods and services with federal funding is subject to the Law for Acquisitions, Leasing and Services of the Public Sector (Ley de Adquisiciones, Arrendamientos y Servicios del Sector Público, LAASP), and its By-Laws (Reglamento de la Ley de Adquisiciones, Arrendamientos y Servicios del Sector Público). Public works financed through federal funding are subject to the Law for Public Works and Related Services (Ley de Obras Públicas y Servicios Relacionados con las Mismas, LOPSR), and its By-Laws (Reglamento de la Ley de Obras Públicas y Servicios Relacionados con las Mismas).[2]

In contrast, procurement of goods and services with state and municipal funds is regulated by the Law for Acquisitions, Leasing and Procurement of Services for the State of Nuevo León (Ley de Adquisiciones, Arrendamientos y Contratación de Servicios del Estado de Nuevo León, LAASNL), and its By-Laws (Reglamento de la Ley de Adquisiciones, Arrendamientos y Contratación de Servicios del Estado de Nuevo León). Some other laws that apply to this procurement regime include the following[3]:

- Organisational Law of the Public Administration of the State of Nuevo León: Organises and regulates the functioning of the public administration of the state, including central and parastatal entities. Among other things, this law establishes the procurement-related powers of the SA.
- Expenditures Law for the State of Nuevo León (Ley de Egresos del Estado de Nuevo León): Issued every year to regulate the allocation, execution, control and evaluation of public expenditures.
- Internal By-Laws of the Secretariat of Administration of the State of Nuevo León (Reglamento Interior de la Secretaría de Administración para el Estado de Nuevo León): Establishes the organisational structure of the SA and the powers of its administrative units.
- Internal By-Laws of the Secretariat of Finance and General Treasury (Reglamento Interior de la Secretaría de Finanzas y Tesorería General del Estado): Establishes the organisational structure of the secretariat and the powers of its administrative units.
- Law for the Financial Management of the State of Nuevo León (Ley de Administración Financiera para el Estado de Nuevo León): Regulates the management of the public finances of the state, establishing the basis for financial planning of the central and parastatal entities.

Finally, procurement of public works with state and municipal funds is subject to the Law of Public Works for the State and Municipalities of Nuevo León (Ley de Obras Públicas para el Estado y Municipios de Nuevo León, LOPNL).

Figure 1.3. Normative framework for procurement in Nuevo León

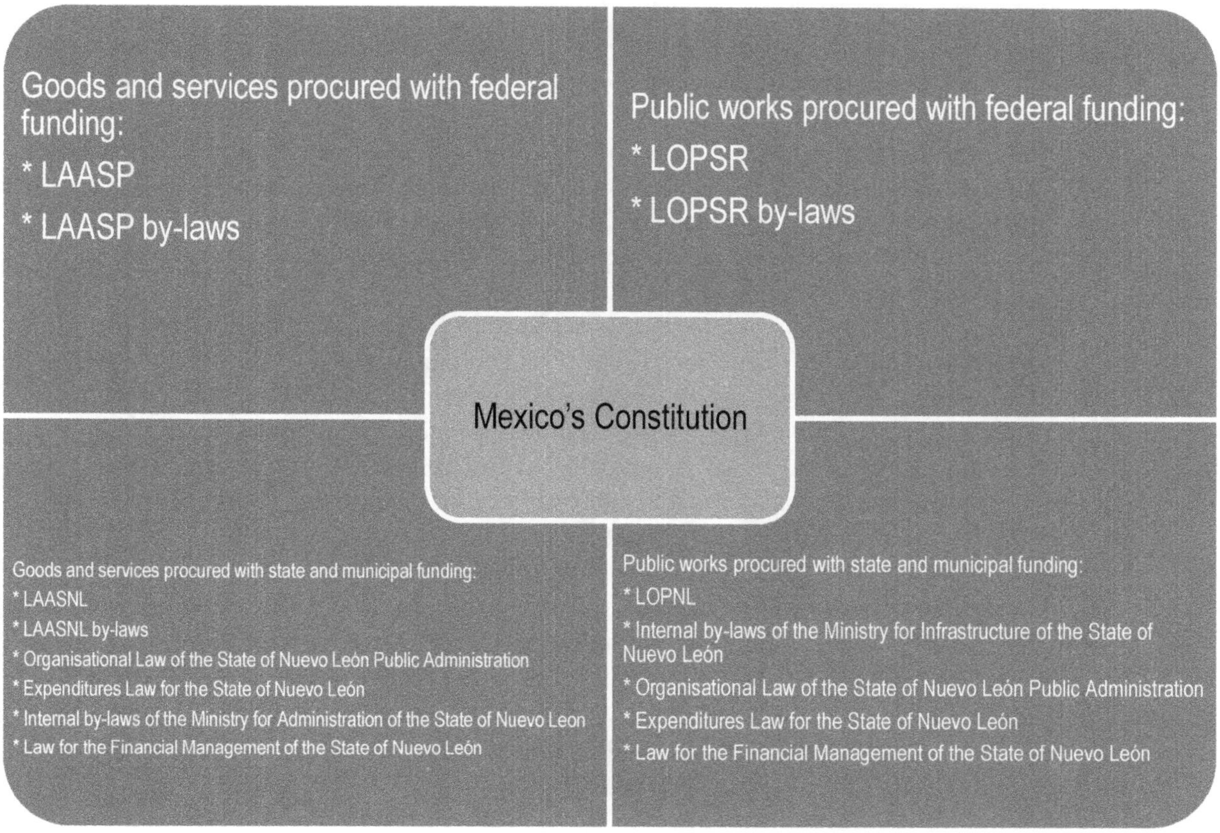

1.3. Centralisation, co-ordination and communication

The European Parliament and Council (European Parliament and Council, 2014[3]) defines a central purchasing body as a contracting authority that:

- acquires goods or services intended for one or more contracting authorities
- awards public contracts for works, goods or services intended for one or more contracting authorities
- arranges framework agreements for works, goods or services intended for one or more contracting authorities.

Centralised purchasing is not a new concept, and it is not a practice that is exclusive to the public sector (see Box 1.1). The rationale for a centralised purchasing system should be examined from the perspective of different stakeholders. These stakeholders include: the users of the UCC's services, such as the procuring entities; the suppliers; and the owner of the UCC, which is usually a ministry or some other public body representing the interests of taxpayers (see Figure 1.4). The main arguments for establishing a UCC are typically the following (OECD, 2011[4]):

- Efficiency and better prices: Centralised procurement, based on the aggregation of purchasing needs of the UCC's customers, provides attractive business opportunities for the private sector. With larger procurement volumes, increasing competition usually follows, driving prices down and leading to more favourable terms for the purchaser. In other words, the potentially large sales volumes that can be expected under centralised procurement mean that economies of scale can be exploited by economic operators. It makes a huge difference for a supplier to produce and deliver large lots under large volume contracts to a small number of customers. This arrangement is preferable to a situation where the supplier has to serve a large number of customers with many small orders, even when the total contract volume is equal.

- Reduced transaction costs in terms of time, expenditures and management of the procurement process, from the first stage of planning and defining needs up to the final stages of contract management, payment and closing files.
- The need for standardisation or increased administrative efficiency within the government administration.
- Procuring entities may lack sufficient capacity to prepare and carry out complex tenders for purchases requiring product or market expertise.
- Professional, centralised purchasing provides certainty to procuring entities with regards to many aspects (e.g., legal, technical, economic and contractual issues). This reduces risks that otherwise would have to be borne by procuring entities. These risks include challenges and complaints, poor quality of products, failure of suppliers and inadequate contractual terms and management.
- Simplicity in terms of the process to purchase goods and services, as well as the use of innovative tools, like framework agreements.
- The use of UCCs facilitates the execution of secondary policy objectives, such as the participation of small and medium enterprises (SMEs) in public procurement, and the promotion of innovation and productive chains. UCCs can also make it easier for the government to transition to green procurement.

Box 1.1. The establishment of centralised purchasing systems

Central purchasing is not exclusive to the public sector. It is widely used in the private sector, both in manufacturing and retailing, among other sectors. The main objective of central purchasing is to reduce purchase prices and purchasing costs in all phases of production and distribution. Most larger companies have central purchasing departments specialising in securing a reliable supply of inputs on favourable terms.

Centralised procurement in the public sector is not new either. Denmark created a UCC for the state in 1976. Since the 1970s, Sweden has relied on a system that co-ordinates central framework agreements with simple procedures, mainly designed for procuring entities within the central government. This system was originally built around 10-15 government agencies, each of which was given the responsibility for a particular product or service area. The system tried to match the product or service area with an agency that had its own large need for the same goods or services.

France also has a long history of centralised public procurement. In 1949, the Ministry of Education established a central purchasing unit for goods and school furniture. In 1968, this entity was named the Association of Public Purchasing Groups (Union des Groupements d'Achats Publics, UGAP).

Hungary, Italy and the United Kingdom (UK) have a more recent history of centralised procurement units. Consip, the central purchasing body in Italy, was established in 1997. It was given the responsibility of running the new Programme to Rationalise Public Spending on Goods and Services in 2000. In Hungary, KSzF was established in 1995. It was given the task of setting up a system for the centralisation of the procurement of certain goods and services. In the UK in the late 1990s, the government took a more co-ordinated approach to the area of public procurement, first with the creation of OGC and then with the creation of its operative branch, Buying Solutions.

Source: (OECD, 2011[4]).

Figure 1.4. A stakeholder's perspective for a UCC

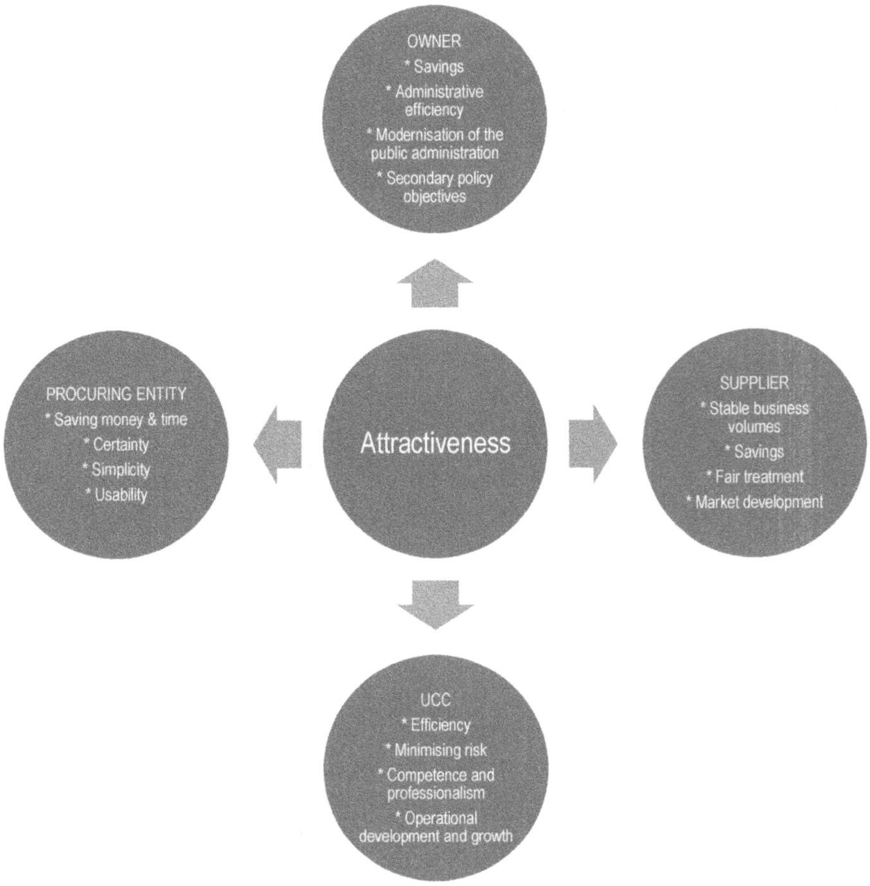

Source: (OECD, 2011[4]).

Notwithstanding the potential advantages mentioned above, centralised procurement also entails risks, such as the following:

- Market concentration and development of monopolistic structures: The large volumes implied by centralised procurement tend to favour large, established suppliers over small or new ones. This may hinder competition and market entry, deteriorating the terms of sourcing. Currently, many OECD countries have an explicit policy that mandates that procuring entities take measures to facilitate the participation of SMEs in public tenders. UCCs may implement specific strategies (i.e., dividing large contracts into smaller lots) to attract SMEs. Smaller companies may also be subcontracted or participate in consortia.
- Commercial risks: A UCC can procure goods or services that do not meet the requirements of the procuring entities. In this case, the procuring entity may not want to go through with the purchase. This risk is bigger when products are not homogeneous and when substitutes exist. Highly standardised requirements by UCCs may not be suitable or acceptable for procuring entities. Therefore, robust co-ordination between UCCs and procuring entities is needed to satisfy all the potential users of UCC services.

- Responsiveness: If not provided with the right level of expertise and resources, UCCs may be slow to respond to changes in markets, potentially neglecting important developments in prices and technologies. This situation is particularly problematic when the use of the UCC is mandatory. It is less troublesome, however, when using the UCC is voluntary.

In order to successfully implement a centralised purchasing system, it is critical to be aware of the advantages and disadvantages of different approaches. Some of the questions to answer when establishing centralised purchasing arrangements are the following (OECD, 2011[4]):

- What kind of business and organisational model can be used for a UCC?
- What goods and services are going to be purchased through the UCC?
- How are the operations of the UCC going to be financed?
- Will the use of the UCC services be voluntary or mandatory for procuring entities?

1.3.1. Business and organisational models for a UCC

There are different ways to design the business model for centralised procurement. Under the "monopoly" model, a central government establishes a central purchasing office to make bulk purchases directly from suppliers. Government ministries and agencies are required to buy goods and services through these central purchasing offices, which have a wholesaling and often also a warehousing function.

Some countries have opted for more decentralised and flexible approaches. In these cases, UCCs still exist, but their legal status changes. In many cases, this means that they are given more financial and managerial autonomy. On top of this, the buyers (ministries and government agencies) are given more freedom to buy goods and services from other sources when the alternative results in better value for money.

Another approach is the use of specialised procurement agencies. Such an agency may specialise in the provision of specific goods or services (e.g., IT products and medical supplies). It may also offer better contracts in terms of price, quality and delivery conditions than a small, non-specialised unit.

Centralised purchasing of certain goods and services is likely to benefit mostly small and medium-sized procuring entities. Large procuring entities, such as ministries or large government agencies, often have sufficient procurement competence and sufficiently large purchase volumes to reap most of the gains that a centralised purchasing system can produce. This is not the case of many small or medium-sized procuring entities. One implication of this is that a government consisting of many small procuring entities may have more to gain from establishing a centralised purchasing system than a government with mostly large procuring entities.

Concerning legal status, UCCs may take the form of publicly owned limited companies or public bodies with considerable autonomy. Unlike private limited companies, the objective of these public UCCs is not to maximise profits. Instead, they are non-profit companies. UCCs are better suited to this organisational form mainly because it provides them with flexibility and a certain degree of freedom. UCCs are less dynamic when they are part of a government administration, are operated within a ministry or as an independent agency. There is some debate on this matter. Some argue that it is also easier for non-profit corporations to attract competent and specialised staff. In addition, they argue that non-profit UCCs are able to focus solely on creating value for their customers, without taking unnecessary political considerations into account. Others argue that because the limited company form is ultimately an organisational model that is meant to be used for profit-seeking firms, it is not ideal for UCCs. Since UCCs do not have the objective of maximising profits, but instead endeavour to create savings for the public sector, limited companies are not the ideal organisational form. Instead, according to this argument, a UCC is best organised as a government agency or a division within a ministry.

The instruments for establishing and regulating the operations of UCCs also differ between countries. Not only are the instruments themselves different, but the mandates given to UCCs by owners vary in many key respects. The operations of UCCs are usually regulated by: a country's budget law or its equivalent; a government decree; a public procurement act, or its equivalent; or a state procurement strategy. Denmark's SKI, for example, is not regulated by a legal instrument. Its establishment, responsibilities and functions are governed by the owners' agreement establishing the company. It is a publicly owned company that operates under private law.[4]

In summary, UCCs operate under very different mandates. It is likely that these differences originate in the variations between countries in terms of legal and administrative structures, traditions and cultures. The operations of Consip (Italy) and KSzF (Hungary), for example, are regulated in detail. In contrast, the UCCs in Nordic countries are given more freedom to plan and manage their operations.

A typical organisational chart of a UCC contains the following main functions (OECD, 2011[4]):

- UCC management
- product and category management
- customer and client market management
- procurement and contracting
- information technology (IT) systems development
- legal services
- financing and accounting.

The department of procurement plays an important role. It is usually divided into several divisions specialising in procurement of information and communication technologies (ICTs) or administrative services, for example. Marketing, customer relations and service to public entities is particularly relevant for voluntary arrangements. Additionally, all UCCs have departments of human resources, finance and administrative support. The IT function is also particularly relevant where all transactions are to be carried out through an e-procurement portal.

National governments are not alone in using centralised purchasing; regional and local governments also practice it. In the latter case, a regional authority creates a central purchasing office to serve ministries and internal entities with procurement services and expertise. Collaborative purchasing arrangements between municipalities in a specific geographic area are not unusual in OECD countries. This is particularly true for goods and services that are in demand in virtually all municipalities, such as fuel and office supplies.

1.3.2. Goods and services to be purchased through the UCC

Goods and services commonly purchased through UCCs are to be of common interest to and should be purchased frequently throughout the public administration, according to the common-interest principle. These goods and services may include: ICT products and services (computers, photocopiers, printers, servers, software); telecommunications products (networks, mobile phones, landline phones); office furniture; travel services; office equipment and supplies; vehicle and transport services; fuel; food; and organisational and human resources development services (OECD, 2011[4]).

Many of the products and services frequently procured through UCCs are considered technically straightforward or standardised. That said, some products and services are highly technical and commercially complex, such as advanced ICT systems. Indeed, UCCs may cover both standardised products and services of non-strategic relevance, and products and services that have a strategic nature.

1.3.3. Financing arrangements for a UCC

A UCC can be financed in several ways. The first alternative is to finance the UCC directly from the government budget, as for ordinary government agencies, which usually receive a lump sum every year that is intended to cover their costs. Another funding possibility is to have service fees. These fees may be levied either on the various government entities that use the services provided by the UCC or on the suppliers to the UCC. The UCC may charge a percentage (usually in the range of 0.6-2.0%) of the suppliers' invoiced turnover. In Hungary and in the case of UGAP (France), for example, the fee is paid by the buyers. In Sweden, Finland, Denmark and the UK, it is paid by the suppliers. The main advantage of user fees is that they provide an incentive for the UCC (i.e., no sales, no revenues). In the cases of Consip (Italy) and SAE (France), these UCCs are financed directly from the government budget.

Proponents of user charges argue that UCCs usually do not make large profits. In this case, user charges are set with the aim of breaking even. Fees are set so that revenues cover costs, including necessary investments. On the other hand, proponents of the public budget model argue that it eliminates the profit risk and provides better incentives for cost-efficiency. Those who do not like this model argue that it removes the incentive to find the most attractive product areas. Moreover, it runs the risk of under-investment in new technology due to the possibility of insufficient public funds.

1.3.4. Voluntary or mandatory scope of a UCC

The extent to which it is compulsory for procuring entities to use the services offered by the UCCs differs significantly among OECD countries. In Italy and Hungary, for example, it is mandatory for central government institutions to rely on the UCC, while for sub-national public-sector entities it is voluntary. Sweden has a semi-compulsory system in which it is possible for procuring entities to purchase from alternative sources if the products offered by the UCC do not meet their needs or if better terms can be obtained elsewhere.

There are advantages and disadvantages to compulsory and voluntary arrangements. In a compulsory system where procuring entities are obliged to rely on the UCC, responsibility for the overall quality of procurement rests with the UCC. This is true whether the quality of a good or service is considered positively or negatively by the procuring entities. Call-off contracts leading to poor supplier performance, inadequate product quality and incorrect prices emanating from poorly designed and awarded agreements by the UCC may lead to serious dissatisfaction among procuring entities. In a voluntary system, the procuring entities can always refrain from using the UCC if it is not considered to be sufficiently usable. Hence, the attractiveness of a UCC is dependent on the extent to which it will satisfy the individual needs of the procuring entities.

Proponents of a system where procuring entities are forced to use the UCC´s services argue that this ensures cost-efficient public sourcing and increases standardisation among authorities. Such a system may further improve tender prices and terms, and would make it easier for the UCC to estimate the expected demand. The terms of this type of system would also create a greater degree of certainty for potential suppliers regarding actual sales. Both of these factors are likely to strengthen competition and produce better prices and other terms. Others argue that such a requirement weakens the incentive of UCCs to be user-friendly and creates the risk of monopolistic behaviour. Indeed, one of the benefits of having a voluntary system is that it provides an incentive for UCCs to offer attractive services on competitive terms. If UCCs fail to do so, there will be no demand for their services; in this case their own existence will be at risk. This is especially true if the revenue of the UCC is tied to the extent to which its services are used by procuring entities. Finally, proponents of a voluntary system argue that it provides better opportunities to properly reflect customer satisfaction with UCC services.

1.3.5. The centralisation process in Nuevo León

As mentioned before, the SGNL is in a process of centralising procurement activities for goods and services in the SA. The tasks in the different stages of the procurement cycle are distributed as shown in the following table.

Table 1.2. Organisation of the procurement function (goods and services)

Activity	Responsible entity
Pre-tendering phase	
Procurement planning	Requesting unit, which is the unit requesting SA the purchase of goods and services
Definition of requisites	SA General Directorate for Procurement and General Services
Market research	SA Directorate for Procurement or Directorate for Maintenance and General Services
Determination of the reference price	Requesting unit
Drafting tender documents	SA Directorate for Procurement or Directorate for Maintenance and General Services
Tendering phase	
Call for tender	SA - Directorate for Open Tenders
Clarification meetings	SA - Directorate for Open Tenders
Reviewing and modifying tender documents	SA Directorate for Procurement or Directorate for Maintenance and General Services
Integrating tender documents	SA Directorate for Procurement or Directorate for Maintenance and General Services
Tender	SA - Directorate for Open Tenders
Evaluation	SA - Directorate for Open Tenders + Procurement Committee + Requesting unit
Signing of the contract	SA Directorate for Procurement or Directorate for Maintenance and General Services + Requesting unit
Post-tendering phase	
Contract management (i.e., extension of the contract, additional items, etc.)	SA Directorate for Procurement or Directorate for Maintenance and General Services + Requesting unit
Payment	Secretariat of Finance and General Treasury

Regarding the procurement process itself, robust co-ordination is required in the different stages of the procurement cycle. This co-ordination should occur between the different directorates of the General Directorate for Procurement and General Services of the SA, requesting units (from the central or parastatal administration) and the Secretariat of Finance and General Treasury. Then, at the policy, planning, control and evaluation levels, the Executive Co-ordinator of the APE and the CTG play an important role. Furthermore, the ASENL plays the role of the external auditor, accountable to the state legislature.

One of the mechanisms to ensure co-ordination at the process level is the Procurement Committee of the APE, which is regulated in the LAASNL and its By-Laws. The members of this committee are listed below.

Participation and voting capacity:

1. Secretariat of Finance and General Treasury;
2. Secretariat for Economic Development;
3. Secretariat of Infrastructure;
4. Office of the State Attorney.

Participation capacity only:

1. CTG;
2. Requesting unit.

The LAASNL establishes that the member of the committee from the Secretariat of Finance and General Treasury presides over the committee and breaks a tie. That said, it is the SA, through the Director for Open Tenders, that leads the committee. This was codified by an amendment to the LOAPENL that was passed in April 2016. The amendment transferred the procurement function from the Secretariat of Finance and General Treasury to the SA. Even though the LAASNL establishes that the SA will play the role of the Technical Secretariat of the Committee, this regulation still needs to be updated to align with the latest reforms to the Organisational Law of the APE, which established the role of the SA as the UCC.

According to Article 16 of the LAASNL, the Procurement Committee of the APE performs the following functions, among others:

- examining the annual procurement programme and the annual or multiyear budget for the procurement of goods, leasing and services, as well as any modification to it
- participating in open tenders and restricted invitation processes, as well as in clarification meetings, events to present and open bids, and in the awarding of contracts
- issuing an assessment of the bids in open tenders and restricted invitation procedures
- assessing the cases of exceptions to open tenders
- proposing rules, criteria and guidelines for the procurement of goods and services.

Besides the Procurement Committee of the APE, there are other committees for entities of the APE which have not signed a co-ordination agreement for the SA to take over their procurement activities. Such committees have the membership listed below.

Participation and voting capacity:

1. Procuring entity, which presides over the committee.
2. Secretariat of Finance and General Treasury. (Given the amendment to the LOAPENL in April 2016, the SA assumes this seat).
3. The lawyer of the procuring entity.

Participation capacity only:

1. CTG.
2. Requesting unit from the procuring entity.

On the side of public works, Article 99 of the LOPNL establishes the Committee for the Award of Public Works Tenders (Comité de Apoyo para la Adjudicación y Fallo de los Concursos de Obra Pública). This committee issues opinions about the awards of public works contracts from open tenders, restricted invitations and direct awards. It also serves as a control mechanism for issues of compliance with the public works legislation. Although the committee's decisions are not mandatory, public officials tend to follow them to avoid potential sanctions for misinterpreting the law. Its members include the following:

- Co-ordinator: The Secretary of Infrastructure, who breaks a tie, if necessary.
- Secretariat: A public official from the Secretariat of Infrastructure, appointed by the Secretary. The Secretariat of this committee participates in proceedings, but has no voting rights.
- Member: Secretariat of the Interior.

- Member: Secretariat of Finance and General Treasury.
- Member: Secretariat of Social Development.
- Observer: CTG, with participation, but no voting rights.
- A representative from the corresponding chamber, depending on the kind of works, associations, professional boards or citizens linked to public works. This representative participates in the proceedings, but has no voting rights.

1.4. Procurement planning

Planning for the procurement of goods and services should be a strategic endeavour. Procurement planning should align with the objectives set forth by the State Development Plan (Plan Estatal de Desarrollo), the Strategic Plan for the State of Nuevo León 2015-2030 and other sectoral, regional and special plans, as applicable to each ministry and agency of the APE. In addition, procurement planning should take into account the resources established in the state's expenditures budget.

Each ministry and the parastatal entity that has an agreement with the SA should produce their Annual Programmes for Procurement, Leasing and Services (Programas Anuales de Adquisiciones, Arrendamientos y Servicios, PAA), bearing in mind the budget allocations indicated in the Electronic Integrated Government Resources System (Sistema Integrador de Recursos Electrónicos Gubernamentables, SIREGOB). PAAs are sent to the SA in January of every year. The SA then compiles a state government-wide programme, which is published by the Electronic System for Public Procurement (Sistema Electrónico de Compras Públicas, SECOP).

Even though the annual programmes of ministries and agencies are posted in the SECOP, the information provided is quite limited. The annual programme entries usually include a code for the good or service, a description, the measurement unit (e.g., piece, box, etc.) and the quantity. However, there is no indication of when the purchase will take place.

1.5. Public finance management and budgeting for procurement

Public procurement does not take place in a vacuum, but should be integrated with budgeting and programming systems for optimal results. Indeed, the 2015 *Recommendation of the OECD Council on Public Procurement* addresses the importance of this integration (see Box 1.2).

Box 1.2. The 2015 Recommendation on Public Procurement

The OECD's 2015 Recommendation on Public Procurement suggests that adherents support integration of public procurement into overall public finance management, budgeting and service delivery processes. To this end, adherents should:

- Rationalise public procurement spending by combining procurement processes with public finance management to develop a better understanding of the spending dedicated to public procurement, including the administrative costs involved. This information can be used to improve procurement management, reduce duplication and deliver goods and services more efficiently. Budget commitments should be issued in a manner that discourages fragmentation and is conducive to the use of efficient procurement techniques.
- Encourage multi-year budgeting and financing to optimise the design and planning of the public procurement cycle. Flexibility, through multi-year financing options – when justified and with proper oversight – should be provided to prevent purchasing decisions that do not properly allocate risks or achieve efficiency due to strict budget regulation and inefficient allocation.
- Harmonise public procurement principles across the spectrum of public service delivery, as appropriate, including for public works, public-private partnerships and concessions. When delivering services under a wide array of arrangements with private-sector partners, adherents should ensure as much consistency as possible among the frameworks and institutions that govern public service delivery to foster efficiency for the government and predictability for private-sector partners.

Source: (OECD, 2015[5])

In September each year, every ministry and public agency in Nuevo León files budget proposals to the Secretariat of Finance and General Treasury. The secretariat then reviews and adjusts the proposals according to the availability of resources and the budgets of previous years, before sending it to the state congress for approval. During fact-finding missions, the OECD team was told that such adjustments are often quite arbitrary. The secretariat does not normally consult with the institutions involved to consider their priorities when making adjustments. This is unfortunate, as such a lack of co-ordination not only affects budgets, but procurement. This can lead to pressing situations, such as the need to speed up procurement processes in the last months of the year to fully execute the budget. Nonetheless, in theory, given that the PAAs are developed in January of every year (after the budget has been approved), there should be enough time to adjust the PAA to the approved budgets. Currently, however, there is no systematic link between the budgeting and procurement processes.

Nuevo León's regulatory framework anticipates multi-year budgeting. The framework requires that the corresponding ministry or entity informs the Secretariat of Finance and General Treasury of its multi-year budgeting needs when filing its budget proposal. In turn, Article 14 of the LAASNL establishes that, exceptionally, and upon authorisation by the Secretariat of Finance and General Treasury, the Procurement Committee may call for, award and formalise contracts whose payments go beyond the fiscal year or start after the fiscal year in which the contract is formalised. As of May 2017, only one multi-year contract was established (for copy machines). Others, for services like catering in state prisons, are under consideration at present.

1.6. Comprehensive organisational procurement strategy

One of the main weaknesses of Nuevo León's centralisation process is that the state has not developed a clear strategy for the procurement function. Indeed, procurement is still seen as a purely administrative activity, rather than a strategic activity and policy tool that can help the government accomplish secondary objectives. When undertaking procurement, public officials in Nuevo León privilege a compliance approach, rather than a value-for-money approach. There are several reasons for this. First, procurement operations in Nuevo León are overregulated because of an incorrect assumption that more regulation leads to fewer opportunities for corruption. Second, recent scandals have sparked high levels of public mistrust of government officials. This has in turn driven these officials to protect themselves by strictly observing the letter of the law – even if it hinders the potential for reaping value for money for the public sphere.

Over the last decade, OECD countries have increasing used procurement as a policy tool to support socio-economic objectives like innovation. The economic crisis that started in 2007-08 forced countries to consider using procurement to drive innovation in order to spur a recovery from the global downturn. This was accomplished, for instance, by countries that encouraged innovative companies to bid for government contracts. Some countries also used procurement to ease the socio-economic impact of the crisis on societies. They did this by providing procurement as a substitute for direct social policies to support employment for disadvantaged groups and communities. These examples are notable because they indicate that a shift has occurred among OECD countries. At present, among OECD countries, the main objective of public procurement is not only to achieve value for money (that is, the value of the items and services procured) but to promote broader government objectives.

Because of its economic significance, public procurement has the potential to influence the market in terms of production and consumption trends. It can do so in a way that is favourable to environmentally friendly and socially responsible products and services. In OECD countries, public procurement accounts for about 12% of GDP and 28% of total government expenditure, on average (OECD, 2012[6]). In Mexico, public procurement accounts for about 5% of GDP and over 20% of total government expenditure.

The centralisation process represents an important opportunity to change the mindset of government officials towards procurement. Unfortunately, in Nuevo León, this process was undertaken without a proper consultation to build buy-in among public officials. Nonetheless, the development of the sectoral plan of the SA (its six-year working plan) opens a window of opportunity not only to develop a new vision for Nuevo León's procurement function, but also to build it through a participative process.

A good strategy clearly defines the functions to be undertaken by the UCC, besides the obvious one of managing procurement operations. The managers of some UCCs believe that providing guidance and advice on how to plan and carry out procurement activities is a necessary organisational function; some may even provide consultancy services. However, where such services exist, the activity is relatively small relative to the UCC's main function. This may have to do with a worry that UCCs will crowd out the private sector or be perceived as a competitor in the consultancy business. As part of its core business, the operational functions of a UCC often include: 1) procurement management and support; 2) market analysis and relationships; 3) development and operation of the business architecture (e.g., an electronic platform); and 4) administration and reporting (OECD, 2011[4]).

1.7. Proposals for action

1.7.1. The SGNL should set a strategy for the centralisation process and communicate it effectively to the whole-of-government

Governments often introduce a centralised purchasing arrangement because they want to modernise and upgrade their procurement systems in terms of efficiency and functionality. However, as is the case in Mexico, governments often lack the experience and knowledge necessary for the operation of a UCC.

The key question is to what extent the centralisation process, and the role of the SA as the UCC, can generate added-value to the public procurement function in Nuevo León in terms of savings, simplification, modernisation and other critical principles. In a study conducted by the OECD in seven European Union countries (Denmark, Finland, France, Hungary, Italy, Sweden and the United Kingdom), the OECD found that, under the right conditions, UCCs do generate added value, but not by default (OECD, 2011[4]). Because certain conditions must be present for UCCs to add value, the question becomes whether these conditions are present in Nuevo León.

The truth is that the SA has to earn its place as a reliable and efficient UCC. This requires an effort by the whole-of-government, not only the SA. Interviews conducted during OECD fact-finding missions revealed that current centralised procurement arrangements are not perceived as efficient or simple. Furthermore, those interviewed stated that ministries and agencies are not aware of what their roles should be in making such arrangements successful. In order for the SA to be successful, it must address these issues. Officials could benefit from studying the economic and non-economic factors that make centralised purchasing systems attractive to shareholders (see Figure 1.5).

Figure 1.5. The factors determining the attractiveness of a centralised purchasing system

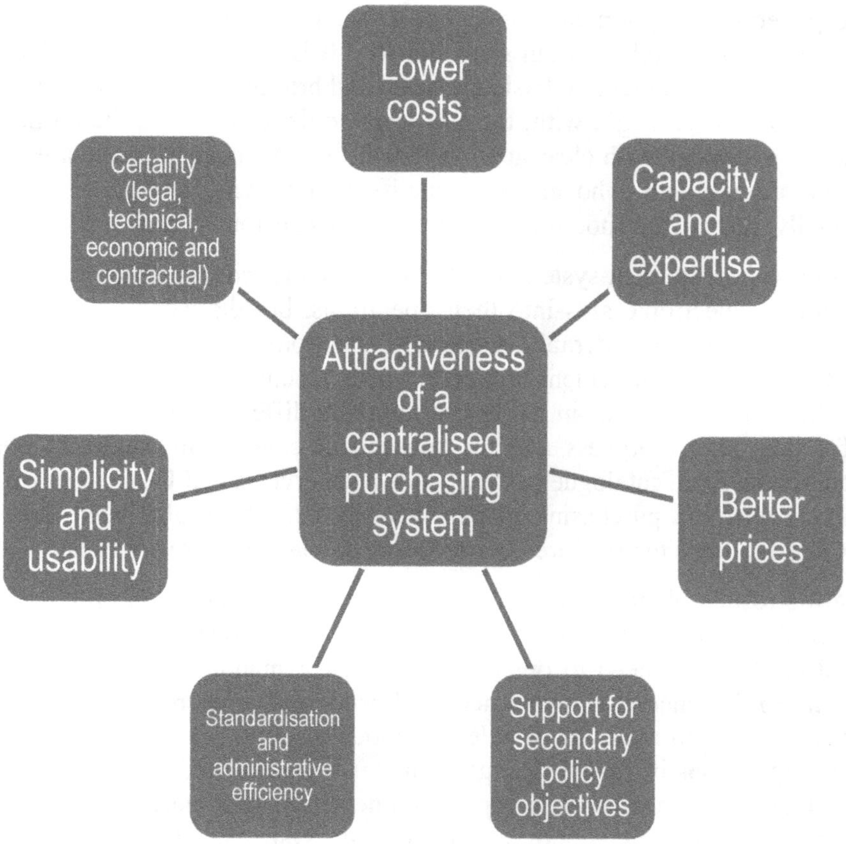

Source: (OECD, 2011[4]).

In this context, it is important that the SA, as any other UCC, develops a strategy with long-term goals and a clearly defined scope for its operations. This strategy should include the services the SA will provide, the products and services for which it will co-ordinate procurement and the entities of the public sector it will target. Requesting units themselves may want to participate in the development of such a strategy, because of their responsibilities with regards to procurement planning.

One of the main arguments behind centralising procurement is achieving cost-efficiency – in other words, obtaining the best possible value for the taxpayer through effective, sustainable procurement. If this can be achieved, governments can use the savings they take in for investment and public services. Some UCCs elaborate efficiency-related goals into sub-goals, such as streamlining procurement processes, the aggregation of demand through framework agreements and the identification of opportunities for savings. Nuevo León's SA has communicated to the OECD that its sectoral plan (under development as of June 2017) will include three objectives:

- cost-efficiency through the standardisation of products and services to be purchased;
- transparency, by applying the four-eyes principle and focusing control activities on one single procurement unit;

- leveraging the purchasing power of the state government to support SMEs and local businesses.

Given the general perception in Nuevo León that the centralised arrangement is not delivering, the SA must take certain steps quickly. It is important that the SA make the model attractive by implementing basic elements and bringing more institutions under the centralised umbrella. To begin with, the SA needs to develop – with the participation of shareholders – a strategy with clear goals. Second, the SA needs to create a workforce of procurement professionals who are also qualified to provide advice to the procuring entities. Finally, this advice should be oriented towards customer satisfaction.

Upgrading the e-procurement system SECOP to make procedures easier is a must. UCCs usually introduce electronic aids into their operations, but the extent to which they use electronic tools differs considerably. Generally, electronic and Internet-based platforms are used to publish procurement notices, tender documentation and award results. However, there are differences in the extent to which different UCCs develop electronic systems for the call-off process and the subsequent contract management phase. The publication of electronic catalogues of the goods and services that UCCs provide seems to be common. Electronic purchasing management systems have also been developed by some UCCs to facilitate the procurement process and make it more efficient.

Improving the results obtained so far in Nuevo León's centralisation process will entail strong political leadership. Indeed, if procurement is to be treated as a strategic activity, government entities will need to operate under a clear mandate, and will need to align political will. For instance, the government will need to advance reforms to the LAASNL and other regulations to remove obstacles for modernisation (e.g., the need to document procurement operations in paper). The government will also need to privilege a value-for -money approach over the current compliance one. It will also need to invest to upgrade the procurement workforce and e-procurement systems. But more importantly, government officials will have to realise that these reforms are worth the effort and, if implemented correctly, will deliver savings that will outweigh the costs.

The OECD has identified certain factors possessed by successful centralised purchasing organisations that obtain savings. The SGNL can learn from this analysis. First, it is important for UCCs to have the support from the owners. The UCC must have a clear mandate to operate. The mandate may be broad or narrow, but it must be clear. Second, good relations with both customers (users) and suppliers are important for building confidence in the operations of UCCs, which in turn are important to motivate tender participation. Third, and related to the second factor, it is important to actually obtain favourable purchasing terms and products, thereby creating legitimacy and loyalty towards the centralised purchasing systems that have been established. Specifically, the more inclined procuring entities are to use the UCC's services, the more attractive it is for potential suppliers to compete for contracts. UCC competence and behaviour are important drivers of success.

Central purchasing also entails certain risks. The most obvious risk is that the UCC will fail to deliver on its promises by not being responsive to the various stakeholders involved (customers, suppliers, and owners), and by failing to deliver attractive terms. Another important risk is a scenario in which the procedural rules in the public procurement legislation become more important than the economic aspect of procurement, thereby making the UCC difficult and expensive for its customers to use. This often results in a rigid compliance approach (OECD, 2011[4]).

1.7.2. The SA should develop an organisational model and a business model which determines the main features of the procurement function of the SGNL

The reorganisation of the APE does not provide a clear organisational and business model for the procurement function. The first issue to determine is what functions will be performed by the SA. For example, the Organisational Law of the APE establishes that the SA has the power to assist ministries and entities in their procurement planning. However, the scope of such assistance is not clear, and any support in other stages of the procurement cycle (e.g., development of technical specifications and contract management) is not explicit. A UCC is not only a procurement manager but, with its extensive experience and knowledge of public procurement, a knowledge centre. In other words, UCCs can be centres of expertise within the government administration. This expertise should be exploited. The owners of a UCC can use it as a tool for the modernisation of the public administration and the implementation of important policy goals. The SA should take this all into account. It should then assess to what extent the UCC is adequately fulfilling other functions, such as market analysis and development of the IT solution for e-procurement. The SA can then consider reforms to upgrade performance.

Second, the SA should determine which goods and services will be covered under the centralised purchasing arrangements. As discussed during this chapter, some goods and services may be better suited for centralised procurement than others. Applying the common-interest principle would help achieve cost efficiency, while also allowing flexibility for items needed by one or only a few entities. Along with this discussion, the SGNL should define which parastatal entities will participate in the centralised arrangement. The current policy is that all parastatal entities should be covered gradually for goods commonly used, but there has been resistance by some to sign the co-ordination agreement.

While the government of Nuevo León has already decided to centralise procurement in the SA, the OECD recommends that the SA develops a specific approach for implementation. Specifically, the OECD recommends that the SA adopt a step-by-step approach in terms of the goods, services and entities centralised procurement will cover. This will provide the SA with realistic possibilities for successfully building the organisation's capacity, infrastructure, and performance – without risking its credibility. The most sensitive stage of an UCC's operations is the start-up phase, since procuring entities may regard the UCC only as a competitor and not as a partner. Building confidence, which is essential for the success of a UCC, takes time. That said, the initial period is often decisive in ensuring a strong outcome. It is important to agree not only on the right first steps the SA will take, but also on the right order of these steps. The main risks are over-ambitious or unrealistic goals set by the owners. Overly aggressive goals jeopardise the possibility of the new UCC becoming a success. Management needs sufficient time, discretion and financial means in order to build the organisation, the infrastructure, the operational models, the systems and the partnerships with the customers (OECD, 2011[4]).

Another determination to make is to what extent centralised procurement will be voluntary or compulsory. Currently, in order for goods and services to be tendered centrally by the SA, participation is mandatory. Since resistance is strong, a voluntary approach would collapse the centralised procurement system. However, as the SA builds up its infrastructure and fixes the reputation of the centralised arrangements, it may apply a differentiated approach. Under this approach, the SA would carefully review goods and services to be centrally purchased from the point of view of the procuring entity's interests in order to determine whether the use of a centralised scheme should be compulsory or voluntary. Some products may be well suited to compulsory use, while others would be much better suited to voluntary use. By transitioning to a differentiated approach, the SA may also improve the attractiveness of its services.

Finally, the SA may want to review the financing of its role as a UCC. This is a difficult issue, as there is no practice in Mexico for a UCC to charge user fees. In addition, given that the centralised system is still in its early stages and trying to gather support, it would not be convenient to introduce user fees in the short term. Furthermore, user fees could spark legal objections. However, again, as the UCC is strengthened, its nature could become more commercially oriented. It could then start to charge some fees – at least to cover basic costs relative to the organisation of tenders. Currently, the SA charges some fees to potential bidders to register to participate in the tender and to obtain the call for tender (even though call for tender information is published in SECOP and newspapers). The rationale behind these fees is to cover publication costs. These fees may hinder the participation of bidders. To offset this burden, the SA could transfer fees to the procuring entities making use of the UCC services, but only if it makes sure the UCC is delivering in terms of savings, cost-efficiency, competence and simplicity.

1.7.3. Obstacles are often found in procurement regulations. Therefore, the SGNL should undertake a careful review of the normative framework applicable to procurement operations

The OECD has identified several obstacles to upgrading procurement practices in Nuevo León's normative framework. For example, during OECD fact-finding missions, public officials argued that they had perceived resistance to the process of migrating electronic procedures. The reason for this resistance was that regulations do not explicitly state that electronic documents are as valid as paper ones, and auditors usually request paper files. This is a clarification that could be incorporated into the LAASNL and its By-Laws. In other cases, the use of specific tools is constrained and subject to complicated procedures. For instance, the use of the points and percentages criterion is established in Article 39 of the LAASNL, but its use by a state entity requires an explicit authorisation by the Secretariat of Finance and General Treasury. This presents a problem, as this secretariat is not where procurement expertise lies. Furthermore, documentation shows that this issue has caused co-ordination issues. Finally, as described previously, the LAASNL still needs to be updated to align with the latest reforms to the Organisational Law of the APE, which established the role of the SA as the UCC. This need to update the LAASNL is reflected in the unclear roles of the SA and the Secretariat of Finance and General Treasury in the Procurement Committee of the APE.

Another concern has to do with overregulating. There is a difficult balance to strike between flexibility and control. Recent scandals at the national and state level in Mexico have led to the faulty assumption that more regulation will lead to less corruption. In fact, the strong compliance approach has limited the ability of procurement officials to seek value-for-money. When reviewing the regulatory framework, the SGNL should bear in mind regulatory burdens imposed on procurement officials. It should then seek controls with clear indicators that allow for the evaluation of the effectiveness of these regulations. Depending on the results, the SGNL could then make these regulations more strict or flexible.

Evaluations of regulations after a period of implementation should be primarily focused on whether the intended outcomes by the regulatory intervention have been achieved. This is the main purpose of retrospective analysis, and it is the systemic application that is recommended in the 2012 *Recommendation of the OECD Council on Regulatory Policy and Governance*. At present, there is not an internationally recognised or agreed-upon guidance for regulatory evaluation. However, the OECD *Regulatory Policy Outlook 2015* proposes a set of evaluation criteria that could form the basis for an evaluation framework (Box 1.3) (OECD, 2015[7]).

Box 1.3. Principles for setting an evaluation framework

General criteria

- Relevance: Do the policy goals cover the key issues at hand?
- Effectiveness: Was the policy appropriate and instrumental to successfully address the needs perceived, as well as the specific problems the intervention was meant to solve?
- Efficiency: Do the results justify the resources used? Or could the results be achieved with fewer resources? How coherent and complementary have the individual parts of the intervention been? Is there scope for streamlining?
- Utility: To what degree do the achieved outcomes correspond to the intended goals?

Additional criteria

- Transparency: Was there adequate publicity? Was the information available in an appropriate format and at an appropriate level of detail?
- Legitimacy: Has there been a buy-in effect?
- Equity and inclusiveness: Were the effects fairly distributed across the stakeholders? Was enough effort made to provide appropriate and equitable access to information?
- Persistence and sustainability: What are the structural effects of the policy intervention? Is there a direct cause-effect link between them and the policy intervention? What progress has been made in reaching the policy objectives?

Source: (OECD, 2015[7])

Most methodologies used in OECD countries for ex post regulatory evaluation concentrate on the unintended consequences of a regulation and on the achievement of policy goals (see Figure 1.6).

Figure 1.6. Methodologies used in ex post evaluation (number of OECD countries)

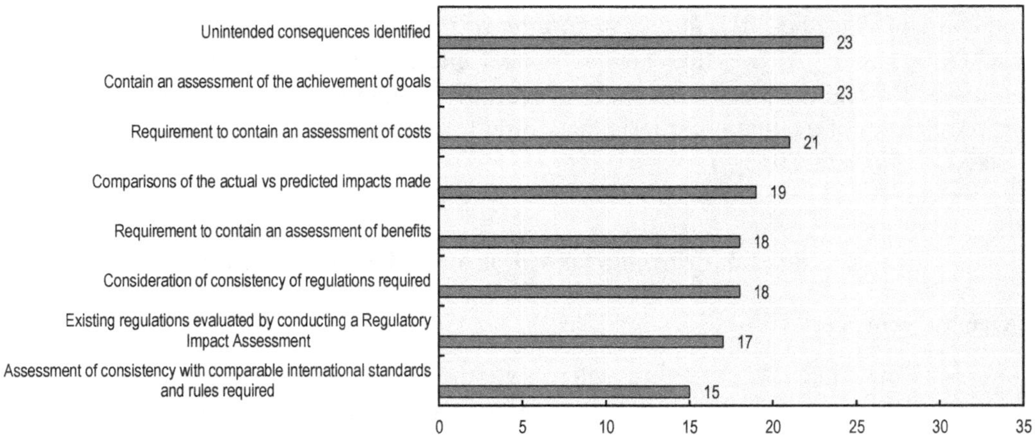

Source: (OECD, 2015[7])

It is extremely important that the government of Nuevo León consult with the populations that will be affected by regulations (both public and private entities) during the review of the normative framework. A common mistake when designing regulatory interventions is to skip the opinions of the target audiences. Consulting with them will not only allow the SGNL to identify the main regulatory bottlenecks in the procurement process, but also design the required reforms. Such consultation will also facilitate the implementation of reforms through the buy-in built during the consultation process.

1.7.4. Improving the co-ordination between the Secretariat of Finance and General Treasury and the SA (and budget and procurement planning) has the potential to streamline procurement operations

During the OECD fact-finding missions, it was evident that procurement is regarded as just another administrative activity in Nuevo León, and co-ordination is weak. In addition, public officials do not see or feel connected to the overall process. Rather, these officials are aware only of their individual experiences in their particular institutions. Blame of others is common, instead of co-operation and looking for co-ordinated solutions. The Secretariat of Finance and General Treasury blames the SA for not putting together the required documents to process payments. The SA blames the Secretariat of Finance and General Treasury for not processing payments in a timely manner and for discretionally changing its procurement and budget planning. The SA blames the requesting units for not making their requests in a timely fashion. Finally, the requesting units blame the SA for complex procedures and delays. Such lack of co-ordination also becomes evident when purchase orders and procurement procedures accumulate at the end of the year. This leads to requesting units spending their procurement budgets to avoid them being slashed for the next fiscal year. This situation is unsustainable. Its solution requires efforts by the entire government. If this can be mustered, the new centralised procurement arrangement can be successful.

Centralised procurement will only deliver if: 1) all institutions in Nuevo León recognise their role in the system; and 2) procedures are made clear and simple. Simplicity will also deter corrupt behaviour. In this case, again, political leadership is critical to getting all the stakeholders to sit at the table to define co-ordination mechanisms, leverage current ones (e.g., the Procurement Committee of the APE) and to accomplish this fast before the centralised arrangements lose all credibility. The Executive Co-ordinator of the APE, along with the SA and the Secretariat of Finance and General Treasury, could create a government-wide task force to address the issues that require robust co-ordination. In some discussions, such as those regarding the delay of payments to suppliers, the participation of private stakeholders could also be beneficial.

While the task force may have a temporary mandate, the co-ordination mechanisms defined in it should be permanent. These efforts must deliver solutions in the short term in order to regain the credibility the centralised procurement plan has lost. A lack of effective and quick action could have a devastating effect, so it is essential that the government acts fast. If it does not, resistance to the new system and pressure to leave it could build, voiding the potential benefits of a UCC.

Notes

[1] However, some tender processes of the PGJE, the SSPE, and the CTG are carried out by the SA. Regarding the PGJE and the SSPE there is an inconsistency between the LOAPENL and the LAASNL. While the former establishes that the UCC is the entity in charge of their procurement operations, the latter gives powers to the PGJE and the SSPE to manage procurement related with security issues.

[2] The Fiscal Co-ordination Law (Ley de Coordinación Fiscal) also applies to the use of some federal resources.

[3] This list is not exhaustive and describes only the main laws and regulations applicable.

[4] In Mexico, public procurement is regulated by the laws mentioned previously, leaving no room for the application of private law.

References

European Parliament and Council (2014), *Directive 2014/24/EU of the European Parliament and of the Council of 26 February 2014 on public procurement and repealing Directive 2004/18/EC*, http://eur-lex.europa.eu/legal-content/EN/TXT/PDF/?uri=CELEX:32014L0024&from=EN. [3]

OECD (2011), "Centralised Purchasing Systems in the European Union", *SIGMA Papers*, No. 47, OECD Publishing, Paris, http://dx.doi.org/10.1787/5kgkgqv703xw-en. [4]

OECD (2012), "Progress made in implementing the OECD Recommendation on Enhancing Integrity in Public Procurement", OECD Publishing, Paris, http://www.oecd.org/gov/ethics/combined%20files.pdf. [6]

OECD (2015), *OECD Recommendation of the Council on Public Procurement*, https://www.oecd.org/gov/ethics/OECD-Recommendation-on-Public-Procurement.pdf (accessed on 18 May 2017). [5]

OECD (2015), *OECD Regulatory Policy Outlook 2015*, OECD Publishing, Paris, http://dx.doi.org/10.1787/9789264238770-en. [7]

Secretariat of Administration (2016), "Reglamento Interior de la Secretaría de Administración para el Estado de Nuevo León", http://sgi.nl.gob.mx/Transparencia_2015/Archivos/AC_0001_0004_0155657-0000001.pdf. [1]

State Government of Nuevo León (2017), "Ley Orgánica de la Administración Pública para el Estado de Nuevo León", http://sgi.nl.gob.mx/Transparencia_2015/Archivos/AC_0001_0002_0164702-0000001.pdf (accessed on 08 November 2017). [2]

Chapter 2. Increasing efficiency and fairness in the solicitation and contract award process in Nuevo León

This chapter provides an overview of the main procurement methods applied in the state of Nuevo León and identifies actions to drive efficiency throughout the public procurement cycle. This includes measures for market analysis, and the adoption of tools like framework agreements and consolidated purchases. While procurement committees already play a central role in Nuevo León, the OECD recommends that the government merge and streamline certain committees. In this chapter, measures are suggested for how these committees can enhance their roles, and in so doing, improve the effectiveness of the procurement process. Finally, this chapter examines how the State Government of Nuevo León (SGNL) can broaden its approach to the application award criteria by applying points and percentages for public tenders.

The structure of public procurement in Mexico has resulted in a two-tier system, as discussed in Chapter 1. All states in Mexico have to follow two distinct public procurement legal frameworks, depending on their source of funding. When using federal funds, contracting authorities (e.g., ministries, administrative units, decentralised bodies) are subject to the federal regulatory framework. When using local funds, requesting units have to follow the system developed at the local level by the state of Nuevo León. Thus, though the primary objective of this chapter is to assess the state public procurement system, it is important to be aware that federal funds are a significant part of overall public procurement in Nuevo León.

With the separation of the Undersecretariat of Administration (Subsecretaría de Administración) from the Secretariat of Finance and General Treasury (Secretaría de Finanzas y Tesorería General del Estado) in 2016, a new entity called the Secretariat of Administration (Secretaría de Administración) was created. It is now responsible for public procurement of goods and services in Nuevo León. The Secretariat of Finance and General Treasury played a significant role in procurement prior to the 2016 the reforms. It did so under a mandate from the Law for Acquisitions, Leasing, and Procurement of Services for the State of Nuevo León (Ley de Adquisiciones, Arrendamientos y Contratación de Servicios del Estado de Nuevo León) which has been in force since 27 March 2013. Due to the reforms, however, the responsibility for the public procurement of goods and services now lies with a unit called the Central Purchasing Body (Unidad Centralizada de Compras, UCC). The UCC is represented by the Secretariat of Administration (SA).

As is common in other Latin American countries, oversight and control of procurement processes will continue to play a significant role in the public procurement system in Nuevo León. However, the reform that the state of Nuevo León is adopting is meant to simplify the procurement process. It aims to do so by centralising procurement under the Central Purchasing Body, and thus increasing the efficiency and effectiveness of the central purchasing body.

Using the 2015 OECD Recommendation of the Council on Public Procurement as a benchmark, this chapter looks at how the state of Nuevo León can improve its public procurement processes. The chapter also examines how the SGNL is encouraging ministries, administrative units, decentralised bodies and public administration entities to drive efficiency throughout the public procurement cycle with the aim of satisfying the needs of the government and its citizens (see Box 2.1). To fulfil this aim, the government must actively assess the needs of public entities, the role of procurement committees and the processes for conducting market analysis. Subsequently, the government must utilise adequate tools to improve procurement procedures. These tools should include aggregation and exceptions to public tendering, though it is important that the government examine the extent to which these exemptions are applied. Furthermore, this chapter describes how the state of Nuevo León can engage more fully in a transparent and regular dialogue with suppliers and business associations. This is crucial, given the importance of stakeholder participation to effective procurement. The chapter asks whether clarification meetings and debriefings are being held at present, as both methods can contribute to a more efficient and fair solicitation and contracting process. Finally, this chapter expands on the importance of developing a more strategic outlook with regards to the assessment of bids which can lead to substantial benefits beyond the lowest price, such as green and sustainable procurement (Box 2.1).

Box 2.1. OECD Recommendation of the Council on Public Procurement

The Council:

VII. RECOMMENDS that Adherents develop processes to drive Efficiency throughout the public procurement cycle in satisfying the needs of the government and its citizens.

To this end, Adherents should:

i) **Streamline the public procurement system and its institutional frameworks.** Adherents should evaluate existing processes and institutions to identify functional overlap, inefficient silos and other causes of waste. Where possible, a more service-oriented public procurement system should then be built around efficient and effective procurement processes and workflows to reduce administrative red tape and costs, for example through shared services.

ii) **Implement sound technical processes to satisfy customer needs efficiently.** Adherents should take steps to ensure that procurement outcomes meet the needs of customers, for instance by developing appropriate technical specifications, identifying appropriate award criteria, ensuring adequate technical expertise among proposal evaluators, and ensuring adequate resources and expertise are available for contract management following the award of a contract.

iii) **Develop and use tools to improve procurement procedures, reduce duplication and achieve greater value for money**, including centralised purchasing, framework agreements, e-catalogues, dynamic purchasing, e-auctions, joint procurements and contracts with options. Application of such tools across sub-national levels of government, where appropriate and feasible, could further drive efficiency.

X. RECOMMENDS that Adherents drive performance improvements through evaluation of the effectiveness of the public procurement system from individual procurements to the system as a whole, at all levels of government where feasible and appropriate.

To this end, Adherents should:

i) **Assess periodically and consistently the results of the procurement process**. Public procurement systems should collect consistent, up-to-date and reliable information and use data on prior procurements, particularly regarding price and overall costs, in structuring new needs assessments, as they provide a valuable source of insight and could guide future procurement decisions.

ii) **Develop indicators to measure performance, effectiveness and savings of the public procurement system** for benchmarking and to support strategic policy making on public procurement.

Source: (OECD, 2015[1])

2.1. Framework for public procurement procedures

2.1.1. Nuevo León needs to address obstacles and delays in the public procurement process, by making purchases of minor goods more efficient

The public procurement system for state-funded goods and services is governed by the Law for Acquisitions, Sales, Leasing and Delivery of Services for the Public Administration of the State of Nuevo León (Ley de Adquisiciones, Enajenaciones, Arredamientos y Prestaciones de Servicios para la Administración Pública del Estado de Nuevo León, LAACSENL). The government has passed three reform bills that have modified the law over the past 30 years. The most recent legislative reform act was passed in 2013. The institutional reforms enacted in 2016 affect the roles and responsibilities of units and entities previously defined by the 2013 legislation, but the legislation has not yet been updated since the 2016 reforms. Despite the new reform laws, the LAACSENL published in 2013 remains vital. Some of its important aspects include:

- the establishment of the principles of efficiency, efficacy, economy, transparency and honesty in the use of public resources
- planning of procurement procedures to contribute to the achievement of goals established in the state's development programme
- the publicity of the Annual Procurement Programme in the Electronic System for Public Procurement (Sistema Electrónico para la Contratación Pública, SECOP)
- consultation of records prior to any contract of consulting services
- regulations establishing the Technical Secretariat (Secretario Técnico) inside the Procurement Committee, which aim to ensure that procurement follows its due process

Public procurement in Nuevo León is not only bifurcated in terms of funding, but also in terms of the type of good or service being procured. Public procurement in the state has to follow two different pieces of legislation depending on the origins of funding. In addition, a clear division exists between procurement of goods and services on the one hand, and public works on the other. The Central Purchasing Body (Unidad Centralizada de Compras, UCC) is the administrative unit responsible for procuring goods and services. The Secretariat of Infrastructure is in charge of planning and building public works. Regulations related to public works in the state are delineated by the Federal Law on Public Works and Related Services and the Law of Public Works for the State of Nuevo León. All aspects related to public procurement purchasing are addressed in this chapter. That said, state public work is rather limited compared to federal public works in Nuevo León.

Nuevo León uses four procurement methods which are each contingent on the size of the budget. They are 1) public tender; 2) restricted invitation (three suppliers); 3) direct award; and 4) electronic reverse auction – which is not contingent on any amount, and is optional. The general rule is that government agencies must use public tenders because they promote greater competition, better prices and higher quality goods and services. However, that is not always the case, as we will discuss later in this chapter. In order to determine which procedure to use, government officials must first determine the amount of funds they expect to spend. See Table 2.1 for the specific amounts of funds that determine each type of procurement procedure in Nuevo León.

Table 2.1. Procurement procedures and range of amounts

Procurement Procedure	Range of purchase UMAs (Measurement Units)	Approximate amount (2015, USD)
Public tender	> 24,000	>$96,000
Restricted Invitation (3 suppliers)	14,400-24,000	$57,600-$96,000
Direct award (3 estimations)	2,400-14,400	$9,600 - $57,600
Direct award	<2,400	< $9,600

Note: This table only considers the largest amount allowed for government agencies according to the budget of Nuevo León.
Source: (The State of Nuevo León, 2013[2])

In many European Union (EU) countries, the threshold for open tender is uniform. Thus, spending does not depend on the budget allocated to each contracting authority (CA), but rather on the total procurement value of each procurement procedure. This arrangement enables better monitoring of public spending. Table 2.2 provides a description of EU thresholds for open tenders.

Table 2.2. EU thresholds for open tenders

Central Government authorities	Works contracts, subsidised works contracts	EUR 5,225,000
	All services concerning social and other specific services listed in Annex XIV	EUR 750,000
	All subsidised services	EUR 209,000
	All other service contracts and all design contests	EUR 135,000
	All supplies contracts awarded by contracting authorities not operating in the field of defence	EUR 135,000
Sub-central contracting authorities	Works contracts, subsidised works contracts	EUR 5,225,000
	All services concerning social and other specific services listed in Annex XIV	EUR 750,000
	All other service contracts, all design contests, subsidised service contracts, all supplies contracts	EUR 209,000

Source: (European Commission, 2014[3])

The state of Nuevo León is now consolidating more power in the Secretariat of Administration (SA) in order to carry out public purchases centrally. The SA currently services 21 central agencies (*dependencias centrales*) and 24 parastatal entities (*entidades paraestatals*) out of a total of 65 with cooperation agreement. The UCC only services the central administration in Nuevo León, not the 51 municipalities. These municipalities are autonomous, and thus can establish their own procurement processes. That said, they have to follow either state procurement laws or the federal procurement legislation, depending on the source of funding.

One of the main challenges facing the SA is how it will improve the process for minor direct purchases. Currently, between 150-300 requirements are registered on a daily basis in the procurement system. The process for getting authorisation to purchase, including establishing that funds are available and making a purchasing order, tend to create delays.

This is true even for very simple and basic purchases of goods and services that are needed immediately. During the OECD fact-finding mission, this issue was raised frequently. The OECD found several examples of public employees purchasing minor goods with their own money because the good was so desperately needed and the procurement process was so inefficient. Part of the problem lies with the centralised structure of the payment system in Nuevo León, as all payments are made by the Secretariat of Finance and General Treasury. Furthermore, the purchasing process within the SA needs to be more effective – from when a request is received through the delivery of goods.

2.1.2. Comprehensive overview of the public purchasing system

Nuevo León needs to improve its data and information systems in order to be able to manage public purchasing in the state more effectively

The 2015 OECD Recommendation on Public Procurement encourages countries to drive performance improvements through evaluation of the effectiveness of the public procurement system – from individual procurements to the system as a whole – at all levels of government, where feasible and appropriate. This requires assessing the results of the procurement process periodically and consistently. It also requires that governments collect consistent, up-to-date and reliable information. Governments must collect data on prior procurements, particularly regarding price and overall costs, for the purpose of structuring new needs assessments. The reason for this is that these data provide a valuable source of insight, and can guide future procurement decisions. Governments should also develop indicators to measure the performance, effectiveness and savings of their public procurement systems. These indicators can aid the government in creating benchmarks, and can also support government efforts to be strategic in public procurement policy making. Therefore, Nuevo León should develop concrete indicators to address key dimensions of the procurement process. See Box 2.2. for examples developed by different OECD countries (OECD, 2015[1]).

Box 2.2. EU thresholds for open tenders

In February 2013, the Leading Practitioners on Public Procurement asked the OECD to help develop a set of indicators to measure the performance of public procurement systems and their evolution over time. Following the Leading Practitioners' meeting, the Task Force on Public Procurement Performance Indicators was formed. The task force identified the four areas listed below for the development of indicators.

Efficiency of the public procurement process: Efficiency in public procurement refers to the proportionality between, on the one hand, the costs and time of each public procurement procedure, and on the other, the value of the contract. Ensuring the best possible ratio of cost and time to contract value will maximize efficiency. Furthermore, it is possible to achieve efficiency gains through the use of consolidation mechanisms and e-procurement.

Openness and transparency of the public procurement process: Openness is understood as fair, equal and equitable treatment of participants in the public procurement process. According to the United Nations Commission on International Trade Law (UNCITRAL), transparency in public procurement involves five main elements: public disclosure of the rules applied in the public procurement process; publication of public procurement opportunities; prior determination; and publication of what is to be procured and how submissions are to be considered; visible conduct of public procurement according to the prescribed rules and procedures; and the existence of a system to monitor that these rules are being followed, as well as measures empowering authorities to enforce these rules, if necessary.

Professionalism of the public procurement workforce: Having a public procurement workforce meeting high professional standards and being capable of achieving strategic government objectives is essential. Key factors for the professionalism of the public procurement function include: sufficient staff in terms of numbers and skills; recognition of public procurement as a specific profession; certification and regular trainings; integrity standards for public procurement and contracting officials; and the existence of a unit that analyses public procurement information so that the government can monitor the performance of the public procurement system.

Contract management and supplier performance: This indicator aims to examine the contract performance phase. Contract performance management activities can be grouped into three areas: delivery management (ensuring that whatever is ordered is then delivered at the required level of quality and performance, as stated in the contract); relationship management (seeking to keep the relationship between the supplier and the contracting authority open and constructive); and contract administration (managing the formal governance of the contract and any permitted changes to documentation during the life of the contract). Consistently monitoring and documenting supplier performance allows public officials to be in a position to require corrective actions from suppliers when they are not in compliance with contract requirements. Performance monitoring can also provide a feedback loop in the selection of potential suppliers, which contributes to improvement of the pre-qualification system. An element for measuring the performance of government in contract management is whether suppliers are paid on time.

Source: (OECD, 2014[41])

Obtaining an overview of the scale of public procurement in the state of Nuevo León requires carefully documented information on the system. Currently, the SA systems are unable to extract information on: the average number of responses received to open public tenders; the proportion of open tenders declared unsuccessful; the volume of purchases for each procurement procedure; the amount spent on state public procurement; or the number of exceptions to public tender, among others.

What can be learned from other OECD projects in the region, specifically Mexico City, is that federal funds amount to between 30-40% of total public procurement. That said, the proportion of federal funds used is higher at times in geographically large states, like Nuevo León. The only data available on public procurement in Nuevo León is from 2012-2014. During that period, procurement surpassed approximately USD 546 million without considering taxes. The yearly average for procurement amounted to USD 182 million per year for the central administration. (This figure refers to funding for goods and services, excluding federally funded projects executed by parastatal entities and municipalities.) In terms of volume, this is not a large sum – considering the size and number of residents in Nuevo León. However, it only represents a part of total public procurement; how large, is unclear. The entities that carry out most of the state's procurement procedures are the Secretariat of Public Security (Secretaría de Seguridad Pública), the Secretariat of Social Development (Secretaría de Desarrollo Social) and the Secretariat of Education (Secretaría de Educación). These ministries are also largely funded by the federal government.

The information available from 2010-2014 clearly shows that direct award is by far the most popular method used in Nuevo León. Between 2012 and 2014, procurement in Nuevo León was, on average, USD 180 million per year with close to 90% being purchased through direct awards. Direct awards have risen in recent years in terms of amount, though they have decreased in terms of number. This might indicate a more frequent use of exceptions. How often direct awards are being applied instead of public tenders is unknown. Public tenders for goods and services rose between 2010 and 2014; in fact, they almost doubled in that period, reaching 113 in 2014. No data was provided on the number of public tenders taking place for goods and services in 2015 and 2016, but according to SGNL officials, the state largely opted for electronic reverse auction in 2015.

It is imperative that the state of Nuevo León have a system that can provide data and information about key public procurement indicators. The SA has been working on developing a matrix of key performance indicators (KPIs), see Table 2.3. The current version of this matrix addresses issues such as level of competition, savings and time, required preparation, and participation in bidding. That said, the current system is unable to produce much of the information needed. The state needs to continue working to refine the KPI matrix. That said, it is essential that the core indicators remain, and that more effort and resources be directed towards upgrading the procurement system.

Table 2.3. The key components of Nuevo León's matrix for performance indicators 2017

Narrative summary		Indicators			Means of verification and source of information	Assumptions
		Indicator	Formula	Frequency		
Goal	Contribute to increasing budgetary savings in the procurement of goods and services through efficient and transparent processes	Rate of change of budgetary savings	(((Budget savings year T - budget savings year T-1) / budget savings year T -1)*100	Annual	Database SECOP	
Purpose	The units have the goods and services contracted with the best conditions of price, quality and opportunity	Rate of variation of the result of evaluation of the level of satisfaction in the contracting of goods and services	(Result of evaluation of the level of satisfaction in the contracting of bins and services year T- Result of evaluation of the level of satisfaction in the contracting of bins and services year T-1) / Result of evaluation of the level of satisfaction in the contracting of bins and services year T-1)*100	Annual	Intranet database	Suppliers meet the quote times and the system works properly
Components	C1. Procurement of goods and services by tender	Average for contracted amounts	Amounts contracted / contracts made	Quarterly	SECOP Database / Contest Management	The suppliers present the technical and economic proposals and comply with the bases of participation
	C2. Updated Supplier Registration	Percentage of verified suppliers	(Verified Suppliers / Supplier Registration) * 100	Quarterly	Supplier Registration Headquarters Database	Suppliers are interested in belonging to the supplier registry
	C.3. Annual Programme of Acquisitions, Leases and Contracting of Services (PAAS) elaborated	Rate of change in consolidated contracts	(Consolidated contracts year T - Consolidated contracts year T-1) / Consolidated contracts year T-1)*100	Quarterly	Information from the Procurement Department	The central government agencies send in time and form its annual programme of acquisitions, leases and contracting services
	C4. Direct purchases of goods and services carried out	Average amount of direct purchases	Amount of direct purchases made / total purchases	Quarterly	Database SECOP	Suppliers quote on time and in form

Source: Information provided by the State of Nuevo León

2.1.3. Use of exceptions from competitive bidding

Nuevo León should develop more comprehensive and clear rules for justifying and approving exceptions to procurement procedures

The OECD Recommendations on Public Procurement (OECD, 2015[1]) state that rules for justifying and approving exceptions to procurement procedures should be comprehensive and clear, such as in cases of limiting competition. The OECD recommends that competitive (open) procedures be the standard method for conducting procurement. It recommends this as a means of driving efficiencies, fighting corruption, obtaining fair and reasonable pricing, and ensuring competitive outcomes. If exceptional circumstances justify limitations to competitive tendering and the use of single-source procurement, such exceptions should be limited, pre-defined and should require appropriate justification when employed. In addition, these limitations should be subject to adequate oversight that takes into account the increased risk of corruption, including by foreign suppliers. See Box 2.3 for examples of exception processes used by countries.

Box 2.3. Use of exceptions from competitive bidding

To ensure a level playing field, exceptions to competitive bidding should be strictly defined in order to avoid abuse. In addition, governments should consider setting up procedures to introduce transparency and integrity measures for exceptions to competitive tendering. Assessment of OECD countries shows that:

- Written justification for the use of non-competitive tendering procedures is required in almost all respondent countries.
- Random reviews or audits of non-competitive procedures are required in three-quarters of respondent countries.
- A higher level of authorising personnel is required for non-competitive tenders in half of respondent countries.
- A small proportion of the countries surveyed require that the amendments to contracts be made publicly available. In addition, a small number of countries require independent validation for large or high-value procurement (30% of respondent countries).

Source: (OECD, 2013[5])

Article 42 of the Nuevo León procurement legislation provides grounds for dispensing with the public tendering procedures. Contracts referred to in Article 42 are supposed to be carried out through restricted invitation procedures. Examples of these cases are provided in sections VIII, IX, X (first sentence), XII and XV of the procurement legislation (see Box 2.4). The sum of operations carried out under Article 42 in sections VII to XVIII are not supposed to exceed 20% of the budget for procurement, leases and services authorised to the agency or entity that is seeking procurement in each budget year. In exceptional cases, the corresponding procurement committee may set a higher percentage than the 20% stated above. The UCC is responsible for the review of exceptions.

Box 2.4. Exception to open tender according to Article 42 of the Law for Acquisitions, Leasing, and Procurement of Services for the State of Nuevo León

The centralized purchasing units may contract acquisitions, leases and services, without subjecting themselves to the public bidding procedure, through the procedures of restricted invitation or direct award, when:

I. The total of each transaction does not exceed the maximum amounts established for this purpose in the State Law on Budget Expenditure to make purchases through restricted invitation or direct award, provided that those transactions are not divided into fractions so they can be included in the hypothetical cases of exception to the public tender referred to in this article;

II. There is no substitute or technically reasonable substitute for goods or services, or there is only one possible offeror in the market or the vendor is a person who owns or exclusively licenses patents, copyrights or other proprietary rights; or because they are works of art, or goods with historic, archaeological or cultural value;

III. In cases declared by the relevant authority as emergency, urgency, or when the public order, economy, public services, public health, security, or environment of any area or region of the federal state may be in danger or disturbed as a consequence of unforeseeable circumstances or force majeure;

IV. There are circumstances that could produce significant losses or additional costs, quantified and justified;

V. Tenders for public security or law enforcement purposes, including the areas of intelligence and the social rehabilitation centres [prisons], when confidentiality or strategic issues can be compromised, as provided for in the relevant laws. The administrative requirements that do not involve security issues are not included in the hypothetical cases referred to in this section, which apply to those subject to this law;

VI. As a result of unforeseeable circumstances or force majeure, it is not possible to obtain goods or services through the open tender procedure in the time required to deal with the event at issue. In this case, the amounts or goods should be limited to what is strictly necessary to deal with the situation, all information should be provided to the Procurement Committee;

VII. A contract awarded through open tender is terminated, in which case the contract may be awarded to the bidder who got the second or subsequent position, provided that the price difference with respect to the proposal initially awarded does not exceed a margin of ten percent. In the case of contracts whose evaluation was carried out through the method of points and percentages, they can be awarded to the second or subsequent tenderer, within the margin aforementioned;

VIII. A public tender has been declared void (provided that the requirements set forth in the call for tenders are maintained), the absence of suitable proposals in a public tender whose non-compliance has been considered as the grounds for rejecting the tenders because they directly affect the solvency of the proposals. In this situation, the restricted invitation will first proceed, unless one of the hypothetical cases stated in sections III, IV or VI of this article occurs; and if the absence of suitable proposals in the tender is declared again, the purchase shall become a direct award;

IX. There are justified reasons for acquiring or leasing goods or the rendering of services from a particular brand;

X. These are purchases of perishable goods, cereals and basic or semi processed food products and stock. Likewise, in the event of used or restored goods whose price is not greater than the one established by an appraisal to be carried out by banking institutions or third parties authorised to do so according to the applicable provisions, issued within the previous six months and valid at the time of awarding the corresponding contract;

XI. Whether it is consulting or advisory services, studies or research. In these cases, the direct award or restricted invitation procedures shall be applied, according to the contracting amounts established by the State Congress for the corresponding fiscal year;

XII. It is the procurement of goods made by the obligated parties referred to in Article 1, sections VI and VII, for direct marketing or to subject them to productive processes that they perform in pursuance of the corporate purpose or line of business expressly stated in the legal action of their incorporation;

XIII. It is the procurement of goods coming from persons who, without being regular suppliers, offer goods under favourable conditions because they are in liquidation or dissolution, or under judicial intervention;

XIV. These are services rendered by a person referred to in section III of Article 8, provided that these are performed by themselves without needing the use of more than one specialist or technician. In these cases, the contracting may be carried out directly or through a partnership or association in which the service provider is a partner or associate;

XV. There are maintenance services of property where it is not possible to define their scope, establish the quantities of work or determine the corresponding specifications;

XVI. The subject matter of the contract is the design and manufacture of a good that serves as prototype to perform the tests that prove its operation. In these cases, the government body, agency, entity or administrative unit may agree that the rights to the design, use or any other proprietary right is constituted in favour of them, as applicable;

XVII. There is specialised equipment, substances and materials of chemical, physicochemical or biochemical origin to be used in experimental activities required in scientific research and technological development projects, provided that such projects are authorised by whoever is assigned by the head of the agency or the governing body of the entity;

XVIII. Acceptance by the Treasury of the State or the respective municipal treasury of the procurement of goods or the rendering of services by way of datio in solutum (transfer in lieu of payment), as provided for in the State Tax Code and other applicable laws;

XIX. When, due to the nature of the negotiation, there are circumstances or characteristics of the contract that make it absolutely essential to use the direct award method, as per the criteria or cases stated in the regulations of this law; and

XX. It is the signing of specific contracts that derive from a framework agreement.

Contracts referred to in this article shall preferably be carried out through restricted invitation procedures, in the cases provided for in its sections VIII, IX, X (first sentence), XII and XV.

Source: (The State of Nuevo León, 2013[2])

During the OECD fact-finding mission, representatives of the state of Nuevo León raised the issue that there are too many exceptions in Article 42. They stated that some exception clauses are used excessively and without proper justification. In addition, there are certain exceptions to the procurement law in Nuevo León that have never been used, but are quite promising. Clause XVI, for example, encourages innovation to take place. Nuevo León could use these kinds of exceptions more, while discouraging exceptions that cause inefficiencies. Several clauses in Article 42 are weak and can be activated easily if procurement preparation or planning is not carried out properly. This issue was also raised by government officials in Nuevo León during the fact-finding mission. They stated that insufficient planning and delays of requests until late in the year lead to a high number of requests for exceptions. As shown in Box 2.5, the number of exceptions to the procurement law in Nuevo León is quite high, compared to exceptions in some of the neighbouring countries in Latin America.

Box 2.5. Exceptions for specific public procurement procedures in Colombia and Peru

In Peru, the regulatory framework allows a number of exceptions that make it possible for a contract to be awarded directly to a specific supplier. Legislation No. 1017 and 30225 on state procurement provide exceptions for the following procurements:

Law No. 1017	Law No. 30225
a) those undertaken between public entities;	1) advertising services provided by the media;
b) in the case of an emergency situation derived from catastrophic events, or from situations that affect national defence and security;	2) consulting services that are the continuation or update of a previous work performed by an individual consultant;
c) in a shortage situation that affects or prevents the public entity from fulfilling its activities;	3) goods and services for research, testing or development of a scientific or technological nature;
d) a procurement that is secret and related to the military or due to internal reasons;	4) the lease of real estate and the acquisition of existing real estate;
e) whenever there is a single supplier of goods or provider of services that does not allow for substitutes; and	5) specialised legal services for the protection of officials, servants or members of the armed forces and police;
f) special services delivered by natural persons.	6) an urgent need to continue implementation of non-performed features from a determined contract or a contract declared void;
	7) training services that have a selection process for the acceptance of the persons interested.

In Colombia, the number of exceptions are more specific, allowing direct awarding in the following cases:

1) manifest urgency;
2) loan agreements;
3) agreements between government agencies (including agreements to undertake jointly the mission of government agencies as well as the actual business between government agencies and state-owned enterprises which affect open competition);
4) goods and services for the defence of government agencies that require keeping data in reserve;
5) trust agreements to be entered into by the subnational level when agencies have started an organisation of debt proceedings;
6) when there is no plurality of bidders;
7) for professional services to support the operations of the government agency;
8) lease and sale of real estate.

Source: (OECD, 2017[6]) (OECD, 2016[7])

In Colombia, the number of exceptions are more specific, allowing direct awarding in the following cases: 1) manifest urgency; 2) loan agreements; 3) agreements between government agencies (including agreements to undertake jointly the mission of government agencies as well as the actual business between government agencies and state-owned enterprises which affect open competition); 4) goods and services for the defence of government agencies that require keeping data in reserve; 5) trust agreements to be entered into by the subnational level when agencies have started a reorganisation of debt proceedings; 6) when there is no plurality of bidders; 7) for professional services to support the operations of the government agency; and 8) lease and sale of real estate.

When discretion in selecting a contracting method is available in Colombia, contracting officials are asked to evaluate both the nature of the procurement as well as broader procurement (OECD, 2016[7]).

The standards set by the OECD on exceptions from competitive tendering call for a more thorough analysis on behalf of the UCC of the exceptions allowed in Nuevo León. There is a need to reconsider the number of exception clauses in Article 42. It is not enough to classify a purchase as a good or service for the security of the state; there needs to be a clear justification of why certain goods should be exempt, despite being purchased by the police. The UCC has to confront the excessive use of non-competitive procurement methods. The UCC should develop specific criteria for evaluating whether a specific tender is eligible for exception. Furthermore, these criteria should be objective, transparent and equitable.

2.1.4. The use of consolidated procedures to achieve value for money

Nuevo León needs to consider ways to ensure that units and parastatal entities with cooperation agreements take advantage of consolidated purchasing, as large procurement volumes generate better prices

The state of Nuevo León practices consolidated purchasing. Consolidated purchasing is when a group of entities can procure goods and services jointly by publishing only one public tender. This allows procurers to take advantage of the economy of scale, and to contract goods and services with the best conditions for the state. The objective of consolidating purchasing is to get lower prices for the goods being purchased. In Nuevo León, the process works as follows. First, the treasury must authorise procurement of the specific goods. Then, these goods must be listed in a catalogue. The UCC justifies the decision to consolidate the purchase on the grounds of evidence based on market research. This research mainly involves receiving quotes from suppliers to create a reference price, while taking into consideration the minimum and maximum quote. The UCC, which is responsible for organising these procedures, also relies on historical prices from previous purchases. From 2010-2014, Nuevo León carried out 35 consolidated purchases, or between 6-8 a year. These consolidated purchases were made for goods and services like stationery, cleaning, toners for printers, hardware, plumbing, drugs, reagent and food. In some ways, the UCC functions like a wholesaler, but it doesn't have a warehouse for products, as they are either kept by the supplier or by certain units that have the ability to store them. All central administration units in Nuevo León are obligated to purchase through the consolidated purchasing process, except for parastatal entities which can join in on their own terms.

As stated above, the objective of consolidating purchasing is to obtain lower prices for the goods being purchased. However, the current processes in the state of Nuevo León are not conducive to achieving this goal. The yearly planning for public procurement is still quite fragmented. Public entities have a certain amount of flexibility within an agreed budget to purchase other goods and services than those initially planned, as long as they stay within the budget. However, that can be detrimental to participation in consolidated purchasing. In addition, the UCC does not engage in long-term planning and additional funding requests to the treasury are frequent during the business year. Currently there is a lack of information prior to consolidating purchasing. This results in limited and ever-changing plans. Additionally, some of the products that the state of Nuevo León purchases are better suited for framework agreements, such as stationery, cleaning, toners, hardware and plumbing (unless units are able to store yearly stock of these goods.) With the current process, units often buy the same product for different prices, which doesn't lead to best buy.

With larger procurement volumes, increasing competition in the market normally follows, affecting prices and other terms in ways that are favourable to the purchaser. The potentially large sales volumes that can be expected under centralised procurement mean that economic operators can exploit economies of scale. Nuevo León's UCC will need to gradually establish itself as a driving force for change and efficiency; one way it can do this is by making a persuasive, evidence-based case for the benefits of bulk buying. Public units need to know that they will reap value-for-money benefits when they buy in bulk. In addition, the UCC needs to do better long-term planning. The government needs to make a real commitment to purchasing from selected suppliers. If it does this, economic operators will be motivated to return to the value chain to ensure better prices from their suppliers. For example, the UCC should consider setting standards for certain products, such as chairs and desks. In this scenario, the UCC would than announce six months in advance that the government would be purchasing 1 000 chairs of type A, 200 chairs of type B and 600 chairs of type C. This kind of specific and long-term planning would give economic operators the time to prepare their offers. It would also allow operators to go back into the value chain, as they would have a guarantee of potentially selling several hundred chairs.

There are no public procurement strategies in place in Nuevo León at present that aim to increase savings and efficiency. The state of Nuevo León is, however, applying consolidated purchasing in a more strategic manner. Going forward, it should continue these efforts, and adopt a few best practices. The UCC should aim to standardise requirements for goods and services. It can do this by applying a method called homologation, which also aims to help the UCC spend less time on the definition of requirements – if some of these requirements have already been defined by a national government entity. One of the challenges Nuevo León is facing is how it can use the bargaining power of the state in a centralised procurement system. The government needs to utilise its full buying power to secure lower prices.

2.1.5. Introducing framework agreements

Nuevo León needs to increase its usage of flexible contractual vehicles providing efficiencies and higher savings, such as framework agreements

Nuevo León does not practice framework agreements. That said, the state's procurement legislation stipulates that the UCC can organise framework agreements with one or more potential suppliers, if evidence presented in market studies shows that such an arrangement would be advantageous. If the UCC decides to adopt framework agreements in the future, officials should bear in mind a few key points. Agreements should include technical and quality specifications for particular goods. Framework agreements must indicate the price and estimated demand. And they must also be authorised by the treasury, according to the state procurement law. Procurement that is subject to a framework agreement may only be purchased outside of this arrangement if the purchasing area can demonstrate that the goods and services are being acquired through better conditions than those found in the framework agreement.

The use of framework agreements by some or all procuring entities at the central government level is widespread among OECD countries. 97% of responding countries reported using framework agreements in 2012, according to the 2012 OECD Survey on Public Procurement (OECD, 2012[8]). Ireland is one of many European countries that have a long tradition of using framework arrangements. In Ireland, the Office of Government Procurement (OGP) has put in place 122 frameworks agreements. These agreements have delivered a total estimated value of EUR 2.5 billion. 89% of frameworks in Ireland were established with a mix of both quality and cost as award criteria. Of those, the median split was 60/40 in favour of quality.

The range of items that are usually covered by framework agreements includes:

1. ICT (information and communication technology) products and services (computers, photocopiers, printers, servers, software), generally the largest product area in terms of purchasing volume;
2. telecommunications products (networks, mobile phones, landline phones, telephone exchanges);
3. office furniture;
4. travel services;
5. office equipment and supplies;
6. vehicle and transport services;
7. fuel (for heating and transport) and electricity;
8. food (foodstuffs, meal tickets);
9. organisational and human resources development services.

In Latin America, framework agreements are becoming popular in countries like Mexico, Peru, Chile and Colombia (see more in Box 2.6). In Colombia, the first framework agreement was put in place in late 2013. It helped public agencies in buying fuel at service stations in Bogota. The framework agreement was a breakthrough for government agencies in Colombia. Prior to the agreement, it took four months to complete an open tender. With the agreement, procurement now takes less than an hour, as officials can place purchase orders via the Colombian State Online Store (Tienda Virtual del Estado Colombiano), an e-procurement platform within Colombia's SECOP suite of e-procurement systems. In addition, after the implementation of the framework agreement, suppliers offered a discount on the reference price for fuel in a greater number of service stations. Furthermore, the government created a fuel supply management system to increase control over fuel expenditure. Colombia Compra Eficiente, the central purchasing body of Colombia, currently offers public agencies 34 frameworks agreements, including insurance, vehicles, janitorial services and cloud services, among others. The total value of purchase orders placed is more than EUR 1.25 billion, and there is a growing trend for subnational-level entities to use these contracts.

Box 2.6. Framework agreements in Colombia and Ireland

Colombia Compra Eficiente has the duty of designing and implementing framework agreements for the use of procuring agencies in the country. Law mandates that central government agencies procure through framework agreements. Other institutions, including Congress, the judiciary system, oversight institutions and institutions at the subnational level, may use the agreements if they deem them useful. Suppliers are awarded work via a public tender carried out by Colombia Compra Eficiente. The awarded suppliers sign a contract where all the technical characteristics and conditions for delivery are delineated. Procuring entities use the Tienda Virtual del Estado Colombiano to ask for quotations and place purchase orders. Thus, the process is seamless and paperless.

Framework agreements in Ireland are aggregated procurement arrangements established through competitive procurement processes. These arrangements are agreements with suppliers or service providers. They set out the terms and conditions under which specific contracts can be made during the period of the agreement. Frameworks agreements are put in place by central purchasing bodies like the OGP. Public sector clients can then modify the amount of goods and services they purchase from suppliers in the framework by means of direct draw down or mini-competitions.

The benefits of framework agreements are plentiful, they:

- *Deliver value for money*: Aggregating different purchasers' potential needs means individual purchasers can buy goods and services at prices below those normally charged. It also means that individuals can buy goods with special added benefits or more advantageous conditions.
- *Are compliant*: Centrally initiated framework arrangements are fully compliant with procurement regulations. Thus, they reduce the potential for fraud or corruption.
- *Are consistent*: The use of these arrangements drives a more consistent and professional approach to procurement processes. This consistency and professionalism helps educate officials and suppliers dealing with the central procurement body, as well as improve their approaches to each tender exercise.
- *Are faster*: Framework agreements remove the need for contracting authorities to conduct full tender exercises or lengthy supplier evaluations. This saves time, and reduces the costs associated with procurement exercises.
- *Have less risk*: Each of the suppliers in a framework agreement has been subject to a rigorous procurement process. This ensures that they offer the type of goods and services required, and that they meet a certain threshold of quality. Framework agreements establish terms and conditions. This fact means that there is no need to re-draft terms or renegotiate when each procurement is undertaken.
- *Leverage scale*: The public sector has substantial purchasing power. Framework agreements harness the opportunity to leverage this purchasing power and thereby ensure that value for taxpayer money is achieved.

Source: Information provided by OGP in Ireland and CCE in Colombia

Framework agreements generally involve the advertisement of an opportunity by a contracting authority (or authorities). This authority then enters into a contract or other arrangements with one or more economic operators for the provision of works, supplies or services over a fixed period. The rationale behind the framework method of purchasing is to achieve savings – both in terms of the cost of procurement and the time spent on the procurement process. It is worth noting that the most significant savings are commonly achieved when purchasing using framework agreements is combined with centralised procurement and e-procurement. In many OECD countries, key tasks of CPBs include aggregating demand and purchasing, managing framework agreements (see Figure 2.1). The roles that are less commonly undertaken by CPBs include co-ordinating training and establishing polices; these are instead some of the main roles of regulatory agencies in Latin American countries (OECD, 2017[9]). (OECD, 2016[10]). The majority of OECD countries make it mandatory for contracting authorities at the central level to use framework agreements. Only Korea and the Slovak Republic make it mandatory for all contracting authorities to use framework agreements. (OECD, 2017[9]). (OECD, 2016[10]).

Figure 2.1. The role of CPBs in OECD countries

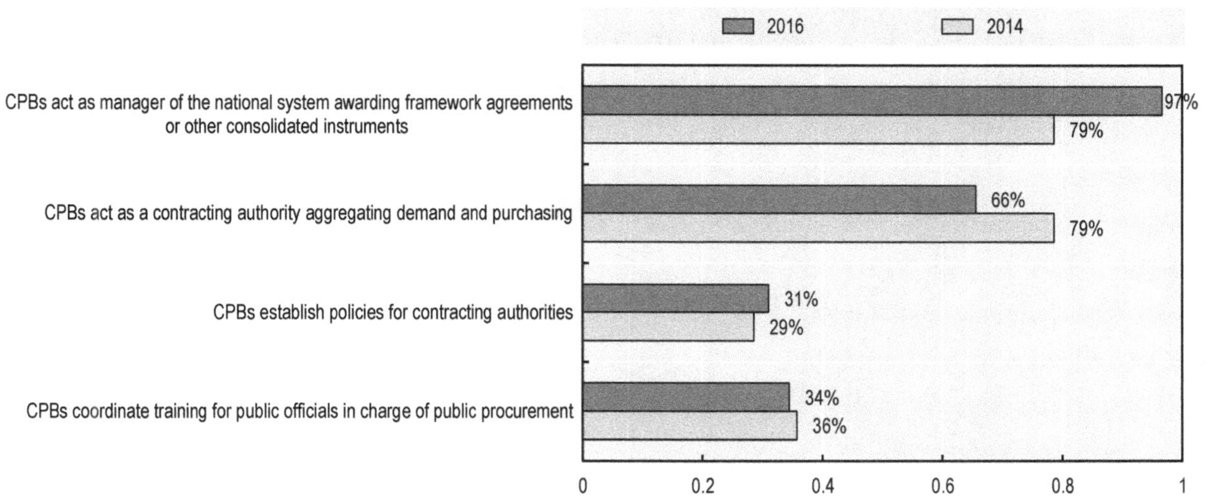

Source: (OECD, 2014[11]) (OECD, 2017[9])

The benefits of framework agreements have already been established. However, Nuevo León's UCC must be aware that framework agreements may not be suitable for all types of purchasing. The most appropriate use of a framework agreement is in a situation where a contracting authority has a repeated need for works, services or supplies, but does not know the exact quantities that are required. In order to assess the suitability of a framework agreement, contracting authorities need to understand the advantages and disadvantages of framework agreements, the different types of framework agreements, how they are set up and how they operate in practice (OECD, 2016[12]).

2.2. The role of the UCC within the public procurement process

2.2.1. Adopting a strategic approach to market studies

Nuevo León needs to adopt more advanced methods for carrying out market studies, by going beyond quotes and reviews of historical prices

The role the UCC within the Secretariat of Administration is key for the successful application of public tenders and other minor purchases. The procurement process is mainly managed by three directorates within UCC (see Table 2.4). Their involvement starts when a requesting unit requires the procurement or leasing of movable property or real estate, or the rendering of services. The request has to be based on specific needs, and must be aligned with the State Development Program. The unit makes a request called requisition. This requisition is then loaded into the Integrating System of Government Electronic Resources platform. Finally, the request is paired with a fact sheet (tech spec) that describes the requested goods or services.

Table 2.4. Functionalities within the State of Nuevo León procurement system

	Requiring Unit	UCC (Directorate of Procurement and General Services)	UCC (Directorate of tenders)	UCC (Directorate of Maintenance and General Services)	Procurement Committee	Winning bidder
Pre-tendering phase	**Participation**					
Procurement planning	•					
Definition of requirements		•				
Market research				•		
Determination of estimated value or reference value	•					
Development of tender documents				•		
Tendering phase	**Participation**					
Tender notice			•			
Clarification about tender documents			•			
Modification of tender documents				•		
Integration of tender documents				•		
Tendering			•			
Evaluation	•		•		•	
Award						
Award approval						
Settlement of disputes in open tenders						
Post-tendering phase	**Participation**					
Signing of the contract	•			•		•
Subcontracting	•			•		•
Additions and reductions	•			•		•
Extension of the agreed period	•			•		•
Complementary contracts						
Mechanisms for settlement of disputes (i.e. conciliation and arbitration)						

Source: Information provided by the State of Nuevo León

After an approval process determining that the procurement can go ahead, the request goes to negotiators within the Directorate of Maintenance and General Services. These negotiators are responsible for conducting market research in order to find the best purchasing conditions for the requesting units. The law specifies that procedures for direct awards that fall under the exceptions to public tenders do not require market research if they fall under sections I, III, V, VII, VIII, XI, XIV, XVI, XVIII and XIX of Article 42 of the Law for Acquisitions, Leasing, and Procurement of Services for the State of Nuevo León. However, every other tender requires market research. These studies must include the following:

- Verification of the existence of goods, leasing arrangements or services and suppliers at the local, national or international level.
- The maximum reference price based on the information to be obtained from states, municipalities, government agencies, public or private organisations, suppliers, or a combination of these sources. Market research may be based on local, national or international information.

The negotiators in Nuevo León mainly apply a two-way approach to market studies. First, they search for bidders that meet the technical requirements in a supplier registry, and then they request quotes directly from these suppliers.

Market studies are vitally important, and should be used in a more strategic way by the state of Nuevo León. They should be undertaken even when there is no legal requirement to do so, particularly for tenders of large value. A thorough understanding of all prevailing market conditions and potential suppliers is essential if contracting authorities want to both buy effectively and detect and avoid bid rigging.

Though main market studies for public procurement are carried out by the UCC, requesting units have to get a pre-price quote during the preparation for the budget. The procedures applied by the requesting units are similar to those of the UCC, as they rely on historical prices or quotes. The UCC and requesting units need to further develop the market studies methodology they apply. Market studies should be conducted by individuals with procurement or research expertise, who are provided with sufficient time and resources. To address this issue, the UCC should establish a guide for the minimum acceptable content for market studies. It can do this by developing a manual which can be used by requesting units and UCC staff when they undertake their market studies. Furthermore, the manual should clearly state that market analysis is undertaken in the planning stage of a procurement procedure, well before the launch of the procedure. That said, market analysis may be undertaken at set times during the year for purchases that are procured on a regular basis.

Nuevo León needs to implement a comprehensive methodology or guide for how to conduct market research. This guide should include ways:

- To increase awareness of the characteristics of the market and of recent market developments or trends that may affect competition for the tender, or may make collusion more likely (e.g. small number of suppliers, standardised or simple products, little or no entry, among others).
- To collect information on suppliers and their products, prices and cost structures. If possible, a comparison of prices offered in business-to-business procurement is recommended.

- To collect information about recent price changes. This will help procurement practitioners be informed about prices in neighbouring geographic areas, and about prices of possible alternative products.
- To collect information about past tenders for the same or similar products.
- To co-ordinate with other public procuring authorities that have recently purchased similar goods, services or works in order to improve understanding of the market and suppliers.

A market analysis is a general survey of the potential in the market to satisfy the defined need of a requesting unit. In order to be successful, this analysis has to be conducted in an open and objective manner, focusing on what general solutions are available in the market – and not just on preferred or favoured contractors. Market analyses may also involve direct engagement with economic operators and other organisations with relevant expertise, such as trade bodies or chambers of commerce. Direct engagement can complement desk-based research, providing first-hand knowledge from the market's economic operators. Direct engagement with economic operators is also commonly referred to as "market sounding", "solicitation of supplier information" or "preliminary market consultation".

2.2.2. Breaking down barriers and improving procurement procedures

Nuevo León should simplify certain phases of the public procurement process to increase competition and maximise value for money

The OECD's assessment of the procurement process in the state of Nuevo León identified several areas for improvement. These include: drafting of technical specifications, creating an approval process for purchasing, drafting of contract documents, notice for submitting tenders, guarantees and the payment process. The latter two subjects are discussed in more detail in Chapter 9.

The UCC receives so called "tech sheets" from requesting units along with a request for a purchase. When carrying out a market analysis, the UCC is also trying to shape the technical specifications of a tender. The collaboration between the UCC and the requesting units is close, with the requesting unit also assessing the bids of technical offers. The way the UCC goes about assessing the technical specifications is mainly by identifying whether a specific product exists, and in what condition the state can receive it. Currently there is limited specialisation within the UCC with regards to specific categories. This means that the work of assessing technical specifications is limited to checking whether certain "tech sheets" are in accordance with legislation. It is important for the UCC to have officials specialised in certain categories, as they will be better able to assess bids. In turn, this kind of educated assessment is likely to reduce the risk of discriminating against some suppliers while favouring others.

The process for initiating a purchase in the state of Nuevo León is quite bureaucratic and needs to be made more effective. A requesting unit with a need has to send a request for requisition to the operations department within the UCC. The operation department (OP) receives the request, reviews and checks whether there are funds for the product. When the requesting unit has signed the classification of the good, the OP guides the process to a specific negotiator. The OP operates as an internal controller, assuring everything is in place for the negotiator to find the best suitable product for the requesting unit. When the negotiator has found a product which the requesting unit agrees to, the negotiator sends the OP documents so that it can start preparing the purchasing order. The purchasing order is then delivered to the supplier. This process for purchasing relatively simple products can take days or weeks, which can result in the requesting unit having to wait and delay some of its activity.

Contractual terms must be clear and specific in order to avoid establishing unnecessary requirements. Furthermore, contractual terms should favour free competition and equality of opportunity in order to increase the number of participants in the tendering process. In many countries where the procurement process is more decentralised than in the state of Nuevo León, central purchasing bodies develop obligatory standardised tender documents for public entities. These documents include guidelines for the setup of tender documents, as well as model contracts. Hence, prior to a tender there are several types of model contracts already available. Legal departments are often responsible for providing procurement entities with an ad hoc tendering model that is in line with strategic sourcing. Once the contract is awarded, the legal department customises the draft contract with the data. Then the contractor or supplier sends this draft contract and data to the legal department, accompanied by supporting documentation to allow for a legal review and continued processing. Within the UCC there is a department that sets up the contracts according to the legislation. That said, no standardised tender documents or model contracts exist.

The state of Nuevo León should develop prototypes of solicitation documents for open competition, restricted invitation and direct award. Central purchasing bodies normally play a significant role in the development of standardised tender documents (see Box 2.7). The government should develop guidelines and policies relating to the creation of model contracts in various forms. These policies should be applicable to public events and formats which are essential for the operation of procurement under the existing regulatory framework. The model contracts should then be included with the solicitation documents for open competition, restricted invitation and an offer for direct awards. Model contracts should include the following elements, at minimum: the type of contract, the identification of risks linked to the project, processes and the execution of the contract, prevention and mitigation, the concentration of contracts in a single supplier, and the scale and complexity of the object of the contract.

Box 2.7. Development of template tender documents in Ireland

The Office of Government Procurement (OGP) in Ireland is responsible for drafting public procurement policies, and for regulating and coordinating the national public procurement system. In addition, the OGP is in charge of the preparation of standardised tender documents, as well as guidance material.

The OGP has created a standard suite of template tender documents to drive best practices and to reflect the new EU Procurement Directives which came into force in 2016. The OGP's website offers a repository of knowledge section that provides an extensive amount of template documents and guidance material. There are currently six model documents available and more are planned. These templates cover the tender process and the contract phase of procedures.

To date, this suite of documents has been used across the public service for the procurement of low-to-medium risk goods and services. The popularity of these template documents is primarily due to their ease of use and clarity. These documents provide a further opportunity to help professionalise, streamline and standardise the procurement function among Contracting Authorities in the Irish state.

Source: (Office of Government Procurement, 2017[13])

The window for submission of tenders in the state of Nuevo León is not overly small, like in other parts of Mexico. For example, in Mexico City, tender documents can be available for only three days after the publication of the tender notice. In Nuevo León, tender documents for open national tenders remain available to the public for 15 calendar days after the date of publication of the tender call in the *State Official Journal* and in one of the newspapers in the region with the most circulation. For open international tenders, Nuevo León allows the tender call to remain available for 20 calendar days after the date of publication in the *State Official Journal* and high-circulation newspaper mentioned prior. For restricted invitation tenders, the time between the publication of the notice and the opening of tenders is 10 calendar days after the delivery date of the last invitation. This only applies to goods and services. Public works allow for 20 calendar days after publication in the *State Official Journal* and high-circulation newspaper listed prior.

No data is publicly available on the amount of time Nuevo León offers suppliers to submit their bids. The OECD was not provided with information regarding this issue by the SGNL. Furthermore, no information is available on the number of suppliers participating in bids. In Europe, the time offered to suppliers before submitting their bids is long, though it can be shortened (see Box 2.8). The state of Nuevo León should consider extending the deadlines set in its regulatory framework to enhance the participation of suppliers in procurement opportunities.

Box 2.8. Time limit for submitting bids in the European Union (EU)

Open procedure

In an open procedure, **any business may submit** a tender. The minimum time limit for submission of tenders is **35 days** from the publication date of the contract notice. If a prior information notice was published, this time limit can be reduced to **15 days**.

Restricted procedure

In a restricted procedure, any business may ask to participate, but **only** those who are **pre-selected** will be invited to **submit a tender**. The time limit to request participation is **37 days** from the publication of the contract notice. The public authority then selects **at least 5 candidates** possessing the capabilities required, who then have **40 days** to submit a tender from the date when the invitation was sent. This time limit can be reduced to **36 days**, if a prior information notice has been published.

Source: (European Commission, Accessed 5 July 2017$_{[14]}$)

2.3. Streamlining and merging procurement committees

2.3.1. Role of the Central Purchasing Committee

Nuevo León needs to ensure that its public procurement committee has an enhanced role in driving efficiency and value for money by leading the implementation of a public procurement strategy

There are a number of procurement committees active in the state of Nuevo León. Their responsibilities vary depending on whether their procurement involves goods and services or public works. These committees operate within two different legal environments – state and federally funded procurement. The main committee for goods and services is the Central Procurement Committee (CPC). Requesting units also have procurement committees, as do parastatal entities. The CPC has the following obligations, according to Article 16 of the Nuevo León's procurement legislation:

- acknowledging the annual procurement programmes (including those of multi-annual nature)
- partaking in every stage of the procurement process, whether public tenders or restricted invitation
- issuing an opinion on proposals submitted by bidders in public tenders and restricted invitations to tender
- analysing and evaluating procurement procedures carried out by any state-level entities
- ruling in cases of exceptions to public tenders
- defining integration and operational procedures of procurement sub-committees
- proposing to the state treasury or to competent public entities indicated in this Law, the establishment of norms, criteria and guidelines regarding the acquisition and leasing of movable property
- commenting on those matters because of their importance

- in the case of municipalities, giving an opinion on matters that, due to their importance for the municipal government, are referred to the CPC by a municipal president or municipal treasurer.

The CPC has the authority to invite representatives of any state-level entities to its sessions when the nature of the procurement process requires their presence. In cases of consolidated purchases or framework agreements, the CPC can also sign coordination agreements between stakeholders. The committee members on the CPC differ from the members on the requesting unit committees, according to Nuevo León's procurement legislation. Both committee formats include representatives that have a say but cannot vote. The CPC tends not to vote, but to reach a unanimous decision. Every procurement committee should have a technical secretary (*secretario técnico*) as the authority responsible for the following functions and actions, according to Article 20 of the procurement legislation:

- prepare the proposals of calls, agendas and the lists of the subjects that will be treated in the sessions
- include in the corresponding folders the necessary documentation, and send it to the members of the committee
- draw up the list of attendees at the meetings of the committee
- take minutes at each session of the committee
- follow-up on compliance with the committee's agreements
- ensure that the committee's file of documents is complete and up-to-date
- assist in the discharge of the functions of the committee.

The composition of the CPC can be seen in Figure 2.2. The members of the committee do not work permanently for the committee; they have day jobs in their respective units. The members are appointed to the committee for an undisclosed time. The committee meets frequently, but it tends to vary between seasons. Early on in the year, the committee might have 2-3 sessions per week. The busiest time of the year is normally at the end of the year. This is when all units are preparing the forthcoming year's budget, and thus need to finish what is left of the current year's budget. This is also when requesting units often realise that they are running out of time to try to get exemptions.

Figure 2.2. Integration of the Central Procurement Committee

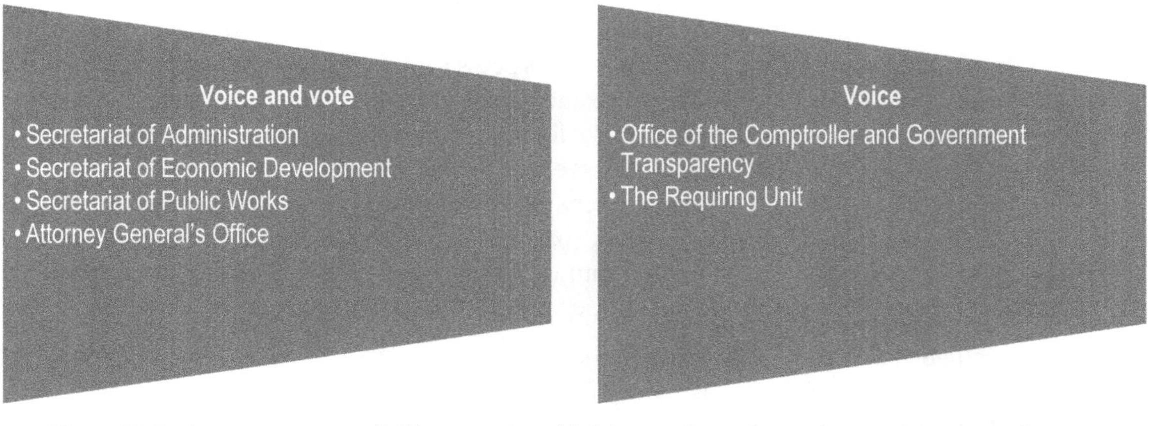

The CPC has a responsibility to be highly active throughout the central state administration's procurement process. Currently, the workload within the UCC is immense. During the OECD fact-finding mission, officials raised questions regarding whether the UCC had the capacity to fulfil its commitments. It is clear that the workload of the CPC is heavy. This is problematic, because it puts the committee at risk of being in a situation where decisions are made despite the fact that not all committee members have had the opportunity to study the documents. A procurement committee should ensure that procurement is being carried out in accordance with the legislative framework, but that should not be the primary objective of public procurement. The primary objective of public procurement is value for money and, second, supporting secondary objectives. The state of Nuevo León should reconsider whether the involvement of a representative from the Attorney General or the Office of the Comptroller and Government Transparency is conducive to the procurement process.

There is currently no public procurement strategy in place for Nuevo León, as discussed in Chapter 1. Nuevo León needs a strong strategy, and it should be the role of the CPC to support the implementation of this strategy. Officials delineate a plan for each year during the annual planning process. However, the plan is ever changeable with units transferring funds between different products, which prevent any coherent plan from being implemented. By developing a strong strategy for the long-term, the UCC can avoid this situation. In addition to reducing the number of committee members and focusing more on the strategy and plans for the forthcoming years, the UCC could also develop a checklist for assessing public tenders based on risk, value and more. A checklist of that sort could help prioritise the workload, leaving certain less risky or minor tenders to the UCC to complete with minimum oversight from the CPC.

2.3.2. Controlling for public works

Nuevo León should consider expanding the role of the Central Procurement Committee by allowing it to address the value and quality of public works tenders

The Law of Public Works for the State and Municipalities of Nuevo León (Ley de Obras Públicas del Estado y Municipios de Nuevo León) is the legislation that governs procurement of public works in the State of Nuevo León. It is distinct from the legislation that governs procurement of goods and services in the state. There is no readily available data on the number of public tenders for state or federally funded public works in the Nuevo León. Furthermore, no data is available on the total state expenditure for public works – or for federally funded work – in the state. In Nuevo León, there is no procurement committee for public works per se. There is, however, a committee (*comité de fallos*) which functions more as an internal control board. The public works process is more decentralised then the procurement process for services and goods, with procurement committees or technical departments carrying out market analyses, drafting tech sheets and more. Currently, there are four large technical departments preparing public works tenders in Nuevo León. They are: the Secretariat of Infrastructure (INFRA), Water and Drainage Services (Agua y Drenaje), the Institute for Education and Sports (ICIFED), and the State Highway Network (Red Estatal de Autopistas, REA). INFRA is obligated to give support to all public entities but not the other aforementioned large technical departments or the parastatal entities.

The committee (*comité de fallo*) for public works is located within the Secretariat of Infrastructure. Its only function is to review the paperwork of winning bids alongside those that get disqualified, and give an opinion. The opinion is given in order to ensure that the legal framework has been adhered to throughout the procurement process for a particular tender. The committee (*comité de fallo*) is composed of representatives; each has the power to give his or her opinion, and to vote. The members of the committee include representatives from the Secretariat of Administration, Secretariat of Finance and General Treasury, the Secretariat of Social Development and the requesting unit. If a vote is tied, a facilitator from the Secretariat of Infrastructure breaks the tie. The Office of the Comptroller for Government Transparency has a voice on the committee, but not a vote.

The committee takes action when the requesting unit has a proposal for who it wants to choose as a supplier for a given tender. That proposal is submitted to the committee prior to making the decision known to the winner. The committee then makes a thorough assessment, looking at all aspects of the tender, from the technical specifications to the economic offer. The committee suggests that the work should be awarded to the lowest bidder. The opinion is only for the requesting unit, it is not publicized; it is an internal control mechanism for the requesting unit. The committee only provides an opinion in the case of state or federally funded public tenders. In the case of direct awards, the committee is not required to issue an opinion.

Though the configuration of public procurement in Nuevo León is not unique, some questions have been raised about its effectiveness. The system is quite complicated with two different legislations, different registries, different e-platforms, distinct standard templates and different awarding criteria. In addition, the 51 municipalities in the state could be working much more closely with the state authorities than they are at present. The committee for public works is an internal control committee, primarily concerned with the correct application of the law. There is no central purchasing body for public works in Nuevo León. That said, INFRA functions as a technical support department. If the State Government of Nuevo León is keen to move towards a more efficient public procurement system, it should modify INFRA's role and expand the role of the Central Procurement Committee by allowing it to address the value and quality of public works tenders, with INFRA providing technical support. The current committee of public works is incapable of that work, but could continue on as an internal control reviewer of public works, as necessary or annually.

2.4. Designing the appropriate evaluation and award criteria

2.4.1. Nuevo León should consider broadening the award criteria by applying points and percentages for public tenders

It is important that Nuevo León manage the public procurement process properly beginning at the early stages. A suitable set of conditions must be provided, including adequate selection and award criteria that will allow for equitable results from the bidding process. Tender evaluation has been identified as a particularly vulnerable step in that process. All evaluation criteria must be directly linked to requirements, be as objective as possible and must be designed not to favour a particular supplier. In Nuevo León, the public procurement legislation establishes that government authorities should use the method indicated in the call for tender for the evaluation of proposals. The criteria for evaluating proposals must be quantifiable and objective. When ministries, entities or administrative units need to obtain goods, leases or services that involve the use of complex, high-technical specialisation or technological-innovation characteristics, the use of the evaluation method of points and percentages may be justified. The evaluation criteria must include at least the following (Article 39):

1. the total cost of the good or service, which should take into account costs incurred from acquisition to disposal, including production capacity, lifetime,

maintenance costs, disposal costs, and, as appropriate, certificates under the applicable legislation;

2. in the case of services, the experience, accredited performance, technical skills, material and human resources of the participant, as well as their administrative systems and the proposed methodology;
3. in the case of consulting, consultants' relevant experience, the quality of the methodology, an assessment of whether the work plan observes the terms of reference, the qualifications of professional staff and the adequacy of the knowledge transfer; and
4. where appropriate, the environmental criteria of the good to be acquired or the service to be contracted, and, in general, criteria referring to the preservation of the environment.

Despite allowing the use of points and percentages for public procurement, the method most used in Nuevo León is binary. The criteria established in procurement calls are supposed to be equitable for all the participants – according to a technical file that includes market research. That is, however, not always the case. During the OECD fact-finding mission, civil society organisations made several serious claims. These claims referenced two types of experiences. One in which suppliers were unfairly discriminated against, and the other in which certain suppliers were shown favouritism despite the fact that they did not fully meet procurement criteria. These practices are not unique to Nuevo León. They are common in many countries, and can significantly hinder competition. It is therefore important to ensure bidders receive equal treatment and equal access to information both during the preparation and evaluation of bids. See Box 2.9 for an example of objective award criteria.

Box 2.9. Objective award criteria

Ensure that award criteria are clearly and objectively defined by:

- Using economic benefit as a basis for evaluation, unless the procurement is of a commodity purchase. In this case the basis of the lowest may be used;
- Specifying the relative weight of each criterion, and justifying them in advance.
- Specifying the extent to which these considerations are taken into account in award criteria when using economic, social or environmental criteria.
- Including any action that the procuring agency is entitled to make with regards to the criteria (such as negotiations, specific conditions, etc.) and recording them.

Source: (OECD, 2009$_{[15]}$)

Best practices for public works tenders are as follows. Once tenders are evaluated, a contract is awarded to the bidder whose proposal observes all the legal, technical and economic requirements stated in the call for tenders. Such a bidder guarantees that it will honour the necessary obligations. It is also the bid that obtained the best result in the evaluation, according to the methodology established in the call. If there is a level playing field, preference will be given to the proposals offering the highest degree of protection to the environment. If a tie persists, preference will be granted to the individuals integrating the micro, small and medium enterprises (SME) sector from the state. This is rarely the case in Nuevo León, though, as public officials usually pick the lowest priced bid – which is not necessarily the best offer.

Nuevo León's binary approach poses challenges to those managing technical specifications. There is a need for high-level capacity among employees when using the binary approach, as this approach does not incentivise companies to come up with new solutions during bidding. By using the binary system, the state of Nuevo León is excluding certain other criteria, such as quality and longevity. This binary system also deters more innovative companies to participate. The state of Nuevo León should consider using the points and percentages criteria in all public tenders. It should weigh criteria's such as: 1) the environment; 2) social goals; 3) improvements to technical requirements; 4) delivery terms; and 5) the experience of key staff, among others. Colombia has practiced this approach for some time (see Box 2.10).

Box 2.10. Points-based evaluation in Colombia

Open tenders in Colombia are evaluated using three criteria: 1) economic; 2) technical; and 3)the nationality of goods and services offered. Economic points are awarded according to the price of the bid. As for technical points, the procuring entity must allocate points based on the quality, delivery time or sustainable sub-criteria. Up to 20% of points must be given to bids of goods and services whose origin is Colombia or one of its trading partners, following the rules set in trade agreements.

For example, in the open tender carried out by Colombia Compra Eficiente to select suppliers for the janitorial services framework agreement, formulas were set to allocate points based on the prices offered by bidders. Bidders provided prices for the provision of persons in charge of cleaning and performing related activities, as well as the price of the necessary products needed to complete these tasks. Technical points were given to suppliers that offered environmentally friendly cleaning products, and to those that committed to hiring victims of war or former guerrilla members.

Source: (OECD, 2016[7])

The award criteria is important to ensure value. The final ranking of tenders is determined by weighting set by the requesting unit in the tender documents. The scoring rules for both technical and financial evaluation are at least as important as the weights in defining the relative importance of all the different award criteria. The combination of weights and scoring rules determines how relevant each award criterion is in contributing to the value of the bid (see Box 2.11 for evaluation scores in Peru). Weights and scoring rules also determine how much more the buyer would be willing to pay for better quality proposals. Hence, behind weights and scoring rules there is value for money. This is why weights and scoring rules should not be set following intuition and common sense, but after sound analysis and simulation exercises. By doing this, officials can avoid unsatisfactory contract awards. The binary approach does not meet most strategic objectives being set today for public procurement. It is important that the state of Nuevo León move forward, but in order to do so, it needs to increase its internal capacity. Only then will the state be able to deliver change.

Box 2.11. Scores depending on evaluation criteria in Peru

In Peru, tender evaluations can be based on price and other criteria established by the entity in the tender documentation. The competition criteria established by the new legislation are referred to as: 1) the environment; 2) social goals; 3) improvements to the technical requirements; 4) delivery terms; 5) the experience of key staff, and more.

	Legislative Decree No. 1017		Law No. 30225	
	Technical score	Economic score	Technical score	Economic score
Goods, services and works	*Minimum weighting*	*Minimum weighting*	*Minimum weighting*	*Minimum weighting*
	60% of the total score	30% of the total score	0% of the total score	50% of the total score
	Maximum weighting	*Maximum weighting*	*Maximum weighting*	*Maximum weighting*
	70% of the total score	40% of the total score	50% of the total score	100% of the total score
Consultancy	*Minimum weighting*	*Minimum weighting*	*Minimum weighting*	*Minimum weighting*
	70% of the total score	20% of the total score	70% of the total score	20% of the total score
	Maximum weighting	*Maximum weighting*	*Maximum weighting*	*Maximum weighting*
	80% of the total score	30% of the total score	80% of the total score	30% of the total score

Source: (OECD, 2017[6])

2.5. Engaging with suppliers prior to and after the tendering process

2.5.1. Nuevo León should consider setting up a formal mechanism for debriefing

The Law for Acquisitions, Leasing, and Procurement of Services for the State of Nuevo León regulates the clarification meeting stage. At least one clarification meeting is required by law, and participation on behalf of potential bidders is optional. Interested parties must submit a written statement expressing interest in participating that includes general information and the name of their representative. Questions and inquiries may be sent through the Electronic Public Procurement System or in physical form depending on the approved format, which is established in the call for tender. The deadline for questions is twenty-four hours before the scheduled clarification meeting date. Each clarification meeting is documented and published in the Electronic Public Procurement System, except when there are any legal restrictions, such as confidential information. In the case of public tenders where the time from the publication of notice and submission of tender is 15 days, the clarification meeting should be held seven days before the submission day.

The state of Nuevo León has no regulatory framework for debriefing bidders. There are also no procedures for debriefing meetings with suppliers. In general, the answers provided by the UCC to contractors are published solely on the Internet. Unsuccessful tenderers may want to know why their tender failed, but they don't have many avenues for obtaining feedback. The amount of information that can be conveyed varies according to the circumstances of the particular contract, but the UCC could give a broad indication of reasons suppliers have been rejected, based on cost and where they ranked in the tender list.

The OECD recognises verbal debriefing as a good practice that is commonly used in many OECD countries to engage with the market and expand the supply base. Implementation of adequate debriefing with the suppliers provides a valuable opportunity for both parties to benefit from the process. Verbal debriefings can improve relationships with suppliers, as well as the quality of their offers, while providing valuable insight to both parties. A debriefing can even be made available to a successful bidder as a first step in establishing a sound working relationship – and a precedent for constructive feedback. However, verbal debriefings must be used judiciously. Debriefings must operate under a clear framework in order to reduce any associated risks and costs. In order to increase the benefits of such debriefings while mitigating any potential risks, the state of Nuevo León should develop clear framework guidelines for debriefings. The OECD recommends that certain generic content be considered during the development of these guidelines (see Box 2.12).

Box 2.12. The benefits of debriefing

Debriefing is beneficial to bidders because it:

1. helps them to rethink their approach in order to make future bids more successful;
2. offers targeted guidance to new or smaller companies to improve their chances of doing business in the public sector;
3. provides reassurance about the process and suppliers' contribution or role;
4. provides a better understanding of what differentiates public sector procurement from private procurement.

Debriefing can also assist Nuevo León by:

1. identifying ways to improve subsequent solicitation processes, including associated communications;
2. making sure best practices and guidance are updated to reflect any relevant issues that have been highlighted;
3. encouraging better bids from suppliers in the future;
4. getting a better understanding of how that segment of the market thinks, enhancing the organisation's market intelligence;
5. helping establish a reputation as a fair, open and ethical buyer with whom suppliers will want to do business in the future; and
6. potentially reducing the number of challenges.

Source: (United Kingdom Office of Government Commerce, 2003[16])

2.6. Proposals for action

The state of Nuevo León is going through a transitional period with the creation of the Secretariat of Administration and the expanded role of the UCC, which will likely grow in coming years. Nuevo León needs to take significant steps in order to move the process forward. This will require legal and cultural changes within the public sector. Nuevo

León's procurement procedures are highly control-oriented. Procurement could be made more effective if officials strive for goals like value for money, while de-emphasising adherence to formalities. Changes in institutions and institutional cultures are needed, not just in Nuevo León, but in Mexico as a whole. That said, there seems to be an understanding among certain units within the state administration about the need to focus on simple and faster processes. This is a good thing. Nuevo León's public procurement system needs to be more transparent, accessible and service-oriented. In order to improve the efficiency and value of the procurement system, the proposals below could be considered.

Framework for public procurement procedures

- Nuevo León needs to address obstacles and delays in its public procurement process, with special attention paid to making purchases of minor goods more efficient.
- Nuevo León needs to improve its data and information systems to be able to manage public purchasing in the state more effectively.
- Nuevo León should develop more comprehensive and clear rules for justifying and approving exceptions to procurement procedures.
- Nuevo León needs to consider ways to ensure that the public entities and parastatal entities with cooperation agreements take advantage of consolidated purchasing, as large procurement volumes generate better prices.
- Nuevo León needs to increase the use of flexible contractual vehicles that provide efficiency and higher savings, like framework agreements.

The role of UCC within the public procurement process

- Nuevo León needs to adopt more advanced methods for carrying out market studies in order to go beyond quotes and reviews of historical prices.
- Nuevo León should simplify certain phases of the public procurement process to increase competition and maximise value for money.

Streamlining and merging procurement committees

- Nuevo León needs to ensure that its public procurement committee has an enhanced role in driving efficiency and value for money by leading the implementation of a public procurement strategy.
- Nuevo León should consider expanding the role of the Central Procurement Committee by allowing it to address value and quality of public works tenders.

Designing the appropriate evaluation and award criteria

- Nuevo León should consider broadening award criteria by applying points and percentages for public tenders.

Engaging with suppliers prior to and after the tendering process

- Nuevo León should consider setting up a formal mechanism for debriefing.

References

European Commission (2014), *Thresholds*, https://ec.europa.eu/growth/single-market/public-procurement/rules-implementation/thresholds_fr (accessed on 05 July 2017). [3]

European Commission (Accessed 5 July 2017), *Tendering Rules and Procedures*, Brussels, http://europa.eu/youreurope/business/public-tenders/rules-procedures/index_en.htm (accessed on 12 June 2017), [14]

OECD (2009), *OECD Principles for Integrity in Public Procurement*, OECD Publishing, Paris, http://dx.doi.org/10.1787/9789264056527-en. [15]

OECD (2012), "OECD 2012 Survey on Public Procurement", OECD, Paris. [8]

OECD (2013), *Implementing the OECD Principles for Integrity in Public Procurement: Progress since 2008*, OECD Publishing, Paris, http://dx.doi.org/10.1787/9789264201385-en. [5]

OECD (2014), "Towards public procurement performance indicators", http://unpublished. [4]

OECD (2014), "OECD Survey on Public Procurement", OECD, Paris. [11]

OECD (2015), *OECD Recommendation of the Council on Public Procurement*, http://www.oecd.org/gov/ethics/OECD-Recommendation-on-Public-Procurement.pdf. [1]

OECD (2016), *Towards Efficient Public Procurement in Colombia : Making the Difference*, OECD Publishing, Paris, http://dx.doi.org/10.1787/9789264252103-en. [7]

OECD (2016), *Government at a Glance: Latin America and the Caribbean 2017*, OECD Publishing, Paris, http://dx.doi.org/10.1787/9789264265554-en. [10]

OECD (2016), "Centralised purchasing systems in the European Union", SIGMA Papers, Brief. 19, http://www.sigmaweb.org/publications/Public-Procurement-Policy-Brief-19-200117.pdf. [12]

OECD (2017), *Government at a Glance 2017*, OECD Publishing, Paris, http://dx.doi.org/10.1787/gov_glance-2017-en. [9]

OECD (2017), *Public Procurement in Peru: Reinforcing Capacity and Co-ordination*, OECD Publishing, Paris, http://dx.doi.org/10.1787/9789264278905-en. [6]

Office of Government Procurement (2017), *Office of Government Procurement in Ireland*, http://www.etenders.gov.ie/ (accessed on 15 June 2017). [13]

The State of Nuevo León (2013), *Law for Acquisitions, Leasing, and Procurement of Services for the State of Nuevo León*, 2013, https://www.pjenl.gob.mx/CJ/Transparencia/01MJ/LAACSENL.pdf. [2]

United Kingdom Office of Government Commerce (2003), *Supplier debriefing.* [16]

Chapter 3. Strategically supporting complementary objectives in Nuevo León

This chapter analyses how Nuevo León strategically pursues complementary policy objectives through public procurement. Complementary policy objectives of public procurement include objectives that reach beyond the traditional goals of public procurement (e.g., advantageous outcomes in terms of efficiency, effectiveness and transparency). They include issues like support for small and medium enterprises, social and green objectives, and support for innovative solutions. This chapter analyses the existing legal and institutional framework in Nuevo León, and the room it provides for secondary policy objectives. In addition, the chapter provides insights into how Nuevo León can link public procurement to its wider strategic development goals. Finally, the chapter explores the benefits of sustainable public procurement, such as better value for money and the achievement of complementary policy goals.

This chapter focusses on the extent to which Nuevo León utilises public procurement strategically to support complementary policy objectives, like support for small and medium enterprises (SMEs), social and green objectives, and innovation. The chapter analyses current efforts, and highlights pathways that Nuevo León can take to achieve a maximum impact with regards to strategic public procurement and complementary policy objectives.

This chapter on specific objectives of public procurement complements the general analysis undertaken in Chapter 1 (analysis of the legal and regulatory framework in Nuevo León) and Chapter 2 (fairness and efficiency). Following these two more general perspectives, this chapter examines public procurement in Nuevo León in the context of its specific, overarching challenges. The review asks whether public procurement is utilised in a strategic manner in the state. It also asks whether public procurement serves Nuevo León's citizens in ways that go beyond the traditional objectives of public procurement.

Complementary policy objectives refer to objectives that reach beyond the scope of a primary policy. Governments around the world are increasingly pursuing complementary policy objectives through public procurement. Aside from objectives like efficiency, effectiveness, transparency and others, public procurement can contribute to achieving more overarching goals. Many leaders know this, and are working to use public procurement to achieve ambitious, complementary objectives. These objectives typically include:

- support for small and medium enterprises
- support for innovation
- "greening", i.e., improving the impact of goods, services and public works on the environment
- improving conditions for marginalised or economically under-represented groups
- tackling other societal challenges (OECD, 2015[1]).

Often, public procurement that is conducted in a way that works towards complementary goals is called sustainable public procurement or strategic public procurement. This chapter uses both expressions interchangeably.

Overall, countries can reap the following the benefits from sustainable public procurement (Clement, Watt and Semple, 2016[2]):

- attainment of policy goals related to sustainability
- better value for money
- reputational benefits
- legal compliance;
- innovation and creative solutions to societal challenges.

This chapter covers three potential areas for action with regards to supporting complementary objectives through strategic public procurement. Officials in the state can begin by:

1. exploring the potential for sustainable public procurement in Nuevo León;
2. finding room for sustainable public procurement in existing frameworks, and utilising it by targeting everyday practices;
3. working towards a policy framework that will support sustainable public procurement.

3.1. Exploring the potential for sustainable public procurement in Nuevo León

Nuevo León could explore the benefits of sustainable public procurement to achieve complementary policy goals. Currently, there is little awareness of the secondary impacts public procurement can have. Furthermore, there is almost no consideration of these topics in the day-to-day procurement practices of the state.

By exploring complementary policy objectives, Nuevo León could expand the positive impacts of public procurement in a targeted way that is meaningful to the region's context. Several issues, such as support for SMEs, can be supported via public procurement.

The OECD describes the working mechanism of strategic public procurement as held in balance with the other goals of public procurement. In other words, complementary objectives must be properly balanced with the primary goals of public procurement. This relationship is described in the OECD Recommendation of the Council on Public Procurement below, in principle V. Overall, the OECD advocates for a three-step process:

1. Identify benefits of strategic public procurement and its limits (i.e., the specific balance of objectives in the individual country context);
2. Set a strategy to guide increased use of strategic public procurement, and define concrete measures that could be beneficial in the given context;
3. Monitor any activities, and adjust where necessary.

Box 3.1. OECD Recommendation of the Council on Public Procurement

The Council:

V. RECOMMENDS that Adherents recognise that any use of the public procurement system to pursue **secondary policy objectives** should be balanced against the primary procurement objective.

To this end, Adherents should:

i) Evaluate the use of public procurement as one method of pursuing secondary policy objectives in accordance with clear national priorities, balancing the potential benefits against the need to achieve value for money. Both the capacity of the procurement workforce to support secondary policy objectives and the burden associated with monitoring progress in promoting such objectives should be considered.

ii) Develop an appropriate strategy for the integration of secondary policy objectives in public procurement systems. For secondary policy objectives that will be supported by public procurement, appropriate planning, baseline analysis, risk assessment and target outcomes should be established as the basis for the development of action plans or guidelines for implementation.

iii) Employ appropriate impact assessment methodology to measure the effectiveness of procurement in achieving secondary policy objectives. The results of any use of the public procurement system to support secondary policy objectives should be measured according to appropriate milestones to provide policy makers with necessary information regarding the benefits and costs of such use. Effectiveness should be measured both at the level of individual procurements, and against policy objective target outcomes. Additionally, the aggregate effect of pursuing secondary policy objectives on the public procurement system should be periodically assessed to address potential objective overload.

Source: (OECD, 2015[1])

As stated in the OECD Recommendation of the Council on Public Procurement (and further detailed in the OECD checklist for its implementation), it is vital that states analyse the extent to which it would be beneficial for them to pursue complementary policy objectives through public procurement. The OECD checklist suggests the following measures (OECD, 2016[3]):

- establish what costs and benefits are concretely associated with the goals to be pursued
- identify which complementary objectives should be pursued by considering national priorities and the primary objectives of public procurement (delivering goods and services to support government policies in a timely, economical and efficient way)
- assess and manage impacts, as well as risks associated with pursuing complementary policy objectives, and hedge especially against the risk of "objective overload" (i.e., attempting to pursue so many complementary objectives that the resulting set of measures becomes unmanageable and inefficient)

- professionalise the public procurement workforce to enable them to handle this strategy

The following sections provide background information on the policy goals that are usually pursued as a part of strategic public procurement, and are relevant to public procurement in Nuevo León. In different policy areas, Nuevo León undertakes individual measures in support of aspects of sustainable development, but it does not appear to have formulated any efforts specifically on public procurement.

3.1.1. Supporting Small and Medium Enterprises

In many countries, SMEs account for a large share of employment and growth. In this context, countries endeavour to support SMEs. Public procurement represents one large source of demand for SME services. However, SMEs frequently face specific obstacles to participating in public procurement. For example, SMEs might lack capacity to bid for and deliver on large government contracts. At times, delayed payments deter SMEs from seeking government contracts due to cash flow constraints. SMEs often have less access to credit, which makes it more difficult to invest, grow or respond to larger orders (Bell and Tayler, 2016[4]) (European Commission, 2014[5]) (OECD, 2016[6]).

Good practices employed by countries to encourage SME participation in public procurement include (OECD, 2016[3]):

- laws, regulations and policies to encourage participation from SMEs in procurement
- removing barriers to SME access to public procurement through:
  - online dissemination and submission of bids
  - utilisation of lots
  - simplified administrative procedures for SMEs
- training and capacity building for SMEs, including online guidance, programmes and workshops, contact points and centralised advisory services
- preferential fees and financial incentives for SMEs (e.g. waiving or reducing fees, shortened payment deadlines)
- systems to monitor SME participation
- awareness raising among public procurers and SMEs.

Experience from Ireland shows how important it is to actively support SMEs in manoeuvring public administration to participate in public contracts (see Box 3.2).

Box 3.2. Secondary policy – the Go-2-Tender training programme for SMEs

Inter-Trade Ireland, an agency under the Department of Jobs Enterprise and Innovation in Ireland (DJEI), provides a number of services to business with the goal of enhancing growth opportunities, innovation and competitiveness. Among other tasks, it offers services targeted specifically at SMEs. These services aim to help SMEs compete in procurement markets.

Inter-Trade Ireland's flagship service in this area is the Go-2-Tender training programme. Go-2-Tender is a two-day practical tender workshop designed for an SME audience that covers key aspects of procurement. During the workshop, SMEs are given knowledge and taught practical skills regarding how to be successful at tendering. Practical skills training includes instruction on how to identify opportunities, how to make bid or no bid decisions and the drafting of successful tenders.

To participate, companies must meet a number of eligibility criteria, such as being classified as an SME, operating in the manufacturing and tradable services sectors, ability to demonstrate export potential, and other attributes. The workshops are conducted by experienced tender specialists, and give insight into the procurement practices of public sector bodies in Ireland. Guest speakers from central government procurement organisations are also invited. In addition to the plenary session, half a day of the workshop is dedicated to mentoring sessions, where participants can choose their topic of interest. Workshops are offered in various locations, and participation fees of EUR 100 apply. In 2016, seven seminars were held across the country. A similar number is foreseen for 2017. Participants can also apply for a follow-up workshop once they have concluded the first Go-2-tender seminar. Since the programme was introduced in 2007, over 900 companies have completed the workshop. These companies won procurement contracts worth EUR 69 million during this same period.

Inter-Trade Ireland also organises Meet the Buyer events, where SMEs have the opportunity to meet public sector buyers face to face. The agency also offers further assistance through FAQs, guides, videos and presentations, as well as dedicated events on emerging trends that impact the procurement environment for SMEs.

Source: Information provided by the Office of Government Procurement (OGP)

According to Nuevo León's state development plan, 99.4% of all companies in the state are SMEs (*micro, pequeñas y medianas empresas*, MIPYMES). These companies employ more than 1 million people (Gobierno del Estado de Nuevo León, 2016, p. 86[7]). In Mexico as a whole, almost 70% of jobs are located in SMEs. (OECD, 2017[8]) These figures illustrate the important role that SMEs have in Nuevo León and the country as a whole. The fact that Nuevo León's economy is one of the largest in Mexico further underscores this point. Nuevo León, in addition to Mexico's federal government, has taken measures in recent years to boost SMEs (Ciudadano,(n.d.)[9]) (OECD, 2017[8]).

Despite constituting such a large share of Nuevo León's economy, Nuevo León's public procurement system has some systemic obstacles that hinder SMEs from participating in public procurement. As reported by several stakeholders, one major issue relates to payments from the public administration in connection with public procurements. These payments are usually delayed. Suppliers reported that they sometimes wait for up to six months for payment after submitting an invoice. Following up on payments can be a cumbersome and time-intensive process, requiring frequent personal visits with the state authorities, repeated submission of documents, and the like. This can be problematic for smaller companies that cannot devote significant capacity to follow up. Smaller companies also suffer more heavily from untimely payments due to their overall lower cash flow. In Nuevo León, there have been instances of suppliers refusing to provide maintenance services to the government after not being paid. In addition, standard practice in procurement proceedings is to ask for a bond – which usually runs around 10% of the contract value. Stakeholders affirmed that this was a large burden for small companies.

Other obstacles for SMEs relate to the quite complex process for registration to bid and to submit documents for participating in a tender. According to Article 24 of the public procurement law, a new registration is necessary every year. Similarly, new, very comprehensive documents have to be submitted in person (and as a paper copy) with every tender. This is required of companies even if these have supplied the exact same goods or services before. While this practice has positive aspects, such as keeping information current, it creates a substantial burden for SMEs.

SMEs have some advantages in the area of public works in Nuevo León, however. The reason for this is that joint proposals are allowed and usually conducted in larger infrastructure projects in the state. Larger projects are usually delivered by consortiums. This allows SMEs to participate even in larger contracts. For public works, the public authorities usually choose local suppliers, given that they usually offer a lower price.

3.1.2. Green procurement

"Green" public procurement refers to "public purchasing of products and services which are less environmentally damaging when taking into account their whole life cycle" (OECD, 2015[10]). Countries increasingly recognise that their purchasing should be aligned with more general strategies to protect the environment, reduce carbon consumption, increase energy efficiency and maintain biodiversity.

Good practices employed by countries to encourage green public procurement include (OECD, 2016[3]):

- laws, regulations and policies in support of green public procurement
- plans for green public procurement with regards to the market (solutions on offer, capacity, etc.) and cost/benefit assessments
- use of environmental standards in technical specifications, such as materials, recycled content; production methods; allowing for submission of alternative solutions; exclusion criteria for non-compliance; etc.
- use of environmental standards in award criteria and contract performance clauses (weighted environmental criteria; eco-labels as a criterion; environmental management systems as criterion)
- systems to monitor green public procurement
- professionalization activities
- awareness raising.

In its State Development Plan, Nuevo León highlights several environment-related aims, including the improvement of air quality and meeting the energy demand in the state. To achieve these goals, Nuevo León will need to invest, for example, in public roads or renewable energy infrastructure ((Gobierno del Estado de Nuevo León, 2016, p. 176[7]).

These measures can be linked in meaningful ways to public procurement. However, as detailed below, the actual public procurement process in Nuevo León gives limited consideration to environmental concerns.

3.1.3. Procurement for innovation

Countries seek to support innovation because innovation triggers economic growth and creates employment. In their efforts to cultivate innovation, countries increasingly emphasise demand-side policies (i.e., creating a demand for innovative solutions) as opposed to supply-side policies (i.e., creating better conditions for innovation to materialise.) Public procurement is one of the most important tools countries have to create and implement demand-side policies (OECD, 2017$_{[11]}$).

Good practices employed by countries to encourage public procurement for innovation include (OECD, 2016$_{[3]}$):

- legal provisions or regulations to encourage inclusion of innovative firms in public procurement
- preferential treatment for innovative companies
    - specific support for innovative SMEs (including purchasing assurance schemes and framework contracts for certified products)
- flexibility in organising tendering processes with the aim of encouraging collaboration across borders or institutions in interdisciplinary projects
- flexibility in the required solution by focusing on addressing needs as opposed to purchasing specific products throughout the entire procurement process (beginning with the planning through to tender documents and contracting)
- incentives to conduct procurement for innovation
- systems to monitor the impact of innovation procurement
- professionalization activities to equip procurers with adequate technical knowledge to conduct procurement for innovation
- awareness raising on the part of procurers and potential suppliers.

Nuevo León allocates 1% of its state budget to support for innovation, science and research. According to the state development plan, a long-standing focus on creating a favourable environment for innovation has contributed to Nuevo León's high living standard, which in fact exceeds the Mexican average (Gobierno del Estado de Nuevo León, 2016, p. 85$_{[7]}$).

In this context of innovation-friendly policies, public procurement could further boost innovation. Currently, Nuevo León's administration does not use public procurement for innovation.

3.2. Fully utilise the existing room in the state's legal and regulatory framework for sustainable public procurement by targeting every day practices

Nuevo León could expand its practical implementation of strategic public procurement in order to achieve complementary policy objectives. At present, Nuevo León's legal and regulatory framework leaves room for the possibility of pursuing complementary policy objectives through public procurement. That said, there is little evidence that procurers are taking advantage of this opportunity. For example, no state procurement processes take into account environmental objectives.

By using the full possibilities of the law to incorporate sustainability into procurement processes, Nuevo León could support the attainment of certain policy goals. This would be true, for example, for policy objectives that are delineated in the State Development Plan. Targeted measures could promote more consideration of complementary policy objectives on a case-by-case basis. In so doing, Nuevo León could begin slowly, first using existing potential without overwhelming the government's limited capacity. At a later stage, officials can begin preparations for an overarching strategy for sustainable public procurement.

3.2.1. Nuevo León's policy framework for complementary policy objectives

An indispensable prerequisite for strategic public procurement is a legal and regulatory framework that allows for incorporating complementary policy objectives. In providing this legal flexibility, countries pursue different avenues. While some countries establish the legal basis for strategic public procurement by structuring the general public procurement law accordingly, other countries adopt specific laws to address one or several complementary objectives. These laws explicitly allow public procurement procedures to make consideration of complementary policy objectives a part of the process. They also regulate public procurement with regards to these objectives in detail.

There is no specific legal, regulatory or other policy guidance in Nuevo León with regards to achieving complementary policy objectives through public procurement. However, several elements of the policy environment speak to the issue of balance in public procurement.

According to the Law for Acquisitions, Leasing, and Services of the Public Sector (Ley de Adquisiciones, Arrendamientos y Servicios del Sector Público, LAASP), the Ministry of the Economy sets the guidelines for government support of SMEs (Article 8). Article 14 grants the government the right to give suppliers with certain characteristics preference. Examples of these characteristics include companies that employ disabled people, companies that have implemented measures to promote gender equality or SMEs that have a certificate from the Instituto Mexicano de la Propiedad Industrial.

Article 39 of the Law for Acquisitions, Leasing, and Procurement of Services for the State of Nuevo León (Ley de Adquisiciones, Arrendamientos y Contratación de Servicios de Nuevo León, LAASNL) describes the selection criteria to be followed when selecting the winning bidder in a public procurement process. Aside from aspects of timeliness, costs, qualifications and work plans or methodology, the legal specifications allow for flexibility in applying award criteria. This flexibility enables Nuevo León to make choices that could produce limited strategic procurement. The flexibility applies with regards to two aspects of the law among many. First, the law allows the state to consider the costs of the entire life cycle of a product when making procurement decisions. Second, the law allows the state to specify environmental criteria, where applicable.

These rules can provide a basis for expanding strategic use of public procurement in Nuevo León. Currently, procurers in the state make little use of this legal flexibility. This appears to be related to challenges resulting from the need to quantify environmental criteria, as well as the priority given to the lowest price criteria. Considerations of price seem to be paramount in awarding tenders; units are advised to award contracts to bidders that comply with the specifications and offer the lowest price. However, a points and percentage system is available for contracting authorities to use in complex or specialised cases.

Nuevo León's points and percentage system could provide a basis for expanding the use of complementary policy objectives. In this case, companies fulfilling certain preferred criteria related to complementary policy objectives would receive more points than those that do not. In order to apply a points and percentage system, contracting authorities would require the authorisation of a higher-ranking entity. Authorisation to use points or weighting of award criteria can be granted by one of the following entities in Nuevo León (depending on the governance level at which the public procurement takes place):

- the Secretary of Finance and General Treasury of the State (Secretario de Finanzas y Tesorero General del Estado);
- the Judiciary Council or the Plenum of the Superior Court of Justice (Consejo de la Judicatura / Pleno del Tribunal Superior de Justicia)
- the Committee for Coordination and Internal Directives (Comisión de Coordinación y Régimen Interno)
- the Municipal Council;
- the supreme organ of any institution.

In addition, the LAASNL contains a provision for procurement cases in which two bidders have equally good proposals. In the case of a draw, contracting authorities can give the bid that is associated with the best environmental criteria preference. If, subsequently, there is still a draw, the bid with the best integration of micro, small and medium enterprises wins. The State Treasury provides guidelines granting support to SMEs.

According to interviews with different stakeholders, officials in Nuevo León have never taken advantage of the room left in the state's legal framework for the purposes of addressing complementary policy objectives. Procurers reported that even if they wanted to include environmental criteria into their procedures, they could not for a few reasons. First, these criteria would drive up prices. Second, cheaper bids still meet the technical specifications set out in the calls for tender. Finally, calls for tenders of larger purchases (which can be restricted via environmental criteria, under the law) have not used environmental criteria due to the budget pressures. Some contracting authorities have considered introducing life cycle costing, but have not yet done so.

While procurers of state-funded projects have not introduced measures to align public procurement with complementary policy objectives, they have done so for federally funded projects. For example, parastatal entities in Nuevo León reported that they had incorporated complementary policy objectives, given that there was a requirement to do so for federal funds. These experiences of applying complementary policy objectives to procurement could be translated to projects conducted using state funds.

It is unclear whether the requirement for approval from a higher-ranking authority represents an obstacle to such measures. That said, the application of a points and percentage system could be facilitated by removing the need for approval, or by simplifying it.

3.2.2. Boosting complementary policy objectives with targeted measures

Countries use different avenues to pursue complementary policy objectives through public procurement. Aside from overarching strategies that can guide implementation of strategic public procurement, it is necessary to consider the complementary policy objectives at hand. Be it green procurement, support for SMEs or innovation procurement, the objective should be considered at all stages of the procurement cycle.

This section serves to introduce a selected set of measures that promise good results in Nuevo León's specific context, without an excessive burden to the public procurement system.

Opportunities for strengthening strategic public procurement as a part of concrete public procurement processes can be showcased by dividing the procurement process into the following stages (Clement, Watt and Semple, 2016[2]):

1. Pre-procurement;
2. Deciding on the procurement procedure;
3. Defining the subject of the contract (subject matter);
4. Selection and exclusion of bidders;
5. Technical specifications;
6. Award criteria;
7. Contract management;

Nuevo León could add considerations of complementary policy objectives to the deliberations that take place at each of these stages. These considerations could be targeted to the specific priorities of certain complementary objectives. They could also be balanced against any capacity constraints or concerns regarding economic efficiency. Based on the existing legal and regulatory framework, adding considerations of complementary policy objectives at the stages listed below could be particularly impactful. The reasons for this are 1) such efforts would be easily accomplished at these stages; or 2) such efforts would build on existing measures (Clement, Watt and Semple, 2016[2]) (OECD, 2016[3]):

3.2.3. Pre-procurement

Currently, procurers in Nuevo León's Central Purchasing Body (UCC) conduct some market research, but it is very limited. Knowledge of the market among procurers is low. Market research plays an important role particularly in the pre-procurement or planning phase. Skilfully handling this phase is extraordinarily important to ensuring implementation of complementary policy objectives. Therefore, a larger emphasis should be placed on developing this phase. Several concrete measures can be beneficial ((Clement, Watt and Semple, 2016[2]) (OECD, 2016[3]):

- Raise awareness of the impact of the planning stage with the officers conducting procurement, and with officers in the requesting unit.
- Advocate that these officers play a stronger role in the central purchasing unit, and task them with working towards complementary policy objectives. Currently, officials do not seem to be aware of the fact that incorporating complementary objectives into the planning phase is an option.
- Provide training and guidance materials on how to conduct needs analyses and how to include complementary policy objectives, such as environmental concerns, into these analyses. Currently, the requiring unit does not seem to work with a needs definition, but rather with requests of specific products. An alternative could be that the requiring unit describes needs, and leaves the matching with specific products to the bidders.

3.2.4. Technical specifications

In Nuevo León, technical specifications are usually determined by the requesting unit, with little influence from the UCC. However, a smart definition of technical specifications represents one of the most important tools for engaging in procurement that is not only beneficial from a needs and price perspective, but also from a complementary policy objectives perspective. If the UCC defined technical specifications in a way that encouraged environmentally friendly solutions, it could steer its requesting units towards choices that would accomplish complementary policy objectives. Box 3.3 provides an example of how environmental standards are considered in public procurement in Hungary.

With regards to technical specifications, Nuevo León could implement the following concrete measures (Clement, Watt and Semple, 2016[2]) (OECD, 2016[3]):

- Train and provide guidance for procurers to include technical specifications that make reference to performance requirements and technical standards or certifications that take complementary policy objectives into account. For example, a technical specification could include a requirement that a product meet a certain environmental standard.
- Raise awareness among requesting units regarding the consideration of these performance requirements and standards.

Box 3.3. Hungary: Including green standards into technical specifications

Context

Hungary's Public Procurement Supply Directorate (PPSD) is an autonomous central purchasing body. The PPSD conducts procurement procedures for several government bodies and institutions. Products and services in the PPSD's portfolio include: communication services and tools, IT systems and services, office technology and services, office furniture, stationary products and paper, vehicles, fuels, travel arrangements, and electronic public procurement services and an electronic auction service.

The PPSD applies green criteria in centralised public procurement procedures, and, where possible, increases the number of environmentally friendly products. The PPSD applies environmental requirements to its procedures and contracts in the following ways: in defining the subject matter, in the technical specifications, in the award criteria and in the contract terms.

Objectives

- increase the use of green criteria in public procurement procedures
- ensure appropriate variety and good prices in cases of environmentally friendly products
- increase the proportion of environmentally friendly products purchased by the PPSD (currently 10% for paper products)
- promote environmental thinking and a change of attitude by means of communication.

Implementation

The green criteria applied by PPSD in the procurement procedures are:

- Paper and stationary products: Environmentally friendly products (envelopes, folders and other paper products for office purposes); and adherence to an environmental management standard (ISO 14001). The technical specifications included environmental labels (FSC, NordicSwan, Blue Angel), ecolabels and recycling.
- IT: EU standards; energy consumption (standby and switched off mode); noise level; waste management (delivery, recycling, extermination); remanufactured products.
- Fuel: EU standards and environmental and sustainability criteria; alternative fuels (biodiesel, bioethanol).

The PPSD publishes information on its website (www.kozbeszerzes.gov.hu) regarding the types of available products it buys and their environmentally friendly features. Contracts and all other documents related to centralised public procurement procedures are also available on this website in PDF format or in databases. The PPSD also conducts presentations and briefings on available green products.

Key lessons:

- The public procurement market is a strategic tool for creating environmentally friendly attitudes, and for promoting environmentally friendly products.
- In order to achieve targets, it is important that environmental requirements work together with economic interests (like cost efficiency and favourable tender prices).
- It is vital that authorities take into consideration products' effects on each other (for instance, the compatibility of the printer and the paper or the fuel and the motor vehicle).
- It is important to define the procurement methods aiming to promote groups of products.
- Raising awareness regarding available green products is an essential factor of success

Source: (OECD, 2015[10])

3.2.5. Award criteria

Even when contracts are not awarded directly, the winner of a tendering process is often chosen based on price-only criteria. Better results can be achieved when officials do the following: 1) choose the winning bidder from a group of bidders; 2) evaluate bids using award criteria that reflect complementary policy objectives. In addition, it is beneficial to expand the use of life cycle costs on a case-by-case basis. Box 3.4 provides an example of how procurers in the Netherlands quantify environmental performance to inform award decisions.

In order to align its awards criteria with complementary policy objectives, Nuevo León could implement the following measures (Clement, Watt and Semple, 2016[2]) (OECD, 2016[3]):

- Raise awareness among procurers and requiring units that direct awards should be a strict exception and tendering the normal case.
- Devise guidance by building on the points and percentages system and on the model of the most economically advantageous tender (MEAT) to select bidders and award points according to complementary policy objectives. For example, a bidder whose product offers a better environmental performance than another could receive more points.
- Raise awareness and provide training on how to implement the points and percentages system to select bidders that comply with secondary policy objectives, such as environmental criteria or lower life cycle costs.
- Provide awards to honour outstanding procurement processes. These awards should honour procurement that used smart award criteria and led to efficient outcomes in terms of both price and complementary objectives.

Different avenues exist in Nuevo León to implement these mechanisms. Some may require legal changes; others can build on existing rules, using additional guidance or training.

Box 3.4. Netherlands: Quantifying complementary policy objectives

Rijkswaterstaat (the Department of Public Works of the Ministry of Infrastructure and the Environment, RWS) developed a methodology for infrastructure projects whereby the functional specification of the tender, together with the quality input from the client, ensured an innovative and high-quality solution. Under this system, the tenderer is also asked to respond to specific quality criteria. The RWS uses the most economically advantageous tender methodology (MEAT), and includes specific sustainability criteria.

The RWS has decided to focus on two criteria when assessing the sustainability attributes of offers, work processes and associated products: CO2 emissions and environmental impact. Two instruments have been developed to measure these attributes: the CO2 performance ladder and "DuboCalc". The CO2 performance ladder is a certification system which allows the tenderer to show the measures it will take to limit CO2 emissions within its company and in its projects, as well as elsewhere in the supply chain. DuboCalc is a life-cycle analysis (LCA) based tool that calculates the sustainability value of a specific design based on the materials to be used. Bidders use DuboCalc to compare different design options for their submissions. The DuboCalc score of the preferred design is submitted with the tender price.

CO2 performance ladder

A tenderer can submit a CO2 performance ladder certificate with its tender submission. The certificate obliges the tenderer to comply with a certain CO2 reduction target according to its method of execution and working processes. Holders of the certificate have their submission price reduced by a value proportional to the effort made to reduce CO2 emissions. The CO2 performance ladder certificate can be provided as evidence at the tender submission stage, but this is not compulsory as long as the certificate is provided within one year of signing the contract.

DuboCalc

Based on an analysis of the entire life cycle, DuboCalc calculates all embedded environmental impacts of material use, from raw material extraction and production up to and including demolition and recycling (the entire life cycle). The ECI value is used in the tendering procedure as follows: the contracting authority provides the tenderer with all the functional requirements and the latest version of the DuboCalc programme. The tenderer designs the infrastructure and calculates the price and ECI value of its product. The ECI value is transformed into a monetary value according to a formula that is prescribed by the tenderer (the ECI value and monetary value are inversely related, and there is a minimum and a maximum for both values). These two prices are offered to the contracting authority. The contracting authority selects the tenderer that has the lowest combined price and ECI value.

Source: (OECD, 2014[12])

3.3. Work towards a supportive framework for sustainable public procurement

Nuevo León's government can translate its strategic priorities for sustainable development to the area of public procurement. Currently, day-to-day procurement practices do not seem to connect to the strategic goals set out in Nuevo León's State Development Plan or its Strategic Plan (Plan Estrategico). As there are no regulations or procedures requiring the consideration of complementary policy objectives, procurers do not consider them – even though they could, legally.

While setting a strategy for strategic procurement requires a considerable amount of resources and knowledge, Nuevo León could begin by working towards providing a better framework and overarching direction for its public procurement function. The state could set priorities for certain procurement areas or sectors. Furthermore, it could provide guidance on how public procurement can contribute to the attainment of the goals delineated by the state's strategic development plan and strategic plan.

3.3.1. Exploring the benefits of a strategy for strategic public procurement

By formulating a strategy, Nuevo León can support the implementation of sustainable public procurement that takes into account complementary policy objectives. Such a strategy can help the state realise a long-term vision for sustainable public procurement with concrete targets. These targets could include responsibilities that are clearly attributed and mechanisms to ensure that the system continuously improves and learns from its own failures and successes (Clement, Watt and Semple, 2016[2]).

Elements of a strategy and of an enabling environment include the following (OECD, 2016[3]):

- legal and regulatory framework that supports the use of complementary policy objectives and ensures that these rules are in line with general provisions for public procurement
- a systematic review of related policies, priorities and goals in the state
- political commitment
- consultation with relevant stakeholders to inform the strategy
- planning based on targets, milestones, expected outcomes and risk assessments
- clear attribution of responsibilities
- dissemination activities
- training
- financial resources
- a monitoring framework.

To bolster this strategy, Nuevo León should develop support documents, such as guidelines or manuals, knowledge management systems and guidance for evaluation. In addition, concrete activities for each complementary goal are paramount to ensuring a successful implementation of a strategy (OECD, 2016[3]). When an overarching strategy becomes too ambitious, opting for sectoral plans or priority setting in defined policy areas can be an alternative. For example, many countries focus on the following key sectors, and set specific targets:

1. construction;
2. ICT;
3. cleaning;
4. food and catering;
5. vehicles,
6. electricity.

Several countries have pioneered strategies for sustainable public procurement in different ways. In addition to other examples in this chapter, Box 3.6 provides an illustration of how a strategy can provide benefits – even if it is targeting only a specific part of a public procurement system (in this case the procurement of one state-owned enterprise in Austria.) On the question of how to successfully involve civil society in creating a strategy for sustainable public procurement, Ireland provides a good model (see Box 3.5).

Box 3.5. Secondary objectives – involvement of civil society in policy development

The Irish government has recognised that the public procurement market can offer small to medium sized enterprises significant business opportunities. In many respects, SMEs are better suited to government contracts as they (by their nature) have flexibility and logistical capability that larger companies do not. Often, SMEs are geographically closest to the place where there service is needed.

The following are examples of the collaborative approach Ireland has taken to assist SMEs:

- The Office of Government Procurement (OGP) established and facilitates quarterly meetings of the SME Advisory Group, chaired by the Minister of State at the Department of Finance or the Minister of Public Expenditure and Reform, so that the voice of Irish SMEs can be heard at the highest level. The OGP engages representatives of the industry, (civil society bodies like the Irish SME Association, Irish business association Ibec, SFA Small Firms Association, Construction Industry Federation, and Chambers Ireland) through the SME Advisory Group. There, all groups can exchange views and identify policy initiatives. Other business-focused public bodies that often attend these meeting include: the Competition and Consumer Protection Agency, Enterprise Ireland, InterTradeIreland and the Department of Jobs, Enterprise and Innovation.
- Recently, the SME Advisory Group created a communications strategy subgroup with the aim of developing a more consolidated and consistent approach to informing SMEs of public procurement opportunities and developments. The aims of this group are to: encourage potential suppliers to build their awareness, understanding and ultimately skills in public tendering; to understand the role respective bodies play in the communications strategy; and to work in partnership with industry representative bodies to considerably improve understanding and awareness of public procurement in the target supplier community. The strategy that was agreed upon by this group includes producing a series of informative YouTube videos explaining specific public procurement topics, the introduction of industry targeted and regional informative breakfast briefing events, and more proactive engagement from industry in promoting and planning events.
- All good organisations must examine the relevance of the services they are providing. In this regard, the OGP has commissioned an external review of the Tender Advisory Service (TAS) model in 2017. The TAS service acts as an impartial broker between suppliers and contracting authorities during a tender process. In so doing, it improves communications and engender a consistent approach to how procurement processes are carried out across the public service. Finally, the SME Advisory Group will review any recommendations arising from the forthcoming external review of TAS before they are implemented.

Analyses show that this approach is working. 95% of procurement expenditure in Ireland goes to firms based in Ireland. The majority of spending is with the SME sector. 68% of OGP framework members are SMEs and 63% of these frameworks have multiple lots.

Source: Information provided by Office of Government Procurement (OGP)

Box 3.6. Austria: Example of an organisational strategy for sustainable procurement (ÖBB Infrastruktur AG)

Context

In 2008, the management board of ÖBB Infrastruktur AG (ÖBB Infra), the Austrian state-owned railways infrastructure company, decided to implement an environmental management system. The system was certified according to ISO 14001, and was established as a major pillar for the sustainable development of the company. A co-ordinator was nominated in July 2009 to deal with sustainability on a corporate scale. Notably, the co-ordinator was tasked with developing guidance on sustainable procurement, as procurement was identified as one of the key areas related to the sustainability performance of the company. ÖBB Infra's annual investment expenditure amounts up to EUR 2 billion (approximately 1% of Austrian gross domestic product). Management decided that procurement should be an important driver of the development of sustainable economic operations throughout the company, so as to reduce the consumption of energy and resources.

Objectives

ÖBB Infra's sustainable procurement strategy aims at raising procurement officers' awareness of the integration of socio-economic criteria into the procurement process. The strategy takes a step by step approach in order to contribute to the following tasks:

- reducing the consumption of resources, utilities and energy
- avoiding waste and pollutant emissions
- increasing quality
- protecting biodiversity
- reducing internal and external environmental costs (e.g. costs for disposal or transport)
- increasing the transparency and plausibility of costs
- fostering innovation
- fair working conditions and income
- creating "green jobs"
- winning suppliers as strategic partners.

The strategy builds on the availability of information about sustainability criteria. It also takes into account internal guidance on specific opportunities, as well as marketing the idea to stakeholders.

Implementation process

A guidance note on sustainable procurement was published in 2011. It contains a short description of the general background of sustainable procurement concepts and the reasons for them, sums up initiatives and strategies in the field, points at the legal requirements, and, most importantly, lists existing national and international eco-labels and their specific relevance for ÖBB Infra (and other infrastructure businesses) and includes an evaluation scheme.

Sustainable procurement is now an integral part of internal training programmes at the company. For example, ÖBB Infra has organised a workshop with external experts for procurement officers, and even offers "rail ecology" seminars. The company promotes practical exercises as a way to gain practical experience, especially in the areas of construction materials and tension weights.

Challenges and risks

A common phenomenon in public procurement is the lack of resources in terms of staff to thoroughly monitor and evaluate the measures taken. In the field of construction materials, the establishment of technical standards is particularly complex and requires the adaptation of contract specifications. This increases the workload for procurement officers. It is therefore necessary to make positive effects visible through continuous dialogue and conversations about best practices. It is also important to develop standardised methods to calculate the total costs of ownership, as they are often neglected in practice.

Key lessons

The success of a project requires the involvement and constant collaboration of all essential persons at all stages. For this particular project, co-operation with recognised organisations (the Austrian Institute for Building Biology and Procurement Service) and suppliers was especially fruitful. This project illuminated several key findings. One was that, as long as external costs and the costs-by-cause principle are not integrated into economic assessments on an obligatory basis, procurement by the lowest costs principle will dominate in practice. In this regard, precise legal requirements could be effective in other cases to promote "green" objectives and ensure that sustainable procurement becomes a standard, rather than an exceptional procurement method. Practice also shows that it is easier and more effective to integrate socio-economic criteria early in the procurement procedure, in the description of the subject of the contract and technical specifications.

Source: For further information see: www.oebb.at/infrastruktur/de/5_0_fuer_Generationen/5_2_Verantwortung_Umwelt/index.jsp (OECD, 2015[10])

3.3.2. Building on Nuevo León's State Development Plan

Aside from the general aspects in Nuevo León's public procurement law, Nuevo León's State Development Plan and Strategic Plan contain references to complementary policy objectives. However, these plans do not address the role public procurement can play in achieving complementary policy goals.

The Development Plan contains three chapters that relate to the following complementary policy objectives:

1. an inclusive economy;
2. human and social development;
3. sustainable development.

A recent review by the comptroller of Nuevo León (Informe de Recomendaciones del "Programa de coordinación permanente en materia de transparencia, eficiencia y calidad en el servicio público de las Adquisiciones, Arrendamientos y Contratación de Servicios del estado") encouraged contracting authorities to consider environmental and social concerns in their definitions of needs. Furthermore, the review recommended that contracting authorities focus on finding more energy efficient solutions, and that they give preference to solutions that produce less waste, water consumption and CO2 emissions (Contraloría y Transparencia Gubernamental, Gobierno del Estado, 2016, p. 22[13]) In addition, the comptroller emphasised the potential negative effects of guarantees on SMEs. The comptroller's report encourages contracting authorities to consider that they might discourage SMEs from participating in public procurement when they cannot comply with requirements for guarantees.

Nuevo León's State Development Plan did not seem to have exerted a perceptible influence on the day-to-day activities of procurers in the state. It would be crucial that officials follow up on individual recommendations, while also reviewing how the overarching goals are linked to public procurement. As a second step, officials should implement measures to support complementary policy objectives that ensure that public procurement processes are aligned accordingly. In addition, it could be worthwhile to explore to what extend the different approaches could be coordinated at a central level, for example by the Central Purchasing Body.

The following aspects could be part of a structured approach or strategy, be it overarching or sectorial (OECD, 2016[3]):

- attribute responsibility to one entity, instead of dispersed institutions that undertake individual activities
- define the objectives, justification and milestones in using public procurement to achieve complementary policy objectives in a centrally accessible strategy document
- develop practical guidance for public procurers in decentralised contracting authorities to facilitate implementation
- raise awareness of this issue among relevant stakeholders, particularly public procurement officials, to achieve a more strategic approach to public procurement
- devote sufficient resources
- develop and implement a methodology to monitor efforts and measure impact of activities related to public procurement and complementary policy objectives.

3.4. Proposals for action

Nuevo León has several overarching plans that speak to complementary policy objectives. The government aims to increase sustainability, spur inclusive growth and contribute to human and social development. In addition, Nuevo León's public procurement rules provide some flexibility with regards to using procurement methods that favour complementary objectives. However, limited coordinated activities have been undertaken with regards to public procurement.

3.4.1. Aligning public procurement with individual activities

Nuevo León could implement the following measures to promote strategic public procurement:

- Develop public procurement strategies that support policy goals such as environmental and sustainability objectives, as well as efforts to supports SMEs.
- Explore how existing public procurement laws, rules and guidance can be aligned with these existing policy goals, and vice versa, such as the specifications in

Article 39 of LAASNL, and consider changes to this article to facilitate the utilisation of procurement methods that allow for strategic procurement.

- Introduce a strategic, overarching policy framework for public procurement.
- Explore to what extend the different approaches are coordinated at a central level, for example by the Central Purchasing Body.
- In the long run, adapt rules and strategies that support a comprehensive policy framework specifically for public procurement. In addition, officials in Nuevo León should explore to what extent a public procurement strategy could translate the policy goals of overarching plans (like the State Development Plan) into concrete actions in the area of public procurement.

Nuevo León could galvanize political leadership in support of employing public procurement to achieve overarching policy objectives. Such efforts could, in turn:

- Win political leadership for strategic public procurement.
- Communicate the importance of public procurement to achieving the goals set out by the State Development Plan.

References

Bell, S. and Y. Tayler (2016), *Government procurement – a path to SME growth?*, http://blogs.worldbank.org/psd/government-procurement-path-sme-growth (accessed on 19 June 2017). [4]

Ciudadano, N.((n.d.)), *Apoyo para fortalecer comercialmente los productos de las Micro,Pequeñas y Medianas Empresas*, http://www.nl.gob.mx/servicios/programa-de-apoyo-al-fortalecimiento-de-las-mipymes (accessed on 19 June 2017). [9]

Clement, S., J. Watt and A. Semple (2016), *A Guide to Implementing Sustainable Procurement The Procura+ Manual*, ICLEI – Local Governments for Sustainability, European Secretariat, http://www.procuraplus.org/fileadmin/user_upload/Manual/Procuraplus_Manual_Third_Edition.pdf. [2]

Contraloría y Transparencia Gubernamental, Gobierno del Estado, N. (2016), *Informe de recomendaciones del Programa de coordinación permanente en materia público de las adquisiciones, arrendamientos y contratación de servicios del estado.* [13]

European Commission (2014), *Public Procurement as a Driver of Innovation in SMEs and Public Services*, http://www.ecpar.org/files/public-procurement-driver-of-innovation.pdf. [5]

Gobierno del Estado de Nuevo León (2016), *Plan Estatal de Desarrollo 2016-2021*, Gobierno del Estado de Nuevo León, Monterrey, http://www.nl.gob.mx/sites/default/files/30jun_pednl2016-2021.pdf. [7]

OECD (2014), "Smart procurement: Best practices for green procurement", OECD, Paris, http://www.oecd.org/gov/ethics/best-practices-for-green-procurement.htm. [12]

OECD (2015), *OECD Recommendation of the Council on Public Procurement*, http://www.oecd.org/gov/ethics/OECD-Recommendation-on-Public-Procurement.pdf. [1]

OECD (2015), *Going Green. Best Practices for Sustainable Procurement.* [10]

OECD (2016), *Checklist for Supporting the Implementation of OECD Recommendation of the Council on Public Procurement*, www.oecd.org/governance/procurement/toolbox/search/Checklist%2004%20Balance.pdf. [3]

OECD (2016), *Financing SMEs and Entrepreneurs 2016: An OECD Scoreboard*, OECD Publishing, Paris, http://dx.doi.org/10.1787/fin_sme_ent-2016-en. [6]

OECD (2017), *OECD Economic Surveys: Mexico 2017*, OECD Publishing, Paris, http://dx.doi.org/10.1787/eco_surveys-mex-2017-en. [8]

OECD (2017), *Public Procurement for Innovation: Good Practices and Strategies*, OECD Publishing, Paris, http://dx.doi.org/10.1787/9789264265820-en. [11]

Chapter 4. Enhancing professionalisation and capacity of the public procurement workforce in Nuevo León

This chapter focuses on Nuevo León's public procurement workforce – that is, the public officials that conduct procurement processes day-to-day. The chapter analyses two areas: First, the chapter evaluates the overarching strategy to increase the capacity of public procurement workers in Nuevo León. Second, the chapter provides insights into how a system of merit-based career progression could help official's better handle evolving challenges. Furthermore, this chapter assesses how general rules for Nuevo León's public service sector have been adapted to a public procurement context, as well as to what extent public procurement is considered a profession in Nuevo León. Finally, the chapter identifies mechanisms Nuevo León could introduce to ensure continuous professionalization of public procurement.

This chapter analyses the capacity of public officials conducting public procurement processes in Nuevo León to do their jobs as defined by law and state regulations. In order for public procurement laws and regulations to take full effect, public procurement officials have to possess necessary skills. In addition, a sufficient number of procurement officials need to be available to handle the number of public procurement processes in Nuevo León.

Good public procurement cannot be realised without knowledgeable and skilled workers. Equipping individual public procurement officials with higher level skills and knowledge can support improvements in other areas. For example, in order for public procurement in Nuevo León to reach its full potential as a strategic function, the state will need highly skilled officials to manage its programmes. Specialised knowledge of all phases of the public procurement cycle is key. All tasks should be executed with skill.

Countries around the world are increasingly striving to hire and train more professional public procurers as they encounter similar challenges (OECD,(n.d.)[1]):

- Public procurement is evolving from an administrative to a strategic function.
- Public procurement rules are complex.
- Public procurement and the public procurement workforce are multidisciplinary.
- Public procurer is not always considered a profession.

Several tried and tested approaches exist to tackle these challenges. Based on these good practices, this chapter proposes two major areas for action:

1. establish a strategic framework for the professional procurement workforce in Nuevo León;
2. establish a system for merit-based career progression for public procurers that are fit to handle evolving challenges.

4.1. Establishing a strategic framework for a professional procurement workforce in Nuevo León

Nuevo León could create and cultivate a public procurement function that is regarded as a profession and cease seeing it as an exclusively administrative function. The state can accomplish this by equipping procurers with the adequate capacity both in terms of skills and number of procurement officials in the system to an adequate level. In so doing, the state will be better positioned to conduct efficient and effective public procurement. Currently, Nuevo León's procurement workforce seems to lack capacity both in terms of numbers and skills. There is no reliable framework for developing the capacity of public procurers, or for conducting training in a strategic and structured manner.

By designing and implementing a framework to develop the capacity of Nuevo León's workforce, the state government could reap the full potential of its purchasers. The framework could consist of a strategy for capacity building and competency-based role descriptions. By developing and conducting systematic capacity-building activities, targeted to the specific needs of Nuevo León's public procurers, the government could increase the efficiency of its purchasers.

4.1.1. Towards professional public procurers

The quality of public procurement is highly dependent on the competencies of the individual procurer. In day-to-day procurement processes, it is the desk officer that takes the crucial decisions that make the difference between effective and efficient procurements and wasteful ones. At the same time, while smaller, less complex purchases require little specialised skill, complex procurement cases can only be negotiated beneficially for the public if the procurer handling the case has the professional knowledge to do so.

Not surprisingly, public procurement is increasingly recognised as a profession in itself. Several international bodies have developed guidance to define and promote what constitutes a professional public procurer. An example from the UK (see Box 4.1 below) illustrates this push of countries to increasingly recognise public procurement as a profession.

Box 4.1. Building a community of procurement professionals in the UK's Government Procurement Service

The Government Procurement Service (GPS) has defined a strategy to professionalize procurement in the government. Though the GPS does not certify procurement professionals, it intends to build a "community of procurement professionals" distinguished by core competencies. These competencies include an understanding of commercial issues, such as profits, margins, shareholders, cost models, total costs of acquisitions and whole-life costs, as well as knowledge and understanding of procurement and contract law.

Procurement professionals are encouraged to engage in professional development on a continuous basis. Professionalizing the GPS helps raise the profile of procurement as a profession. It also presents procurement as an attractive career option. The UK has worked to increase capacity in the profession via entry schemes, and by creating skills frameworks to help raise standards. All of these efforts support the development of skills and capability.

Source: (OECD, 2013[16])

The OECD Recommendation of the Council on Public Procurement (OECD, 2015[2]) considers three aspects of public procurement when measuring the capacity of a procurement workforce (see also Box 4.2):

- high professional standards for knowledge, practical implementation and integrity
- attractive, competitive and merit-based career options specifically for public procurement officials
- collaborative approaches with knowledge centres.

Box 4.2. OECD Recommendation of the Council on Public Procurement

The Council:

RECOMMENDS that Adherents develop a procurement workforce with the *capacity* to continually deliver value for money efficiently and effectively.

To this end, Adherents should:

i) Ensure that procurement officials meet high professional standards for knowledge, practical implementation and integrity by providing a dedicated and regularly updated set of tools, for example, sufficient staff in terms of numbers and skills, recognition of public procurement as a specific profession, certification and regular trainings, integrity standards for public procurement officials and the existence of a unit or team analysing public procurement information and monitoring the performance of the public procurement system.

ii) Provide attractive, competitive and merit-based career options for procurement officials, through the provision of clear means of advancement, protection from political interference in the procurement process and the promotion of national and international good practices in career development to enhance the performance of the procurement workforce.

iii) Promote collaborative approaches with knowledge centres such as universities, think tanks or policy centres to improve skills and competences of the procurement workforce. The expertise and pedagogical experience of knowledge centres should be enlisted as a valuable means of expanding procurement knowledge and upholding a two-way channel between theory and practice, capable of boosting application of innovation to public procurement systems.

Source: (OECD, 2015[2])

The OECD Methodology for Assessing Procurement Systems (MAPS)[1] (OECD,(n.d.)[3]) includes an indicator regarding a public procurement system's ability to "develop and improve" (Indicator 8.) This indicator includes references to a system's ability to provide training, advice and assistance with regards to public procurement. It also includes a sub-indicator that calls for procurement to be considered a profession. The sub-indicator includes assessment criteria that require a country to have:

- a recognition of procurement as a specialised function as described by a diversified competency framework
- competitive appointments and promotions
- evaluation of staff performance and adequate promotion.

A supplementary MAPS module (currently under development) spells out elements of approaches to a comprehensive professionalization approach for public procurement.

These more overarching concepts must be realised through concrete measures. International best practices usually recommend the following elements of a system to promote public procurement capacity building (see for example (OECD,(n.d.)[4])).

- strategies to outline capacity building and professionalization activities, supported by a concrete action plan that outlines steps towards implementation

- tools to define and track roles and associated knowledge or skills, such as competency frameworks, job profiles and certification systems
- clear responsibilities (i.e. who is in charge of capacity building with regards to public procurement specifically)
- tools and activities to increase the knowledge or skills of the public procurement workforce (e.g. training)
- incentives (i.e. the definition of a clear career trajectory combined with attractive and merit-based remuneration and progression)
- analytical systems to identify needs and monitor impact
- adequate financial resources for capacity-building activities
- advisory services or helpdesks
- exchanges with knowledge centres outside of public procurement institutions.

Many of these measures have been combined into a well-rounded overarching strategy that guides New Zealand's efforts to enhance the capacity of its public procurement workforce (see Box 4.3). Box 4.4 details an example from Ireland, where template documents have improved the quality of tender documents.

Box 4.3. Key initiatives to professionalize and empower the public procurement workforce in New Zealand

Key initiatives New Zealand has adopted in order to professionalize and empower its public procurement workforce include:

- Developing a model to assess the capability of procurement in agencies.
- Assessing agency procurement capability on site, and providing action plans for development.
- Requiring agencies that are not targeted for onsite assessment complete a self-assessment using measures described in the procurement capability model.
- Developing standard role competency requirements for procurers, and implementing these requirements in government agencies.
- Benchmarking key agency performance against the private sector.
- Increasing hiring of skilled and qualified procurement professionals to fill the skills gap.
- Ensuring government procurement salaries reflect market norms.
- Contracting agencies to allocate resources to reform procurement practice.
- Identifying opportunities for procurement in shared service centres.
- Including procurement professionals in works project teams.
- Establishing a small team of strategic procurement experts (also known as a commercial pool) to support high risk and high value projects across the government.
- Allocating resources to support public-private partnership projects.
- Determining procurement training needs and source providers.
- Mandating that agencies use tools provided to assess procurement capability and capacity.
- Mandating that agencies ensure that procurement staff are trained in order to fill identified skill gaps.
- Providing e-learning to support procurers to gain a professional procurement qualification.
- Targeting key procurement personnel within agencies to fast track their professional procurement education.
- Developing and launching career development plans for procurement personnel.
- Developing a New Zealand procurement academy.
- Encouraging and subsidising public sector procurement professionals in gaining recognised procurement qualifications.
- Launching a graduate programme in procurement.
- Facilitating temporary transfers and career progression planning between agencies for procurement professionals.
- Establishing and facilitating a procurement leaders group (for officials aged under 35 years) to cultivate future procurement leaders.
- Developing the course "Demystifying Procurement", a two-day introductory course to procurement in a public-sector context. Alternatively, this course is available for learning on line.

Source: (OECD, 2016[5])

Box 4.4. Development of template tender documents in Ireland

Ireland's Office of Government Procurement (OGP) is responsible for drafting public procurement policies, and regulating and coordinating the national public procurement system. In addition, the OGP is in charge of the preparation of standardised tender documents, as well as guidance materials.

The OGP has created a standard suite of template tender documents to guide best practices, and to reflect the new EU procurement directives that came into force in 2016. The OGP's website offers a section that serves as a repository of knowledge. The section provides an extensive amount of template documents and guidance materials. There are currently six model documents available, and more are planned. These templates cover the tender process and the contract phase of procedures.

To date, the government has asked that this suite of documents be used across the public service sector for procurement of low-to-medium risk goods and services. The popularity of these template documents is primarily due to their ease of use and clarity. These documents provide a further opportunity to help professionalise, streamline and standardise the procurement function of contracting authorities in the Irish state.

Source: Information provided by the Office of Government Procurement (OGP)

4.1.2. Building on Nuevo León's general capacity strategy for the public sector to also make public procurement more professional

Many countries develop strategies to systematically increase the capacity of their public workforce, often specifically for the area of public procurement. Such capacity strategies for the public sector and specifically for public procurement can offer benefits as they aim to systematically increase the capacity of public procurers. This, in turn, leads to a more economical use of resources, as well as to good management and more efficient procurement. A strategy is important, as it helps officials to prioritise activities. Ideally, the government would opt first for an assessment of the procurement workforce, highlighting strengths, weaknesses, gaps and building blocks that should serve as the starting point for any capacity-building measures. A second step to determine priorities should consist of a careful consideration of the country context, as well as the maturity of the procurement system. In addition, a strategy can incorporate steps that involve stakeholders, or the gathering of resources (OECD, 2016[6]).

Nuevo León does not have a specific strategy for enhancing its public procurement workforce. However, the Strategic Plan for the State of Nuevo León 2015-2030 (Plan Estratégico para el Estado de Nuevo León 2015 - 2030) addresses the need to develop the state's public-sector workforce. The plan addresses not just public procurement officials, but public officials in Nuevo León in general. In 2015, Nuevo León's Effective Government and Transparency Commission (Comisión de Gobierno Eficaz y Transparencia) introduced seven "pillars" for talent development in the public sector (see also Figure 4.1).

1. connection between talent strategy and business needs;
2. attraction and retention of talent;
3. recruitment, hiring and bringing new employees on board;
4. motivation and recognition of performance;

5. creation of leaders;
6. development of the organization;
7. creation of a culture of talent.

Figure 4.1. Seven pillars for talent development

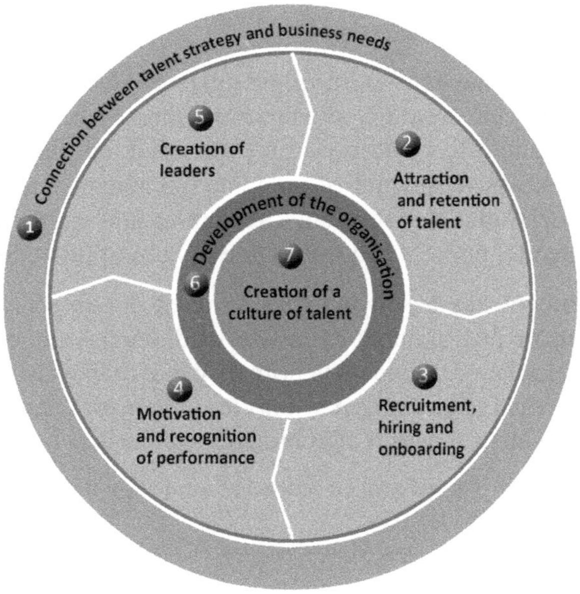

Source: (Consejo Nuevo León, 2015[7])

This strategy includes the formation of competency standards for all public positions, staff training programmes and talent retention surveys, according to the state's strategic plan.

Nuevo León's State Development Plan contains a related commitment. Action item 2.1.4 under the objective, "Develop effective public governance", describes the strategic goal of promoting professional career services that are linked to performance evaluation and recognition of merit (Gobierno del Estado de Nuevo León, 2016, p. 60[8]).

In this context, it could be beneficial for the government to consider measures that formally structure capacity-building efforts for the public procurement system. As mentioned above, a dedicated advisor or a unit should be tasked with analysing capacity-building needs and responses specifically with regards to public procurement. This unit could also be tasked with developing guidance material and trainings, as needed. Ireland, for example, could serve as a model for developing guidance materials (see **Box** 4.5 below).

Box 4.5. Development of national procurement guidelines in Ireland

One of the primary objectives of establishing the Office of Government Procurement (OGP) in Ireland was to improve the professionalism of the staff involved in procurement. The Irish state spends approximately EUR 8.5 billion every year on goods and services. In this context, it is essential that the public service operates in a co-ordinated and efficient way. Procurement is a key element of the government's public service reform.

The OGP is currently finalising national guidelines for goods and services of low and high value in public procurement tendering competitions. These guidelines will be published as a dynamic document. This means that they will be available electronically. The document will contain links to relevant information, as well as policy and template documents.

The purpose of these guidelines is to promote best practices and consistency of application of the public procurement rules in relation to the purchase of goods and services. The guidelines have been written in plain language with the goal of providing a clear description of the rules. The guidelines form part of the OGP National Procurement Policy Framework, which consists of five branches:

- legislation (directives, regulations)
- government policy (circulars, etc.)
- general guidelines;
- the Capital Works Management Framework
- detailed technical guidelines, template documents and notes that are issued periodically.

Source: Information provided by Office of Government Procurement (OGP)

In Nuevo León, several units are in charge of human resource activities. That said, the state does not have an active team or official in charge of bringing human resource activities to public procurement. In general, the Directorate for Human Resources (Dirección de Recursos Humanos) in the Undersecretariat of Administration (Subsecretaria de Administración) is in charge of questions related to professional development and performance review in the administration, including in the area of public procurement. Human resource matters are handled by the central administration for the entirety of Nuevo León's public officials, including those employees working on public procurement. In total, the central administration's Human Resources Directorate handles 18 000 files. All guidelines, tools and practices on human resource management are handled at this level; they also apply to everyone working on public procurement.

The Centralised Purchasing Body (Unidad Centralizada de Compras, UCC), in cooperation with the Office of the Comptroller for Government Transparency (Contraloría y Transparencia Gubernamental, CTG), is in charge of creating job profiles and trainings for public procurers. In 2015, the Commission for Effective and Transparent Government (Comisión de Gobierno Eficaz y Transparencia) set guidelines for professional development with the aim of achieving an effective and transparent public sector (Consejo Nuevo León, 2015[7]).

4.1.3. Being aware of strengths and weaknesses

Any training strategy to professionalize the public procurement workforce should be developed based on a realistic analysis of the strengths and weaknesses of the workforce (OECD, 2016[6]). Different frameworks exist to assist in conducting a detailed assessment of the workforce's strength and weaknesses. Some examples include a procurement capacity development guide by the United Nations Development Programme (UNDP, 2010[9]) and a toolkit for the same purpose by the European Commission (European Commission, 2011[10]).

One of the main strengths of the procurement workforce in Nuevo León is that officers usually focus on legal compliance and strive to ensure that public procurement processes follow the rules in all areas. This requires a thorough knowledge of the applicable laws and regulations in the state, which most officials have. Officials in Nuevo León are aware of the laws, regulations and guidelines that govern their areas of work. These officials do not only understand regulations as they relate to expected behaviour, they also understand the legal basis of these rules, which is a strength. However, it has to be noted that this close attention to legal compliance may be counterproductive, as officials sometimes end processes out of fear of not being able to meet a high level of legal compliance. They fear reprisal, or simply want to "be on the safe side", i.e. they refrain from doing anything that is associated with the slightest risk of violating a law.

To some extent, weaknesses in Nuevo León's procurement system relate to systemic factors. One of the most-stated challenges mentioned by public procurement officials in the state concerned the number of highly skilled procurement officials available to manage purchases. There are two facets of this challenge: the number of officials available to conduct public procurement, and their skills. These two facets are interlinked and cannot be separated. While a certain number of officers is needed to conduct different types of procurement-related activities (from more administrative, low-skilled tasks to complex high-skilled tasks), the staff also needs to be equipped with the right skills to be effective. Management not only needs to hire a given number of people to do a job, it also needs to ensure a sufficient level of knowledge. That is the only way the organisation can ensure efficiency and effectiveness. Across the board in Nuevo León, there seems to be a lack of sufficiently skilled public procurement officials. This results in overtime work or delays during peak periods, and also in inefficient procurements. Staff sometimes have knowledge gaps, or are sometimes allocated to the wrong processes. The administration is aware of this capacity gap, but training to increase capacity costs time, and managers are reluctant to free up their staff for training courses.

On a cultural level, public procurement is considered an administrative function, not a strategic function in Nuevo León. This means that the perception of the tasks to be delivered and the related incentive structure favours administrative behaviour. As a consequence, Nuevo León's workforce – in both its skills, attitudes and motivations – is not equipped to approach complex procurements strategically.

Aside from these systemic, overarching factors, OECD interviews with procurement officials in Nuevo León identified knowledge gaps with regards to concrete aspects of public procurement. A more comprehensive and targeted analysis of these knowledge gaps could shed substantial light on the source of the issue (OECD, 2016[6]). During OECD interviews, procurers and suppliers cited a need for additional knowledge or training with regards to negotiations (of prices and terms), as well as a need for procurement-specific knowledge (as opposed to government-specific knowledge).

Training could address these issues. In some instances, public procurers report, there have been challenges related to basic education, such as basic language skills with young hires.

4.1.4. Implementing targeted measures to build capacity, including training

The following section focusses on avenues to increase the competencies of individual public procurers.

Options range from more structured approaches like formal, academic training, to more ad-hoc and unstructured approaches like exposure or mentoring from senior to junior officials (Train4Dev, 2011[11]) (Pearson Jenny, 2011[12]). Table 4.1 provides an overview of different approaches to building capacity, their applicability and their strengths and weaknesses

Table 4.1. Different approaches to build capacity, their applicability, strengths and weaknesses

	Description of the learning process	Level & application	Strengths	Challenges
Coaching and mentoring	Tailored and contextual learning process Coaching: generally focused on workplace challenges; time-bound Mentoring: generally a long-term process of supporting an individual's career and personal development	Individuals and groups at various levels; ideal as follow up to training	Provides focussed / tailored guidance	Ideally: separation from line management structures, focus on specific skills
Degree-level study	Specialised university study at masters' and doctoral levels	Individuals; young / midlevel professionals	Positive and quantifiable impacts	Long absence from work (need cover); difficulty adapting and applying new knowledge to workplace; risk of brain drain
Distance learning	Programmes offered by universities or institutions for participants to follow from home	Individuals For contexts in which high quality training is not available locally and where travel/relocation is not an option (financially or personally)	Provides training opportunities while maintaining geographical, financial, and time-flexibility	Students are isolated; needs high level of intrinsic motivation and study skills; needs good quality and affordable Internet access
E-Learning	Technology-supported or web-based learning systems. E-learning can happen across distances and borders or within one organisation and therefore not necessarily at a distance.	Individuals and groups highly technical content geographically dispersed groups	Individual and flexible learning opportunities; can be very cost effective	Students are isolated; needs high level of intrinsic motivation and study skills; needs good quality and affordable Internet access
Experiential learning	Processes to support individuals to learn from their experiences, such as action learning, critical incident analysis, on-the-job training, work-based learning, work/job shadowing, etc.	Individuals and groups Can also be used to monitor training achievements	Departs from the participant's own level of experience; grounds learning into workplace practice; works well for those not academically inclined	Can create resistance where this learning style does not match the culture or expectations; difficult to deliver theoretical or fact-based knowledge
Exposure	Exposure visits take people to see what others are doing in work situations similar to their own; attending conferences and other events provide exposure to new knowledge, ideas and influences within sectors	Individuals and groups	Makes learning about new ideas more practical and grounded in reality; stimulates the spread of good practice and the fertilisation of innovation	Exposure can be expensive and not cost effective (e.g., international travel); clear learning objectives need to be specified and followed up effectively
Knowledge management	Process by which organisations generate value from their intellectual and knowledge-based assets by documenting what staff and stakeholders know about the organisation's areas of interest, and then sharing that collected data back to those who need it to enhance their performance	Groups, organisations and sectors, particularly in multidisciplinary areas	Enhances communication and connection within systems to ensure that they are using all the available knowledge assets to best effect	Can be very complex and time consuming to implement; requires constant attention and updating; can become overly technical and dependent on data management system
Partnerships and networks	Mechanisms through which diverse actors with mutual interests come together; can include twinning	Organisations and sectors	Provides opportunities for sharing knowledge and experience across borders	Can be difficult to co-ordinate and keep functional; power relations can become unbalanced, having a negative impact on opportunities for learning

Source: Adapted from (Pearson Jenny, 2011[12]) (Train4Dev, 2011[11])

As recommended by the OECD checklist on public procurement capacity, a team should be dedicated to overseeing capacity-building measures. This unit should be tasked with analysing needs for capacity development, such as training, and then with determining and developing appropriate activities in response. This should not only include structured assessments of the procurement workforce, but also the development of guidelines for trainings and training programmes, as well as certification schemes. (OECD,(n.d.)[4]).

Trainings warrant a specific mention. The OECD recommends the following elements (OECD,(n.d.)[4]):

- Training curriculums that consider the multidisciplinary nature of public procurement, including an emphasis on integrity aspects.
- Formal on-the-job training programmes.
- Measures to ensure that trainings are accessible. For example, trainings should include advertising measures, provide sufficient funding and use flexible learning methods.
- Certification for trainers to ensure quality trainings.
- Review and feedback loops to keep trainings up to date.

In Nuevo León, there does yet not seem to be any systematic training related to public procurement. The state offers training related to transparency, ethics and integrity issues. The new ethics code will be accompanied by training – highlighting the areas of the general ethics code that are relevant for public procurement. In addition, it offers training to help individuals use the federal public procurement platform, Compranet. The training includes a 300-page manual. Compranet accounts are issued only upon successful completion of this training. Public procurers mentioned a similar course with regards to the Electronic System for Public Procurement (Sistema Electrónico de Compras Públicas, SECOP). When asked about a general course on public procurement, procurers cited a non-mandatory training in 2008. With regards to the control and audit function, Nuevo León currently offers no training to audit officers. That said, the government is currently analysing whether and how training specific to audits and the audit of procurement should be introduced.

Officers currently training Nuevo León's public service employees have strong expertise in human resources and labour psychology. They are a good foundation to build on, but Nuevo León would benefit from hiring additional trainers with procurement-specific expertise. At present, trainings appear to be organised around general human resources tools and techniques. Available specialisations include change management, how to handle time and conflicts, and psychological factors. However, no current trainers seem to have experience that is specific to public administration or work in government. In fact, many seem to come from the private industry. This raises questions, for example about the extent to which private sector experience can be directly translated to the public sector. At present, the government does not have trainers who have sufficient knowledge of public procurement to conduct meaningful training on these issues.

In addition to these general efforts, some organisations in Nuevo León have made individual efforts to provide training. Certain contracting authorities reported offering specific trainings, like the Water and Sewer Services of Monterrey (Servicios de Agua y Drenaje de Monterrey), which uses external trainers. Some municipalities conduct ongoing training sessions related to customer service.

Nuevo León's public procurement system does not conduct training activities related to bringing new employees on board. Many public procurers reported that new hires usually acquired knowledge about their new public procurement role on the job. They did this by reviewing the laws, previous cases and guidance on procedures, as well as by engaging in some self-training online. Nuevo León provides limited introduction to general operations and procedures as stated in the Operation Manual Book to new government employees. However, each position also has an operations manual. The government is currently developing a manual for the Ministry of Administration.

Nuevo León's Human Resources Directorate has recently increased efforts to provide training. The state has embedded a Professionalization Institute within the government that is in charge of educating instructors on general topics in the administration. The Professionalization Institute selects trainers for this work following an evaluation that narrows the field to only four or five individuals. These trainers then provide face-to-face training and online training. However, the majority of the training courses seem to still be in the planning phase, attempting to match the training to different levels of competences. In addition, the government does not have trainers in the area of public procurement.

4.2. Establish a system of merit-based career progression for public procurers that are fit to handle evolving challenges

Nuevo León could build a more professional workforce in the medium and long term by setting up a structured system for career progression. Currently, no competency-based framework guides different procurement roles, associated hiring, evaluation or promotion processes. There is no structured, transparent system for hiring public procurers, and no transparent process to decide on promotions.

By setting clear requirements for new hires and promotions in the public procurement system, Nuevo León could ensure sustained, high-quality performance from its procurers. At present, the state is undergoing an exploratory, 360-degree evaluation of its public procurement workforce, whereby not only subordinates are reviewed by managers, but managers are reviewed by subordinates. Expanding this evaluation, and linking it to career progression could ensure that the best performers are rewarded for good work. Overall, career progression in the public procurement system (as in the entire public administration) should build on a competency framework. This competency framework should be rooted in transparency, and should provide incentives for good performance and for retaining good staff. This is particularly important in a situation of budget constraints, where the administration cannot make new hires and every peso spent on public procurement has to be as effective as possible.

4.2.1. Smart human resources management in times of budget constraints

Public procurement is increasingly considered a strategic function. International guidelines, such as the OECD Recommendation of the Council on Public Procurement, recommend this (OECD, 2015[2]). In trying to make public procurement more strategic, procurement officials face increasingly complex tasks that require specialised knowledge. Therefore, one of the first measures public procurement officials should take to cultivate highly skilled procurement personnel is hiring officials with required competencies that can hit the ground running.

Nuevo León's challenges in the area of public procurement capacity are related to the state's immense budget deficit and austerity measures. While stakeholders (both on the government and supplier side) report shortages of a sufficient number of qualified procurers, there is no room to increase the procurement workforce due to budgetary constraints. Currently, the public service is reportedly dismissing public employees. Not enough funds are available to pay all the benefits that public officials are normally entitled to.

Overall, there is awareness among high-level officials that the average professional profile of the current public procurers in Nuevo León's central purchasing unit is less than ideal. Most procurement personnel are subject to the same general specifications all public servants must meet in the state, per the Law on the Civil Service in Nuevo León. However, there is no defined specification for the area of public procurement. Therefore, most of the procurers in the UCC do not have a specific background in public procurement. As a consequence of this, capacity is lacking, particularly with regards to market research (i.e. retrieving quotes) and tender design (drafting the call for tender and structuring public consultations).

As a remedy, the state has increasingly tried to absorb procurement personnel from decentral agencies into the UCC. It has done this in order to push for the greater centralisation of purchases. Human resources management at the level of the central administration is currently developing a proposal to identify personnel needs as a consequence of centralisation. It is also exploring to what extent capacity needs in the UCC can potentially be covered by absorbing personnel from decentralised purchasing units.

All public officials – and public procurement officials – should be hired via transparent and structured processes. These processes should establish that the skills and knowledge of the applicant match the competence level that is needed for the particular role. The OECD recommendation and associated checklist for public procurement implementation and capacity highlight the benefits of structured, competency-based hiring and promotion (OECD, 2015[2]) (OECD,(n.d.)[4]).

At present, however, Nuevo León does not seem to require advanced, procurement-specific skills when hiring procurement officials. To be hired, applicants only have to have one year of procurement-related experience. Other hiring criteria consist of formalities and procedural issues, such as submission of specific forms, passing a health check, etc. Several procurement officials mentioned that having contacts within the political leadership was necessary to be hired in Nuevo León's public service.

As stated earlier, candidates for public procurement positions have to have at least one year of experience related to public procurement. In addition, they have to provide documentation establishing their identities, criminal records, medical and psychological examinations, and similar documents. For negotiators, hiring managers request experience in purchasing and skills, like computer proficiency and negotiation and communication skills. There are no other requirements beyond these more administrative requisites.

In addition, compared to the private sector, Nuevo León's public sector is unattractive as an employer, mainly due to lower pay. Most of the employees (111, as of 2017) are employed under limited-term contracts (*empleados base*). The employees are unionized, and have been employed since the previous administration in Nuevo León. Only three employees are employed as officials (*honorarios asimilables a sueldo*). The turnover rate is 4.3%. These factors present challenges, particularly with regards to attracting highly skilled, highly effective individuals that might have more attractive offers from the private sector. A comparison between the average monthly salaries of Nuevo León's public procurement workforce and the average Mexican salary illustrates these challenges (see Figure 4.2) In this context, it has to be noted that more that 60% of the workforce are on a assistant level or below, and, accordingly, earn less than the levels of analyst and above (see also Figure 4.4).

Figure 4.2. Average monthly salary of employees in Nuevo León's central administration, Acquisitions and General Services unit (Adquisiciones y Servicios Generales), 2016, per category, Mexican pesos

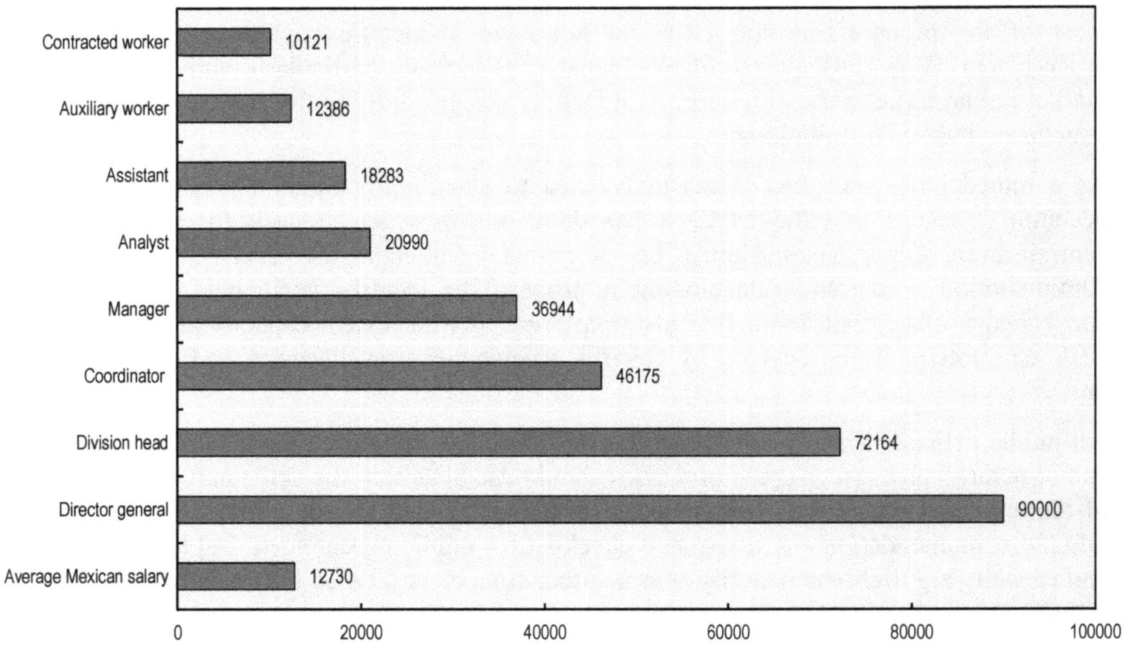

Source: Central Administration, Nuevo León; OECD: average annual wages.

To structure the hiring of procurement officials, certification systems have proven useful, for example in the United States (see Box 4.6 below).

Box 4.6. Certification of capabilities for procurement in the United States

The American Purchasing Society (APS) is a professional association of buyers and purchasing managers in the United States. It was the first organisation to establish a nationally recognised certification for buyers and purchasing professionals. APS offers three different certification programmes:

1. the Certified Purchasing Professional Programme directed at professionals who have demonstrated the skills to successfully implement improve purchasing and supply chain practices as part of a business solution in an organisation;
2. the Certified Professional Purchasing Manager Programme aimed at those in managerial positions and those who have managerial experience; and
3. the Certified Professional Purchasing Consultant Programme aimed at certified purchasing professionals who either consult or teach purchasing to people outside their own employer.

Source: (American Purchasing Society, 2016[13])

4.2.2. Building on elements of Nuevo León's public procurement roles

While Nuevo León has public procurers in a variety of different contracting authorities, the core of the state's public procurement workforce is located in the General Directorate for Acquisitions and General Services. This unit in Nuevo León's central administration consists of 114 persons.

Article 75 of Nuevo León's Acquisition Law (Ley de Adquisiciones) provides the legal basis for the formulation of profiles for public officials working on public procurement in different roles, as well as performance evaluation and training. The Central Purchasing Body (UCC) is tasked, together with the Comptroller of the State, with creating guidelines for the creation of job profiles as well as training. Profiles, training programmes and performance evaluation are to be published in the SECOP, and in the corresponding transparency portal.

Section II (Article 19) of the Interior Regulation (Reglamento Interior) contains guidance on human resource management in the public administration in general. This guidance appears to be applicable to the public procurement system as well.

As opposed to working with isolated role descriptions, countries increasingly use competency frameworks to organise their public procurement workforces. The competency frameworks build on competencies that are represented in different procurement roles to a different extent. Employees can increase their competencies and move from one level to another (see Box 4.7). In Scotland, competency frameworks have been applied in order to develop the skills of public procurers (see Box 4.8).

Box 4.7. What is competency management?

Competency management is a way of defining the abilities employees need to have, as well as the behaviours they should practice to do their jobs well. Competency management links several human resource management activities to ensure that an organisation is staffed by people who perform effectively. The use of competency management in OECD countries has increased steadily in recent years, and has been linked to demands for increased flexibility and autonomy in workforce management.

Source: (OECD, 2015[14]) (OECD, 2011[15])

Box 4.8. The Scottish procurement competency framework

The procurement competency framework of the Scottish government identifies the skills and competency levels required by all staff involved in the procurement process. It has been developed by the cross-sectoral people and skills working group to support the delivery of the recommendations in the Review of Public Procurement in Scotland (2006) which related specifically to people and skills. The framework is intended to compliment, not replace, existing personal development tools in organisations.

The framework identifies thirteen key competencies candidates should have:

1. Procurement process: has the sufficient knowledge and understanding in sourcing and tendering methods to carry out duties associated with role.
2. Negotiation: has the ability to negotiate within the scope of the role.
3. Strategy development and market analysis: has the strategy development and market analysis skills necessary to carry out duties associated with role.
4. Financial: has the financial knowledge and understanding needed to carry out duties associated with the role – elements include appraisal of suppliers' financial positions, total costing and the compliance frameworks that exist for public sector finance and procurement.
5. Legal: has sufficient understanding of legislative frameworks relating specifically to procurement to carry out duties associated with role.
6. Results focus: is aware of how personal and team objectives contribute to the success of the organization, and continually demonstrate commitment to achieving these.
7. Systems capability: has the knowledge and understanding of systems and processes utilised in the procurement of goods and services. Specific system competencies may be localised to specific systems.
8. Inventory, logistics and supply chain: has the knowledge and understanding of materials management solutions to carry out duties associated with role. Elements include inventory, logistics, warehouse management, etc., Knowledge and understanding of supply chain management techniques is also important, and is not restricted to organisations holding stock.
9. Organisational awareness: clearly understands roles and responsibilities, how procurement should be organised and which units within the organisation are in charge of it.
10. Self-management: responds quickly and flexibly when required, supporting others while striving to improve skill application in line with organisational requirements.
11. Leadership: contributes to the achievement of team goals by providing support, encouragement and clear direction when appropriate.
12. Communication: openly shares relevant information and communicates in an effective and timely manner using a variety of means.
13. Relationship management: identifies different types of customers and stakeholders and formulates strategy for managing relationships.

Source: (OECD, 2013[16])

Introducing a competency-based system to manage public procurers from a human resources perspective can offer benefits in Nuevo León as well. It can contribute to a clearer understanding of expectations of employees on different levels and in different roles. In addition, such a competency framework can identify officials who need training and development (Scottish Government, 2016[17]).

In creating a competency-based system for the area of public procurement, Nuevo León can build on two elements: the current division of labour between different colleagues in the General Directorate for Acquisitions and General Services, and the efforts at the central administration level to develop a more professional civil service.

For practical purposes, the implementation of a competency-based system should start at the central level. However, it can easily be translated to the purchasing units within other contracting authorities. Officials in the General Directorate for Acquisitions and General Services are distributed between different roles; the requirements for professionalization differ accordingly. The following roles are differentiated (see also Figure 4.3 below for an organisational chart):

- The Directorate for Procurement (Dirección de Adquisiciones) is tasked with public procurement that relates to goods, while the Directorate of Maintenance and General Services (Dirección de Mantenimiento y Servicios Generales) is in charge of the procurement of services. Both units are tasked with duties before and after the actual public tendering process (e.g. they conduct market studies, determine needs and set evaluation criteria). They also sign contracts with selected bidders.
- The task of administering the competition lies with a separate unit, the Directorate of Public Tenders (Dirección de Concursos). This unit is in charge of planning and conducting the selection process. This includes choosing the selection mechanism (e.g. open tender, exception, reverse auctions, among others), communicating all required information in a timely manner, interacting with the bidders and handling the electronic communication related to the procedure.
- Operations Control (Jefatura de Control de Operaciones) provides administrative support to the public procurement system in Nuevo León. The unit receives requests, supervises a national warehouse, checks whether necessary rules and requirements are being complied with, manages invoices and payments, and archives documentation.
- Communications (Jefatura de Administración y Comunicación) is tasked with communications around public procurement both internally in the administration and externally. That means that this unit provides guidance to contracting authorities and gathers information from them, including data and statistics about their public procurement processes. In addition, the unit engages with the wider public via social media.

Figure 4.3. Organisation chart of Nuevo León's Central Purchasing Body

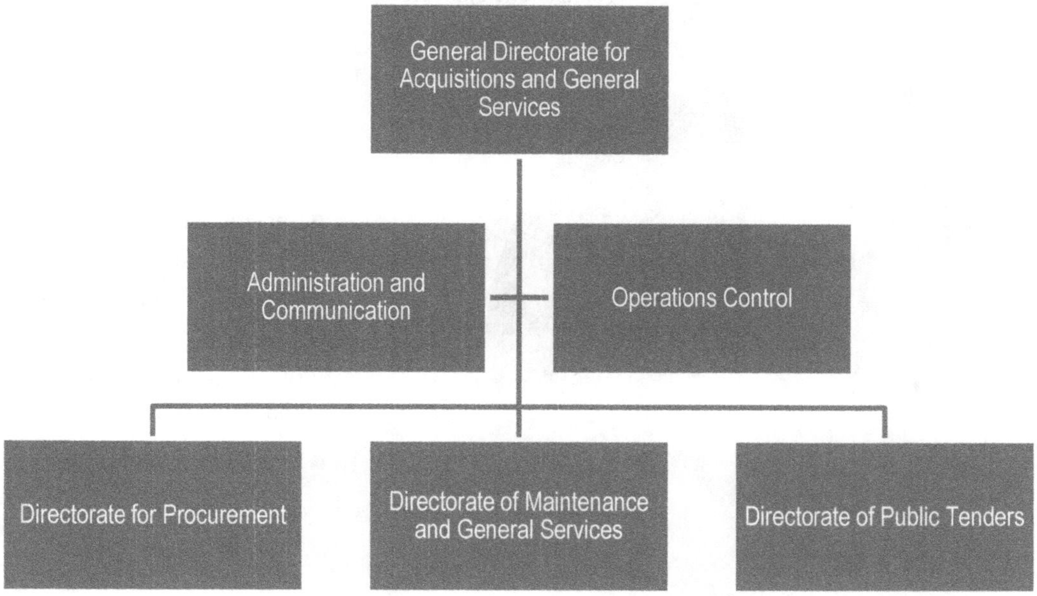

Source: Information provided by the State of Nuevo León

Table 4.2 and Figure 4.4 provide an overview of the proportion of these different roles:

Table 4.2. Areas in Nuevo León's public procurement workforce

Role	Number of Employees
Dirección General de Adquisiciones y Servicios Generales (General oversight)	1
Dirección de Adquisiciones (Directorate for Procurement)	11
Dirección de Mantenimiento y Servicios Generales (Directorate for Maintenance and General Services)	28
Dirección de Concursos (Contest Management)	9

Source: Information provided by the State of Nuevo León

Figure 4.4. Distribution of roles in Nuevo León's public procurement workforce

Number of employees

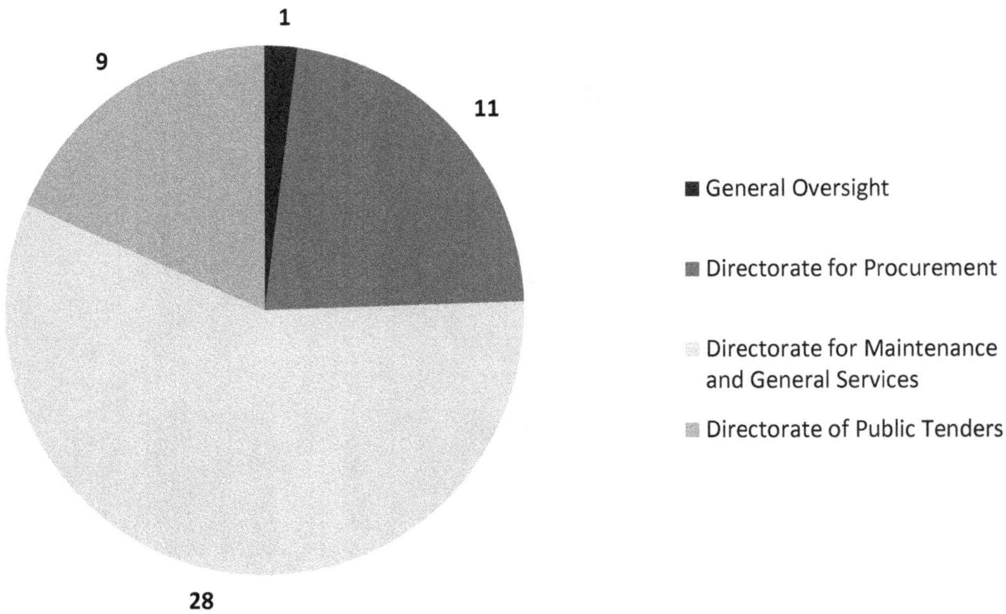

Source: Information provided by the State of Nuevo León

Across the functional divisions within Nuevo León's public procurement workforce, in terms of hierarchy and pay grade, there are 20 different levels, grouped into seven categories. Currently, Nuevo León has employees in the following categories:

- one contracted expert (level 3)
- 41 auxiliary workers (levels 4-5)
- 21 assistants (levels 6-7)
- 28 analysts (levels 8-9)
- 9 managers (levels 10-12)
- 5 coordinators (levels 13-14)
- 1 division lead (level 18)
- 1 director general (level 20)

There is a lower number of managerial positions; workers at the assistant level are in the majority. Taken together, these assistant-level workers take up more than half of the procurement workforce. During the analysis it remains unclear, however, how exactly the responsibilities are defined at each level. However, the relatively low number of roles with an analytical, rather than administrative focus suggests that the system does not consider procurement to be a profession that requires a defined set of qualities or strategic focus. Rather, procurement is seen as a system with a bureaucratic or administrative focus. Figure 4.5 summarises the proportion of job types according to the different categories.

Figure 4.5. Number of employees in the General Directorate for Acquisitions and General Services, per category, 2016

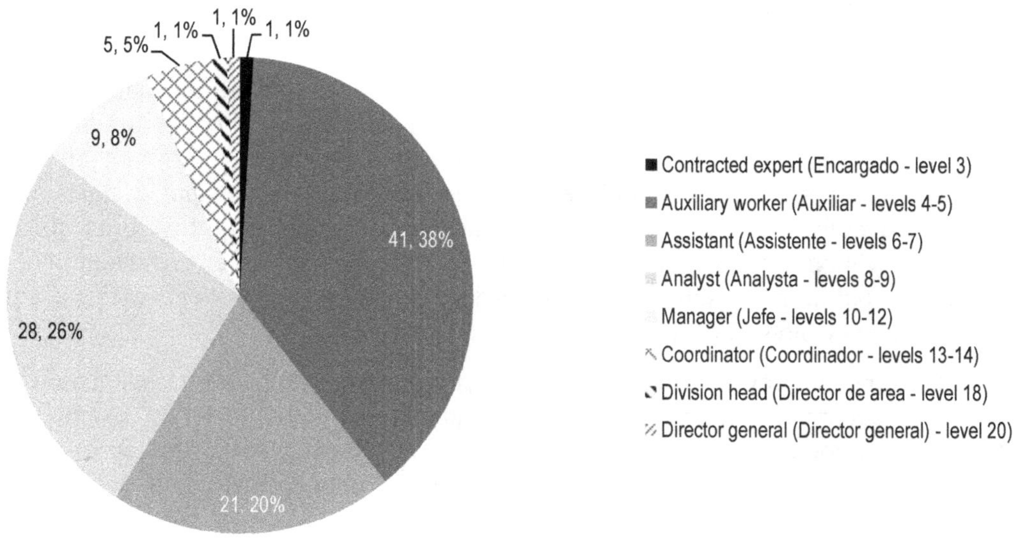

Source: Central Administration, Nuevo León.

A competency-based framework for human resource management of Nuevo León's public procurement function could build on these roles. In so doing, the framework could describe the competencies that each role should have, according to the different hierarchy levels in each division.

In addition, general efforts by human resources management at central administration level could be translated into the area of public procurement. The Human Resources Department has been developing a framework that describes the specific competences of individual officials. This appears to allow HR to match existing capabilities with the requirements of the different roles. It also appears to help with developing and targeting training measures. The Human Resources Department is tasked with developing the trainings. There are no specialised trainings for roles such as audit or risk management. There does not appear to be a certification mechanism for public procurers.

The human resources department for the central administration in Nuevo León is currently developing a competency model. Previously, Nuevo León drew on a catalogue of profiles, and officials have rotated from one position to another based on their skills (matching with the roles to be filled). The new system of competencies will be focused around four different norms and behaviours. The four pillars are:

1. a culture of legality: the capacity to understand, respect and promote legal standards and institutional culture to create an environment of trust and harmony between the public official and the citizens;
2. leadership focus on service: capacity to form, guide, develop and participate in teams while focusing on the service;
3. results orientation: capacity to direct actions towards the achievement of expected objectives with speed and a sense of urgency, to set challenging goals maintaining high levels of performance by committing to on-the-job learning and professional development;
4. innovation for transformation: capacity to innovate, with efficiency, austerity and sustainability, throughout all government processes.

In addition, the model will have three levels:

1. governor to director level;
2. staff reporting to the leadership level;
3. professionals who do not have a reporting manager.

Currently, the human resources department in Nuevo León's central administration is finalising the content for these four pillars. It is doing so in collaboration with the departments leading the different government agencies, as well as with an external certification expert. Once established, trainers will be selected and budgets will be secured to deliver training around the competency model. In a first pilot stage, the competency model will undergo an evaluation. There is no specific consideration of roles specific to public procurement. Conflict of interest has not been identified as a topic of the competency model or training.

In continuing the development of the competency framework and its adaptation to the public procurement function, Nuevo León's administration could follow examples from international good practice, as described in the OECD checklist on public procurement and capacity. It is recommended that competency frameworks for public procurement have the following elements (OECD,(n.d.)[4]):

- a description of the specific functions, skills and competencies needed to implement the organisation's mission with regards to public procurement
- coverage of a multidisciplinary portfolio of expertise necessary to deliver public procurement (i.e. knowledge of the underlying laws as well as professional, technical and personal effectiveness skills – including negotiation, risk management, teamwork, communication, leadership and the management of people, projects and large resources, as well as integrity and information technology)
- description of expectations and prerequisites for each job.
- delineation of the different jobs and levels in terms of knowledge and practice requirements.
- a mandate that officials put in place and undertake regular professional development to refresh knowledge and build new skills to ensure that procurement officials meet high professional standards of knowledge and competence.

4.2.3. Ensure that there is a merit-based career progression based on transparent rules and evaluations

Requirements for public procurers should be commensurate to the complexity of procurement cases they deliver. Countries that follow international best practices are working towards giving public procurement a more strategic role. Individual public procurers in these countries are expected to deliver these changes – and will only be able to do so with more advanced skills (OECD, 2015[2]).

In this context, retaining talent in the public sector is a paramount aim (OECD, 2015[14]). To do so, being a public procurer has to become an attractive career option, (OECD,(n.d.)[4]):

- recognizing public procurement as a strategic function with defined professional and hierarchical levels (by describing jobs, qualifications, competencies)

- establishing procurement-specific careers paths with vertical and horizontal mobility, including between public institutions and sectors
- engaging in recruitment and promotion based on the competency frameworks
- paying adequate, transparent salaries and making competitive, performance-based promotions
- certifying public procurement expertise
- giving regular performance evaluations.

In Nuevo León, there are elements of a structured, professional public service. However, the government gives limited consideration to the specific functions and requirements of the public procurement workforce.

Some of the recent developments could be expanded to specifically suit the public procurement function. As mentioned briefly before, the Human Resources Department has recently implemented a feedback and performance review system allowing for 360-degree evaluation of all public servants. This evaluation is intended to increase the professionalization of public workers on all levels. The 360-degree review allows HR to give employees grades on a scale from 0-10, with 10 being the best score. Four competence areas are assessed:

1. leadership and management (directivas y gerenciales);
2. vocation and commitment to the public service (vocación y compromiso con el servicio público).
3. basic or general competencies (básicas o generales).
4. technical or specific (técnicas o especificas), only to be filled by director level.

The tool will be managed online, and is based on self-evaluations as a first step. It contains definitions of each competency and a description of the behaviour that should be observed as part of this competency. Following the 360-degree review by individuals online, the Human Resources Department will discuss the results of the evaluation with the managers. In addition, the programme provides the expectation that human resources, together with managers, creates a training plan for the entire year, as well as specific follow up to be delivered. Two of these evaluations will be carried out per year (in the beginning of the year and at the end.)

The 360-degree review was implemented to identify priorities for certain areas. As part of the roll out of the 360-degree reviews, the Human Resources Department provided face-to-face trainings on the tool in the spring of 2017, and offered limited support online. The tool was tested in a pilot phase in the central administration, with results expected for May 2017.

This performance review system could, in combination with a structured competency framework, provide the basis for a merit-based career path for public procurers in Nuevo León. At present, public procurers have no career trajectory that is based on professional considerations or specialisation. Employees are assigned to different positions based on considerations of grade or seniority. Issues like specialisation or procurement-specific performance do not seem to play a role. As a consequence, specialisation within the public procurement workforce at the central level has not been pursued. Within the same unit (*dirección*) procurers usually conduct the same tasks. These are at times specialised in an ad-hoc fashion based on recurring needs. For example, while one procurer conducts all procurements related to the maintenance of buildings (cleaning services, renovations, carpenter services, paint jobs, etc.), another one focuses on the information technology infrastructure (voice, IT, data, etc.) There is no specialisation according procurement types or methods.

There is no structured system at the moment to manage promotion in Nuevo León's public service, including public procurement. Based on current role descriptions, there seem to be initial guideposts that allow officials to identify whether an individual is performing above, below or at average levels. However, the descriptions of the competencies per level, as well as the specifications underlying the 360-degree review, are often not clear enough to allow for a robust assessment of an individual's performance or position.

Once hired, promotions throughout Nuevo León's public sector are made based on criteria that are unrelated to the official's job performance. In fact, there are no clearly stated criteria. This disenfranchises good performers and keeps underperformers in the workforce, taking up resources without delivering. In addition, civil servants reported that the workforce overall was aging and increasingly unfit (e.g. unable to handle computers.) This is because it is difficult to dismiss officials. In times of budget constraints, younger employees with more flexible contracts are dismissed first.

4.3. Proposals for action

Nuevo León has taken first steps to build the capacity of its public officials to be effective in their positions. The State Development Plan sets out the framework for what constitutes a public service professional. A 360-degree review mechanism and competency frameworks are being introduced. However, gaps remain with regards to specific measures for public procurers. Nuevo León could build on its recent progress through the following proposals:

4.3.1. Systematising capacity building efforts to ensure a comprehensive approach

Nuevo León should improve the foundation of its efforts to increase the capacity of its public procurement workforce by ensuring all avenues are followed:

- Nuevo León should develop a professionalization strategy by:
  - summarising approaches to professionalising the public procurement function in a professionalization or capacity-building strategy.
- The state should utilise all avenues for capacity building. It can do so by:
  - developing and providing training courses for public procurement officials that are specifically targeted at different profiles
  - introducing a help desk function that provides support for contracting authorities in case of doubt
  - introducing an incentive scheme tied to a clear career path for public procurement officials. This can be accomplished by:
    - launching twinning arrangements to learn from more advanced colleagues in the region or in the organisation
    - co-operating with academic institutions and others.
- Nuevo León should create clear aspirations by introducing a certification mechanism that:
  - communicates clear goals that have to be fulfilled in order to receive a certificate
  - and offer incentives based on the certification scheme.

- The state should respond to needs for specialised knowledge by:
  - providing targeted training in those areas that require additional skills, such as in complex procurement procedures or when incorporating complementary policy objectives.

4.3.2. Offer targeted capacity building beyond the public procurement workforce

To ensure maximum effectiveness of capacity building measures in the area of public procurement, Nuevo León could target suppliers by:

- Offering measures that will help suppliers build capacity. These can include:
  - increasing the success of public procurement procedures by increasing the market's ability to respond to contracting authorities' demand in terms of offers
  - providing training for companies on how to respond correctly to a tender, how to avoid mistakes, etc.
- Raising awareness around public procurement issues. The state can accomplish this by:
  - communicating changes in rules and requirements
  - and communicating opportunities for capacity building.

Note

[1] http://www.oecd.org/governance/ethics/benchmarking-assessment-methodology-public-procurement-systems.htm

References

American Purchasing Society (2016), *Purchasing Certification Programs, webpage*, https://www.american-purchasing.com/page.php?PageID=6 (accessed on 15 November 2017). [13]

Consejo Nuevo León (2015), *El Nuevo León que queremos. Plan Estratégico para el estado de Nuevo León 2015-2030.* [7]

European Commission (2011), *ToolKit for Capacity Development*, Office for Official Publications of the European Communities,, https://ec.europa.eu/europeaid/sites/devco/files/guidelines-toolkit-capacity-development-2010_en.pdf. [10]

Gobierno del Estado de Nuevo León (2016), *Plan Estatal de Desarrollo 2016-2021*, Gobierno del Estado de Nuevo León, Monterrey, http://www.nl.gob.mx/sites/default/files/30jun_pednl2016-2021.pdf. [8]

OECD((n.d.)), *Public Procurement Toolbox: Capacity*, http://www.oecd.org/governance/procurement/toolbox/principlestools/capacity/ (accessed on 03 July 2017). [1]

OECD((n.d.)), *Methodology for Assessing Procurement Systems*, http://www.oecd.org/governance/ethics/benchmarking-assessment-methodology-public-procurement-systems.htm (accessed on 19 June 2017). [3]

OECD((n.d.)), *Checklist for Supporting the Implementation of OECD Recommendation of the Council on Public Procurement: Capacity.* [4]

OECD (2011), *Public Servants as Partners for Growth*, OECD Publishing, Paris, http://dx.doi.org/10.1787/9789264166707-en. [15]

OECD (2013), *Public Procurement Review of the State's Employees' Social Security and Social Services Institute in Mexico*, OECD Public Governance Reviews, OECD Publishing, Paris, http://dx.doi.org/10.1787/9789264197305-en. [16]

OECD (2015), *Achieving Public sector Agility at Times of Fiscal Consolidation*, OECD Publishing, Paris, http://dx.doi.org/10.1787/9789264206267-en. [14]

OECD (2015), *OECD Recommendation of the Council on Public Procurement*, http://www.oecd.org/gov/ethics/OECD-Recommendation-on-Public-Procurement.pdf. [2]

OECD (2016), *Roadmap: How to Elaborate a Procurement Capacity Strategy*, http://www.oecd.org/governance/procurement/toolbox/search/Roadmap-Procurement-Capacity-Strategy.pdf. [6]

OECD (2016), *Towards Efficient Public Procurement in Colombia: Making the Difference*, OECD Publishing, Paris, http://dx.doi.org/10.1787/9789264252103-en. [5]

Pearson Jenny (2011), "Training and Beyond: Seeking Better Practices for Capacity Development", *OECD Development Co-operation Working Papers*, No. 1, OECD, Paris, http://dx.doi.org/10.1787/5kgf1nsnj8tf-en. [12]

Scottish Government (2016), *The procurement competency framework*, http://www.gov.scot/Topics/Government/Procurement/Capability/proccompfw (accessed on 04 July 2017). [17]

Train4Dev (2011), *Enhancing Learning for Effectiveness*, http://www.learn4dev.net/wp-content/uploads/2015/07/Enhancing-Learning-for-effectiveness_T4D_Guide.pdf. [11]

UNDP (2010), *Public Procurement Capacity Development Guide*, http://www.undp.org/content/dam/aplaws/publication/en/publications/capacity-development/undp-procurement-capacity-assessment-users-guide/Procurement%20Capacity%20Assessment%20Guide.pdf. [9]

Chapter 5. Implementing electronic mechanisms to support Nuevo León's procurement system

This chapter discusses information technology (IT) tools and the public procurement system of the State Government of Nuevo León (SGNL). It focuses specifically on the availability of these tools, and how they can be utilised by Nuevo León's public procurement system. The chapter analyses the degree of implementation of IT services, and their use in public procurement activities as compared to the recommendations set by the 2015 OECD Recommendation on Public Procurement. Furthermore, the chapter assesses how the use of an e-procurement system in the SGNL is bringing it closer to achieving some of the major objectives of public procurement, such as transparency and efficiency. Finally, the chapter addresses how the SGNL could further reap the benefits of the e-procurement system as well as data and information that could be collected through IT systems in order to improve the functioning of the public procurement system overall.

Governments around the world are increasingly incorporating information and communication technologies (ICTs) into their daily activities and operations. ICTs are also incorporated into public procurement processes through implementation of e-procurement systems.

E-procurement is an effective tool for improving administrative procedures, and, perhaps more importantly, it can also help officials uphold several principles that are central to public procurement. These core principles include transparency, access, efficiency, integrity and accountability. Implementation of a sound e-procurement system allows timely diffusion of information with lower transaction costs to relevant stakeholders. These stakeholders include: contracting authorities; tenderers; other suppliers in the market; oversight bodies, such as control and audit authorities; civil societies; and citizens. The use of ICTs can facilitate the participation of more suppliers, especially small and medium enterprises (SMEs), in public procurement processes. This occurs because e-procurement can give procurers and suppliers improved market access with reduced marketing costs. Increased competition helps governments find the goods, services and works they need. It can also result in better terms and conditions for procurers, and increased value for money of purchases. Over the course of the whole process, e-procurement systems also provide better traceability of information and higher transparency, which in turn enhance integrity and accountability of actors and the system as a whole. *The OECD Recommendation of the Council on Public Procurement* (henceforth referred to as the OECD Recommendation) recognises the diverse benefits governments can derive from harnessing digital technologies throughout their procurement cycles (Box 5.1).

Box 5.1. OECD Recommendation of the Council on Public Procurement

The Council:

VIII. Recommends that Adherents improve public procurement system by harnessing the use of digital technologies to support appropriate **e-procurement** innovation throughout the procurement cycle. To this end, Adherents should:

i. Employ recent digital technology developments that allow integrated e-procurement solutions covering the public procurement cycle. Information and communication technologies should be used in public procurement to ensure transparency and access to public tenders, increasing competition, simplifying processes for contract award and management, driving cost savings and integrating public procurement and public finance information.

ii. Pursue state-of-the-art e-procurement tools that are modular, flexible, scalable and secure in order to assure business continuity, privacy and integrity, provide fair treatment and protect sensitive data, while supplying the core capabilities and functions that allow business innovation. E-procurement tools should be simple to use and appropriate to their purpose, and consistent across procurement agencies, to the extent possible; excessively complicated systems could create implementation risks and challenges for new entrants or small and medium enterprises.

Source: (OECD, 2015[1])

The State Government of Nuevo León (SGNL) has begun taking steps to digitise its procurement processes. Some of these steps include online publication and digital storage of procurement information and increasing use of e-reverse auctions. As previously discussed, e-procurement systems could contribute to economic development in the state. E-procurement could make the system more transparent and efficient. Coupled with the economic power of central purchasing, e-procurement could help spur economic development. Furthermore, an e-procurement system could help Nuevo León build a more effective and transparent government. These two goals are core objectives of Nuevo León's State Development Plan (Plan Estatal de Desarrollo) for 2016-2011, and the Strategic Plan for the State of Nuevo León 2015-2030 (Plan Estratégico para el Estado de Nuevo León 2015-2030). This chapter analyses the implementation of e-procurement systems in the SGNL. It then discusses ways in which e-procurement can result in diverse benefits, such as transparency, accountability, efficiency and performance management.

5.1. Developing informational e-procurement platforms that can better store and disseminate public procurement information

5.1.1. Increasing transparency of the public procurement system through the use of e-procurement

An adequate degree of transparency is essential to a well-functioning public procurement system. Because of this, many OECD countries have placed transparency at the heart of recent reforms of their public procurement systems. The 2013 OECD report, *Implementing the OECD Principles for Integrity in Public Procurement: Progress since 2008* recognised this trend. The report described how many countries seek to ensure a degree of transparency "that does not impede the effectiveness of public procurement" (OECD, 2013[2]). In order to increase transparency, many countries have implemented e-procurement systems.

Publishing and disseminating public procurement information has been one of the main motivations for the implementation of e-procurement systems in OECD countries, including in Mexico. In 2016, the state of Nuevo León approved the Law on Transparency and Access to Information of the State of Nuevo León (Ley de Transparencia y Acceso a la Información Pública del Estado de Nuevo León). It extended the transparency and access to information law that was already on the books to more public agencies and institutions. This was a great step forward in terms of ensuring transparency in the public sphere. This reflected the changing perception on public information. As the anti-corruption NGO Transparencia Mexicana explains, "In Mexico, public information has increasingly been conceived as the property of citizens, rather than as a prerogative of politicians" (Transparencia Mexicana, 2012[3]).

At present in Mexico, transparency in public procurement has been widely recognised as "an effective deterrent to corruption" (Transparencia Mexicana, 2012[3]). Increased transparency ensured through the use of e-procurement systems enables oversight of public officials' procurement decisions by more stakeholders. Thus, e-procurement systems provide greater accountability. The crucial role transparency plays in procurement systems is further described and also highlighted in the OECD Recommendation (Box 5.2).

Box 5.2. OECD Recommendation of the Council on Public Procurement

The Council:

II. Recommends that Adherents ensure an adequate degree of **transparency** of the public procurement system in all stages of the procurement cycle.

i. Promote fair and equitable treatment for potential suppliers by providing an adequate and timely degree of transparency in each phase of the public procurement cycle […]

ii. Allow free access, through an online portal, for all stakeholders, including potential domestic and foreign suppliers, civil society and the general public, to public procurement information […]

iii. Ensure visibility of the flow of public funds, from the beginning of the budgeting process throughout the public procurement cycle […]

Source: (OECD, 2015[1])

While the installation of an e-procurement system can increase accountability and oversight, it is not a cure-all. As the anti-corruption civil society organization, Transparency International, puts it, "the establishment of an e-procurement system as a stand-alone reform is unlikely to bring about positive transformational results. Transparency and accountability must be built into e-procurement specifications and design in order to allow for a meaningful analysis of the information generated" (TI, 2014[4]). In this sense, implementation of an e-procurement system should not be an end in itself. Governments must take measures to ensure that transparency, accountability and information analysis are built into all steps of the process, thus contributing to the sound functioning of the public procurement system overall.

Public procurement information recorded by the Electronic System of Public Procurement could be more clearly presented and made more easily searchable

Nuevo León's Central Purchasing Body (Unidad Centralizada de Compras, UCC) centralises purchasing in the state, and conducts all public procurement processes of goods and services for centralised entities. It also conducts procurement of goods and services for some decentralised entities with which it has signed a cooperation agreement. The Electronic System of Public Procurement (Sistema Electrónico de Compras Públicas, SECOP) publishes information related to public procurement processes that are carried out by the UCC via open tender, restricted invitation, e-reverse auction and framework agreement.

The SECOP has the objective of: 1) disseminating relevant information to potential suppliers, such as calls for tenders, clarification meetings and minutes of procurement events; 2) being the means by which electronic procurement procedures are developed; 3) promoting transparency and monitoring of public sector acquisitions, leases and services; and 4) generating the necessary information that allows adequate planning, programming and allocation of the budget for public procurement and the creation of all reports related to the evaluations. In view of these objectives, the main webpage of the SECOP[1] displays links to the following information (see Figure 5.1):

- laws and regulations applicable to public procurement of the SGNL
- current and past public procurement opportunities by open tender
- current and past public procurement opportunities by restricted invitation
- communiqués on framework agreements
- e-reverse auction portal[2]
- annual procurement programme
- registry of studies
- registry of suppliers
- registry of social witnesses.

Figure 5.1. Display of the main page of the SECOP

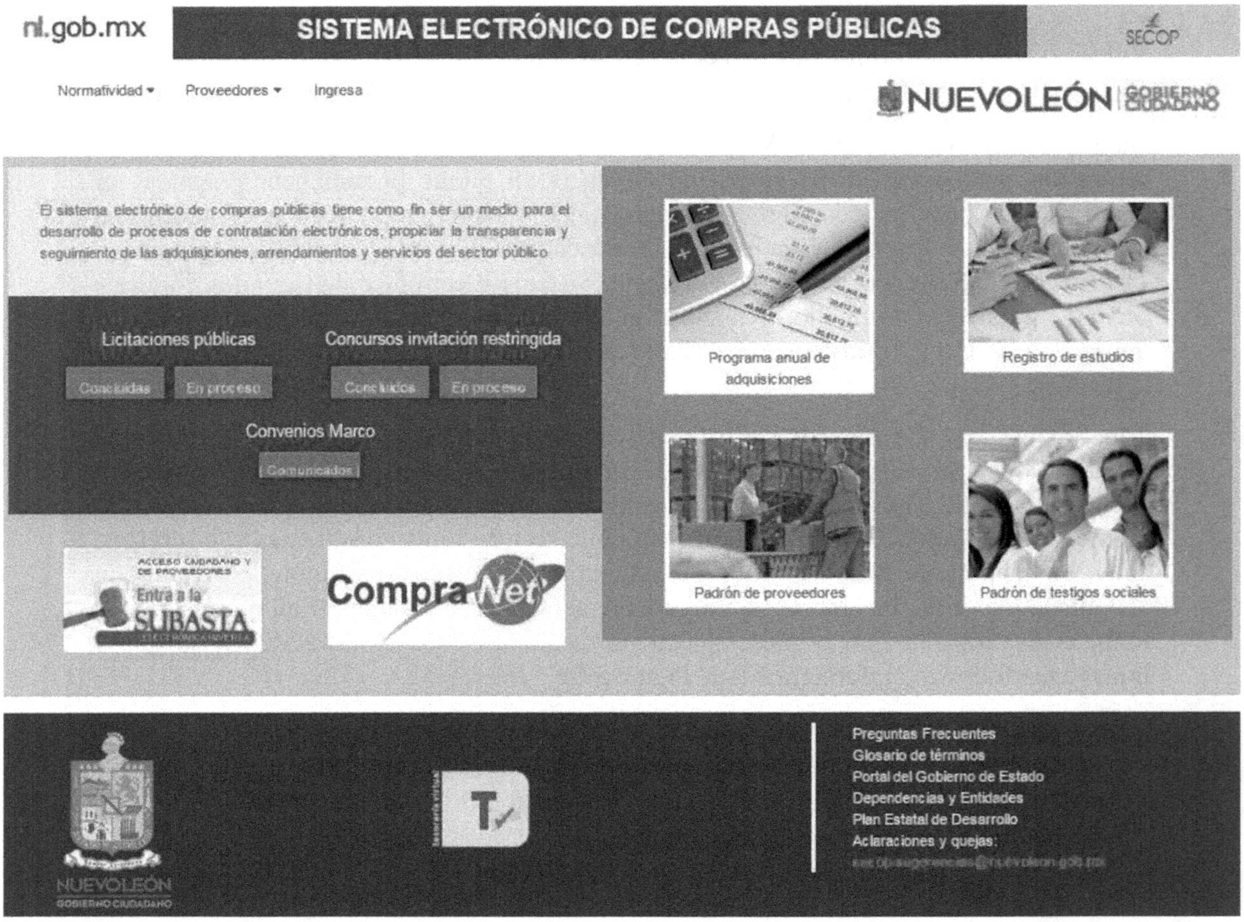

Source: (State Government of Nuevo León,(n.d.)[5])

These webpages contain information related to all the public procurement processes that have been carried out since the implementation of the SECOP in 2016. Each page on public procurement processes provides the complete list of subjects related to each type of procedure, along with a set of documents in PDF format. This list contains specific information on the procurement process; the number of the process, which also indicates the year of the process; and a description of the process. The description of the process includes information on whether it was open to international participation, whether it was carried out in a physical way or electronic way, and a short description of the good or the service that was (or will be) procured. This list is also complemented with links to documents that are associated with each process. For instance, for all concluded open tenders, one can consult the SECOP website for information regarding: the call for tender, technical specifications, minutes from clarification meetings, the opening of the proposals, evaluations by the procurement committee and the final judgment and award notice.

The way the SECOP website presents information could be altered to better reflect what the SGNL wants to communicate to its stakeholders. Currently, the number of tender processes the SECOP publishes on line is relatively low compared to other national e-procurement platforms. Yet, it is still difficult for users to access the information they need without prior knowledge about a specific process. For example, in order for any party to look for information on a public procurement process, it needs to plug in which procedure was used to carry out the process. Furthermore, the interested party needs to know whether the process of interest has been awarded, as well as the year it was undertaken. Put simply, it is difficult for interested parties to search the website if they do not have prior knowledge. Thus, the SECOP website's current layout does not facilitate access to information for those without information on specific processes. In light of these facts, the SGNL should consider what information would be of interest to its stakeholders, and how this information could be best communicated to them. For instance, some search functions and filters could be added to the lists of processes. In addition, some key information regarding the public procurement process overall could be displayed on the SECOP main page and on each page using PDF forms.

The SGNL could consider improving how it communicates annual procurement programmes

Publication of an annual procurement programme is obligatory for governmental entities in Nuevo León. Article 12 of the Law on Acquisition, Leases and Service Contracts of the State of Nuevo León (Ley de Adquisiciones, Arrendamientos y Contratación de Servicios del Estado de Nuevo León, LAASNL) stipulates that the annual procurement programmes of all governmental entities need to be made available on the SECOP and its websites by 31 January of each year. These programmes are meant to serve only as prospective references. They do not create any commitment, and can be modified with any additions, changes or by cancelation after informing respective procurement committees.

Currently, annual procurement programmes of 16 central government bodies are published on the SECOP. The programmes are published in PDF format, which can be consulted and downloaded directly from the platform. This way of displaying programmes only allows interested parties to search by individual entity and to look for the good or service of interest. Furthermore, the annual procurement programmes do not specify which year they correspond to.

The way the SECOP presents information needs to correspond to the communication objective of the information. For example, both government entities and suppliers rely on information provided by annual procurement programmes. These programmes help government entities plan their procurement activities for the forthcoming year and organise their spending in more structured and predictable ways. These programmes also possess crucial information for suppliers. Suppliers need this information in order to be informed about upcoming procurement opportunities so that they can organise bids. Thus, the presentation of information about annual procurement programmes needs to contain information that are useful both to government entities and suppliers.

Nuevo León's current communication methods are not optimal, especially in achieving the latter objective of informing suppliers. Most suppliers do not know which entities need their goods and services. Furthermore, a one-year range (as delineated by the annual procurement programmes) is too broad for suppliers to plan effectively. In light of these facts, the SGNL could assess what information, and how much advance notice suppliers need to increase their participation and access to public procurement opportunities. During the OECD fact-finding mission to Nuevo León, shareholders asserted that certain suppliers approach government entities individually in order to understand their needs and upcoming procurement opportunities. This creates information asymmetry between public officials and suppliers, as well as among suppliers. In order to reduce this information asymmetry and facilitate and increase participation of suppliers, the SGNL should communicate better with all suppliers, not just the select few that have the means or drive to reach out in person. The SGNL can improve its communication by creating annual procurement programmes based on assessments of suppliers' needs. The Annual Procurement Plan List in the Australian Government procurement information system, AusTender, could serve as a model for these changes (Box 5.3).

Box 5.3. AusTender - Annual Procurement Plan List

AusTender, the Australian government procurement information system, provides suppliers one central point to find publicly available business opportunities and planned procurements advertised by the Australian government.

On AusTender, suppliers can browse annual procurement plans by agency, or search procurements by keyword, category, date of approach to market and/or agency. If, for example, a supplier sells office equipment, it can filter procurements by this category and then browse planned procurements across the government. Suppliers can also add procurements of interest to their AusTender "watch list" in order to receive updates and notifications.

Source: (Australian Government,(n.d.)[6])

As a long-term strategy, the SGNL could publish public procurement information from all governmental entities, including information from parastatal entities, on a single portal

In addition to the SECOP, the government of Nuevo León uses a few other channels to publish information related to public procurement opportunities. It is mandatory in the state that information related to public procurement processes that are not carried out by the UCC be recorded on the State Transparency Portal[3]. The information that gets recorded on the Transparency Portal is similar to the information available via the SECOP. In particular, the portal provides public procurement information by entity, including tender notices, direct awards of public works, purchase orders and e-reverse auction processes. While there are some key differences between the Transparency Portal and the SECOP, both follow very similar publication requirements. The complete list of information available at present via the Transparency Portal can be observed in Figure 5.2 The display method of this portal poses similar problems to those of the SECOP. Unless interested parties have information on a specific process, the display is not easy for users to navigate.

On the Transparency Portal, purchase order records are put together by each state government body and agency and published on a monthly basis. The equivalent of this information is not yet available on the SECOP. Certain data records available for download via the Transparency Portal contain different types of information per entity and are not presented in a uniform way.

The SGNL could consider developing a single portal through which all information related to public procurement can be accessed. Such a portal should include all information from central government bodies, as well as decentralised agencies. This could enable the government to better communicate procurement information. It would also foster greater transparency by allowing a larger base of stakeholders to access the system and gain knowledge about public procurement in the state.

Figure 5.2. The public procurement transparency portal of the SGNL

Source: (State Government of Nuevo León,(n.d.)[7])

5.1.2. Managing supplier information via the Unique Registry of Suppliers and Contractors (Padrón Único de Proveedores et Contratistas)

The registry should store information on suppliers and contractors using a structured, electronic format so as to decrease the amount of information it has to provide during each procurement process

For any potential suppliers to participate in public procurement, they need to be registered in the state registry first. In 2017, the SGNL launched the Unique Registry of Suppliers and Contractors (Registro Único de Proveedores y Contratistas, RUPC*)*. The RUPC[4] unifies the registration processes for suppliers of goods and services and suppliers of works. Previously, suppliers of goods and services were registered through Registry of Suppliers (Padrón de Proveedores), while contractors of works were registered through the State Registry of Contractors *(*Registro Estatal des Contratistas).

Under the current framework, suppliers and contractors complete their registrations on a single portal, providing general information including:

- information on the legal representative of their organisation, legal identity documents and general information regarding the company, its address and their proof

- federal taxpayer registration number and supporting documentation
- declaration of economic activities
- geographical location and photographic proof
- résumé and previous experiences
- certification
- financial information based on annual declarations.

On the main dashboard, they can follow the progress of the registration.

RUPC registration is free; however, the amount of documentation that is required of suppliers and contractors to register and participate in state public procurement opportunities is quite substantial. Suppliers and contractors are given a registration certificate that allows them to participate in public procurement processes only once the registration is complete. The Secretariat of Administration reviews and validates the registration process for suppliers of goods and services, while the Secretariat of Infrastructure (Secretaria de Infraestructura) reviews and validates the registration process for contractors of works.

The SGNL should consider ways to lessen the administrative burden for suppliers and contractors once the registration is complete. For instance, the information suppliers and contractors provide within the RUPC could be stored in a structured format that is easily retrievable during public procurement processes. If contracting authorities, especially the UCC, could retrieve general information on each supplier from the RUPC, it could lessen the administrative burden both on suppliers and on public authorities. This is especially true with regards to having to verify the consistency of information during each process. If the SGNL chose to take steps to keep general information on each supplier easily available, it would also be important to ensure that this information was updated on a regular basis.

5.2. Increasing the efficiency of the public procurement system through the use of electronic mechanisms

In addition to facilitating storage and timely diffusion of public procurement information, integrating digital technologies into the public procurement function increases the efficiency of the system. This is the case because data technologies encourage standardisation and automation of procurement processes, as well as savings in terms of transactions, administrative costs and time. Furthermore, in many countries around the world, governments adopt digital procurement tools to increase efficiency. These tools, also acknowledged in the OECD Recommendation as increasing the efficiency of public procurement systems (Box 5.4), are increasingly provided on e-procurement systems in OECD countries.

Box 5.4. OECD Recommendation of the Council on Public Procurement

The Council:

VII. **Recommends** that Adherents develop processes to drive **efficiency** throughout the public procurement cycle in satisfying the needs of the government and its citizens. To this end, Adherents should: […]

iii. Develop and use tools to improve procurement procedures, reduce duplication and achieve greater value for money, including centralised purchasing, framework agreements, e-catalogues, dynamic purchasing, e-auctions, joint procurements and contracts with options. […]

Source: (OECD, 2015[1])

This section discusses how the SGNL could further increase efficiency of the public procurement system through existing e-procurement solutions, as well as electronic tools that the SGNL could further utilise for this end.

5.2.1. Setting strategic objectives for the e-procurement system

Implementing new electronic procurement tools should be linked to strategic objectives

After inheriting the current version of the SECOP from the previous administration of the SGNL, the current administration began to develop a 2.0 version of the SECOP. The new administration's objective is to use the platform to unify, simplify and digitise the system for registration of suppliers of goods and services, as well as contractors. The administration also hopes to improve the SECOP in order to streamline public purchases and contracting in the state.

The SGNL is increasingly devoting efforts to reaping the benefits of the e-procurement system that go beyond transparency. For instance, the state government has expressed a desire to increase the efficiency of the public procurement system. The development of the e-procurement system in the SGNL supports this objective through simplifying and streamlining the procurement procedures. Colombia has made similar efforts (see Box 5.5). The SGNL should ensure that e-procurement developments are in line with the overall development plan of the state, and that e-procurement is not linked to one specific government administration. By doing so, it could ensure the continuity of the system – not only in the minds of public officials, but also for the suppliers that participate in public procurement process.

Box 5.5. E-procurement in Colombia

Colombia passed a law in 2007 that made it mandatory for every procuring entity to disclose documents related to procurement on an electronic webpage called the Electronic System for Public Procurement (Sistema Electrónico de Contratación Pública, SECOP). Following the passage of this law, interested suppliers could check the SECOP for business opportunities for free. This boosted competition in tender processes.

Colombia Compra Eficiente launched SECOP II in 2015. SECOP II is a fully transactional e-procurement platform conceived as an evolution of the first SECOP. On this platform, suppliers can create a profile and receive updates of new business opportunities. Interaction with procuring agencies is performed through SECOP II. Bids are submitted electronically, and data is disclosed in real time for any interested party. Modules for the publication of annual procurement plans and for contract management have also been included in the new platform. SECOP II improves overall efficiency as it increases competition and reduces transaction costs related to procurement processes. Furthermore, SECOP II operates in tandem with the budget system of the central government.

Note: SECOP II can be accessed through https://www.colombiacompra.gov.co/secop/secop-ii.
Source: Information provided by Colombia Compra Eficiente

5.2.2. Use of e-procurement to cover the whole public procurement cycle

The SGNL could consider expanding its use of the e-procurement system to cover the whole public procurement cycle so as to reduce paper-based processes and support public procurement operations

Automation of the procurement process replaces face-to-face interactions by placing them on electronic platforms; this increases the system's efficiency by reducing transaction and administrative costs, as well as time. Furthermore, replacement of processes requiring the physical presence of public procurement officials with automated electronic processes reduces the room for integrity breaches. Transactional e-procurement platforms that allow interaction with the system are thus highly useful to both contracting authorities and suppliers.

Most of the obligations regarding the use of e-procurement systems in the SGNL are related to the publication of information. Currently, public procurement processes in Nuevo León generally take place via face-to-face interactions not via electronic means (except for the cases of e-reverse auction).

Use of e-procurement systems is pervasive among OECD countries, though the degree of implementation varies. As is true with the SGNL, e-procurement systems in many OECD countries are most commonly used to publish and store public procurement information. The functionalities that are more often provided by OECD countries' e-procurement systems include announcing tenders, notifying suppliers of contract awards and providing tender documents. The functionalities that are related to transactional aspects of e-procurement systems – such as electronic submission of invoices, online catalogues and ordering – are provided by e-procurement systems in a minority of OECD countries. The grand majority of OECD countries simply use e-procurement systems to support electronic submissions of bids.

Figure 5.3. Functionalities provided in e-procurement systems of OECD countries (2016)

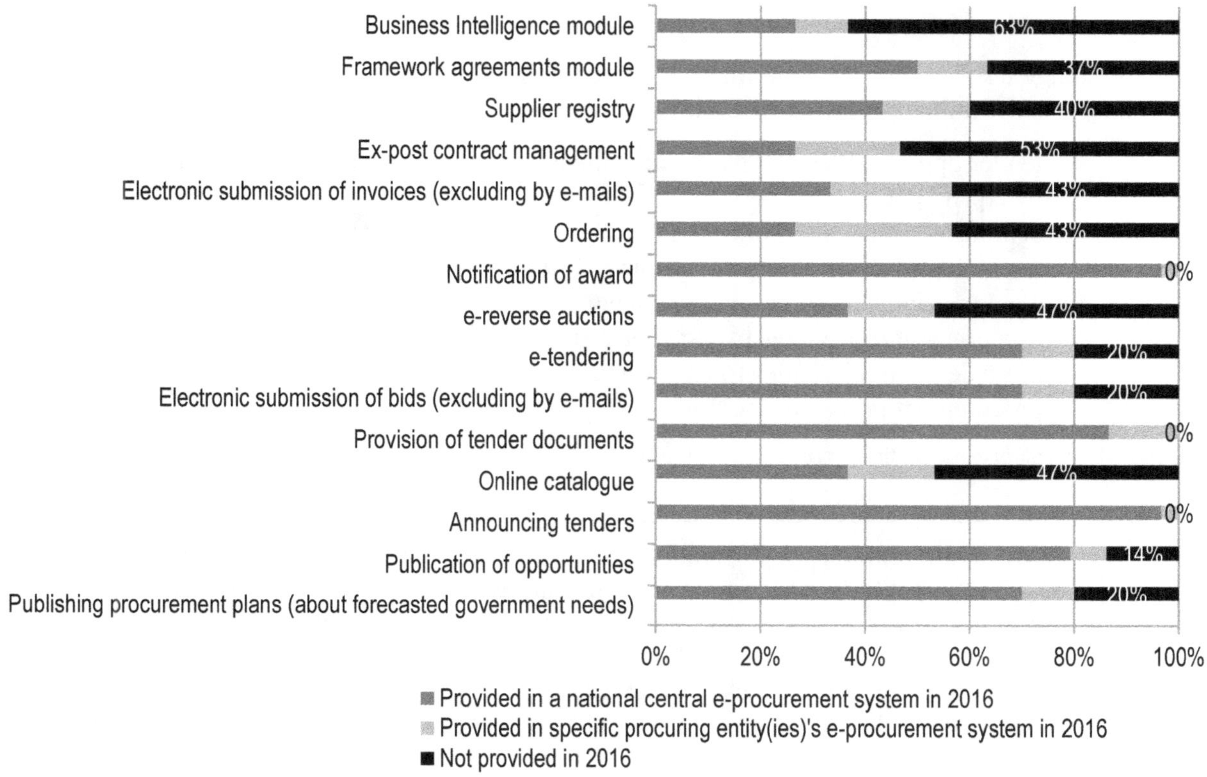

Source: 2016 OECD Survey on Public Procurement, unpublished.

OECD countries are increasingly making their e-procurement systems more transactional. For example, Canada, Israel and Slovenia have all announced plans to implement electronic submission of bids. Furthermore, the European Commission has developed initiatives to support the transition to an e-procurement system that covers the whole public procurement cycle for all European Union (EU) member countries. This move includes mandatory e-submission of bids in EU member countries by 2018.

Box 5.6. E procurement initiatives in the EU

The European Union has taken initiatives towards an end-to-end e-procurement system. Going beyond electronic tools, procurement digitalisation rethinks various pre-award and post-award phases with the aim of making procurement processes simpler for businesses to participate in and for the public sector to manage.

In achieving this end, the new rules on e-procurement in the EU are to be gradually introduced with the following timeline:

- tender opportunities and tender documents will become electronically available by April 2016
- central purchasing bodies should move to full electronic means of communication including electronic bid submission by April 2017
- e-submission should be made mandatory for all contracting authorities and all procurement procedures by October 2018
- more detailed provisions to encourage interoperability and standardisation of e-procurement processes are forthcoming.

Source: (European Commission,(n.d.)[8])

The SGNL could exploit opportunities to further digitise its public procurement operations. The state could take measures to accomplish this by digitising submission of requisition from the state government bodies and agencies to the UCC, ordering, invoicing and contract management. These processes are already recorded digitally, but they exist mostly in PDF format as scanned copies of documents. Replacing this paper-based process with digital technologies could, in particular, improve administrative delays and burdens on public officials and suppliers. It could also further standardise and streamline public procurement operations.

5.3. Use of the e-procurement system to support data collection, and the use of data to improve the public procurement system

A well-implemented e-procurement system enables and facilitates timely collection of comprehensive and reliable data. Statistical information on procurement using these data is essential in evaluating the policies and functioning of the system. The OECD Recommendation underlines the importance of "driving performance improvements through evaluation of the effectiveness of the public procurement system from individual procurements to the system as a whole, at all levels of government where feasible and appropriate" (OECD, 2015[1]). It further details that, in order to achieve this end, countries should "assess periodically and consistently the results of the procurement process. Public procurement systems should collect consistent, up-to-date and reliable information and use data on prior procurements, particularly regarding price and overall costs, in structuring new needs assessments, as they provide a valuable source of insight and could guide future procurement decisions" (OECD, 2015[1]).

5.3.1. Assessing the performance of the public procurement system

Automatically collecting and centralising public procurement data from the SECOP and other related systems according to a pre-defined performance framework could help the SGNL assess and evaluate the performance of its public procurement system

The SGNL's public procurement system has undergone a significant reform. This reform focused not only on institutional changes, but also on how the public procurement function was viewed in the state. Previously, the procurement process was viewed as an administrative "tick-the-box" exercise. The reform allowed the SGNL to implement various measures to transform public procurement into a strategic tool. These measures aim to help procurement officials make efficiency gains and create value for money, as discussed in previous chapters. While this transformation is still underway, it is of utmost importance that the SGNL collect meaningful data and use them to assess the performance of the public procurement system.

Currently, the SECOP does not contain functionalities that allow for automatic aggregation of data. Rather, data are rather collected on manual basis in Excel files. At the same time, the SECOP includes a registry of studies. This registry is supposed to include studies based on data and information collected through electronic means. However, no reports or studies have been generated with data collected through the e-procurement system. The registry only lists one study. It is called the Consultation on Preparation of the State Development Plan, and is listed as published in January 2016. That said, the study is not accessible via Internet (Figure 5.4).

Figure 5.4. SECOP's registry of studies

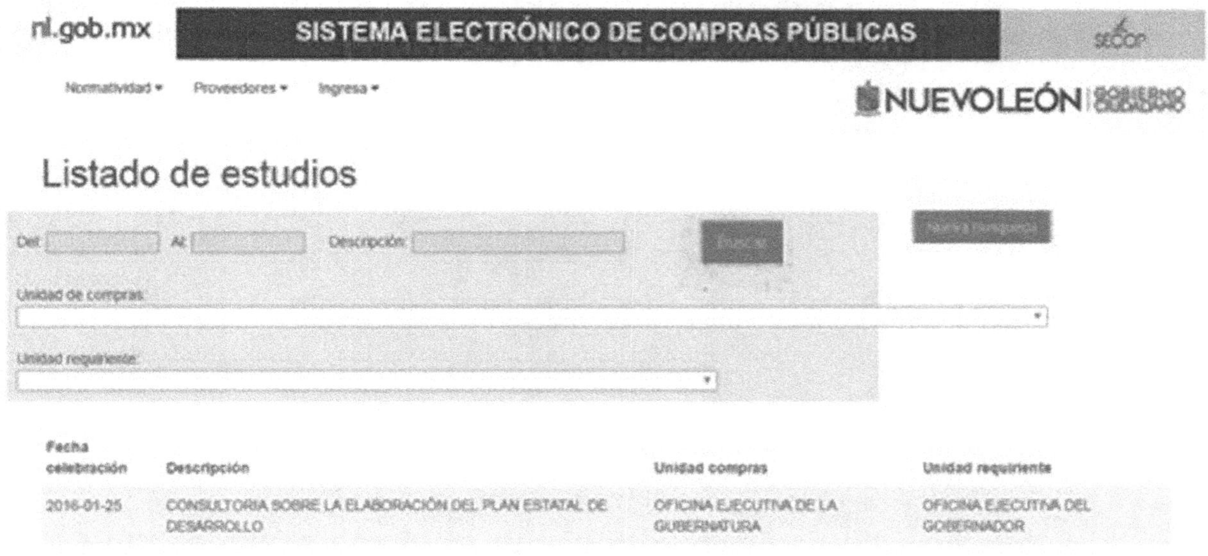

Source: (State government of Nuevo León,(n.d.)[9])

OECD countries increasingly use the data that are generated through e-procurement system in order to assess the performance of their public procurement systems and to communicate information about their systems to different stakeholders. This means that these systems cannot be not limited to internal use by their governments. Countries increasingly publish data in order to communicate with the diverse stakeholders of the public procurement system, including potential suppliers, civil societies, academics and citizens. The case of Korea's public procurement data system (Box 5.7) provides an example of such use and the communication of public procurement data.

Box 5.7. Korea's public procurement data system

Almost 70% of public procurement transactions in Korea occur via the Korean On Line E-Procurement System (KONEPS). The remaining transactions, including defence procurement, procurement transactions by other public enterprises that use their own e-procurement systems and some manual transactions, are not currently practised in a centralised way. In 2013, Korea's Public Procurement Service (PPS) launched the Public Procurement Data System to close this gap. The project aims to provide policy makers and citizens with complete procurement transaction data across the entire public sector in order to enable a better understanding of the procurement market. The project also includes an analytical study of policy results.

Proper legal authority for the project was established by modifications made to existing procurement laws, including the Government Procurement Act (July 2013) and the Enforcement Decree on the Government Procurement Act (January 2014). These modifications gave the PPS the legal authority to request data, and to establish deadlines for government agencies to submit the requested procurement data.

Total public procurement in Korea encompasses procurements that occur in both electronic and non-electronic ways. Electronic procurement is carried out on KONEPS and 23 other electronic procurement platforms for specific procuring entities. Thus, data integration includes linking of the 24 e-procurement systems, as well as central collection of manual records. A report will be prepared to present the data collected per government bodies, companies, and projects. Data will also be presented in infographics in order to facilitate end user comprehension.

The data integration faces some difficulties due to administrative burdens that affect approximately 28 000 government agencies. Delays in concomitant projects in some government agencies to improve their electronic systems, which were intended to facilitate the data integration, can also slow progress. In order to alleviate the administrative burden on the collection of manually kept data, the Korean government is discussing linking data integration to other financial information systems, including the Educational Financial System, the Local Government Budget and Accounting System, the Local Pubic Enterprise Budget and Accounting System and the National Budget and Accounting System. Additionally, some difficulties have arisen due to the disparity of the information collected at each government agency and across different e-procurement systems. In response, the government provided new code mapping to agencies where data were collected by different standards.

Provision and publication of data statistics on total public procurement on a monthly and annual basis, and 103 specific reports based on the data, are expected to increase the availability of data for companies and the public. It is the hope of the Korean government that the availability of these data will enhance government and budgetary transparency. The reports will be made available on line.

Source: (OECD, 2016$_{[10]}$)

The SGNL could consider making further use of public procurement data and information in order to assess the functioning of its public procurement system. This would necessitate identifying a performance framework for the SGNL's public procurement system. According to this framework, the SGNL could then define the areas where collection and aggregation of data is needed. As acknowledged in Chapter 2, the

Secretariat of Administration is defining a set of key performance indicators for the public procurement system. These indicators would provide a performance framework against which the state's public procurement system could be assessed according to certain objectives and priorities. Colombia's development of key performance indicators for its public procurement system (Box 5.8) could provide some insight. In developing Nuevo León's framework, the communication between different authorities – including those who define the indicators and those who manage the IT system – would be crucial. The reason for this is that all parties must have a common understanding of the objectives and priorities of the system, as well as the administrative implications and any questions of feasibility.

Box 5.8. Key performance indicators of the public procurement system of Colombia

11 key indicators across four key target areas

Along with the development of SECOP II, Colombia's current e-procurement, Colombia has recognised the importance of developing key performance indicators that can be derived from information available within SECOP II and other related systems. 11 key indicators across four key target areas have been identified and defined.

Indicator	What does it measure?	Description
	Value for money	
Opportunity of the contracting process	The level of budgetary commitments in a fiscal year	Ratio between the commitments and the appropriation during the fiscal year, which does not include staff costs, budgetary transferences and debt expenses
Changes in value according to specifications	The variation in the value of the contracts between the initial value established in the tender documents and the final value awarded	Average difference between the estimated value of the selection and the final value of the contract
Average time of the selection process according to the award mechanism	Difference in time of the selection process by award mechanism	Period of time between the signature date of a contract and the starting date of the process
	Integrity and transparency in competition	
Average of new contractors	Percentage of new contractors in a public entity regarding the former year	Ratio of new contractors of a public entity to the number of contractors working in the public entity in the previous year
Concentration of the contracts' value by contractor	The concentration of resources by contractor that perform for a public entity through public procurement	Concentration of a public entity's budget by contractor measured by the Gini coefficient
Percentage of contracts awarded to plural bidders	Frequency of awarded contracts to plural bidders by a public entity	Ratio of the contracts and the value of the contracts awarded by a public entity to plural bidders
Percentage of contracts awarded in non-competitive processes	Percentage of public contracting that is done under non-competitive processes	Percentage of awarded contracts without a competitive process, not including inter-administrative contracts, reserve spending of the defence sector and professional services
	Accountability	
Percentage of public entity users of the SECOP	SECOP use by the public entities that are obligated to use it	Percentage of public entities using the SECOP
Percentage of public entities that publish their annual acquisition plans on the SECOP	The progress in the compliance of the publication of the Annual Acquisition Plan on the SECOP	Percentage of public entities that publish their Annual Acquisition Plan every year on the SECOP
Percentage of publicity of the contracting processes in the SECOP	The level of publication on the SECOP of the contracts signed in a fiscal year	Percentage of the value of the procurement processes that a public entity publishes on the SECOP
	Risk management	
Percentage of contracts with modifications in time or value	Proportion of contracts modified after their signature regarding the total of contracts done by a public entity	Proportion of contracts modified in the value or in the duration of their performance after their signature

Source: (OECD, 2016[11])

5.3.2. Use of data to improve the public procurement system

Analysing historical public procurement data and annual procurement programmes could help the UCC better manage public resources spending and exploit opportunities for efficiency gains

As discussed in previous sections of this chapter, publication of procurement plans not only benefits suppliers by informing them and helping them prepare for upcoming procurement opportunities. It also aids public authorities to better plan their spending activities.

Current annual procurement programmes used in Nuevo León include the product or service code, a description of the good or service, the procuring unit and a quantity. These programmes are available on the SECOP in PDF formats. They are not binding, and state government bodies and agencies can modify them throughout the year. The Administration and Communication Headship of the Ministry of Administration is responsible for collecting projects for annual procurement programmes from various agencies and administrative units of the state government. However, during the OECD fact-finding mission, officials asserted that insufficient analysis was carried out on annual procurement programmes.

In addition to considering how the government communicates with shareholders about annual procurement programmes, the SGNL needs to think about how annual procurement programmes could be used to improve the public procurement system. Together with historical data on public procurement spending, they could be further analysed to explore more consolidation opportunities. These programmes could also be used to monitor gaps in terms and conditions, especially prices, of similar goods and services. Furthermore, in cases where a relatively high number of changes are made to annual procurement programmes, the UCC could provide guidance to help the government bodies and the agencies plan their purchases. Such guidance from managers could also help officials within the UCC have more predictability with their work flow.

Detailed management of product and service categories could further help the SGNL bring value for money to public procurement

Interviews carried out during the OECD's fact-finding mission identified some hesitation among suppliers to register with the RUPC. One main reason was that suppliers believed the government offered an uncompetitive business relationship in comparison to the market – mainly because of delayed payments. Sometimes, decentralised agencies in Nuevo León have their own lists of suppliers who are not registered with the RUPC. Agencies use these suppliers because they can offer more competitive terms and conditions for the goods and services being procured. In order to ensure sound functioning along with the centralisation of public procurement, the UCC needs to be able to establish competitive terms and conditions between the state government bodies and agencies that they procure for, and the suppliers. More detailed management of product and service categories through the e-procurement system, and improved data collection could aid the SGNL to achieve this end.

Collecting data in a more structured and systematic way, as stressed in this chapter, could help the SGNL identify the types of procedure that are more suitable for each product and service category. Data collection could also help the SGNL establish more competitive prices. In order to do so, information needs to be managed by different product and service categories. Subsequently, public procurement authorities could be assigned to manage, accumulate and further develop knowledge according to established product and service categories. Furthermore, the SGNL is currently developing an e-catalogue module on its e-procurement system to support purchases of goods and services of smaller value. For this development, it would be crucial to have a sound understanding of the market, as well as the needs of the government bodies and agencies for each product and service group.

5.4. Proposals for action

The SGNL has made important progress in the use of electronic mechanisms to support public procurement processes. Publication of public procurement information through the SECOP has increased transparency of the public procurement system. Despite these advances, however, this chapter has discussed the SGNL's lack of strategy with regards to communicating information on the e-procurement system. This is important, as the SGNL needs to make diverse public procurement information available to various shareholders via this platform.

In addition to transparency, the SGNL is also exploring further opportunities to gain efficiency through e-procurement systems. The state government has unified suppliers' and contractors' registration processes and started developing e-catalogues. Data collection in a structured and automatic way could help the SGNL increase the efficiency of the public procurement system. In particular, it would be crucial for the SGNL to use data to assess the functioning of the public procurement systems in a more sustained way.

In this regard, the SGNL could consider undertaking the following actions in order to reap certain benefits from using electronic mechanisms:

Develop an informational e-procurement platform that can better store and disseminate public procurement information

1. Increase transparency of the public procurement system through the use of e-procurement
   - Public procurement information recorded on the SECOP could be more clearly presented and made more easily searchable.
   - The SGNL could consider improving how annual procurement programmes are communicated.
   - As a long-term strategy, the SGNL could publish public procurement information of all governmental entities, including that of parastatal entities, on a single portal.
2. Managing suppliers' information: The Unique Registry of Suppliers and Contractors
   - The registry should store information on suppliers and contractors in an electronic and structured format so as to decrease the amount of information requested for each process.

Increase efficiency of the public procurement system through the use of electronic mechanisms

1. Set strategic objectives for implementation of the e-procurement system

- The implementation of new electronic procurement tools should be linked to strategic objectives.

2. Use e-procurement for the whole public procurement cycle.
   - The SGNL could consider further use of e-procurement system to cover the whole public procurement cycle so as to reduce paper-based processes and support public procurement operations.

Use e-procurement system to support data collection and the use of data to improve the public procurement system

1. Assess the performance of the public procurement system
   - Automatically collecting and centralising public procurement data from the SECOP and other related systems according to a pre-defined performance framework could help the SGNL assess and evaluate the performance of its public procurement system.
2. Use data to improve the public procurement system
   - Analysing historical public procurement data and annual procurement programmes could help the UCC better manage public resource spending, and exploit opportunities for efficiency gains.
   - Detailed management of product and service categories could further help the SGNL bring value for money to public procurement.

Notes

[1] http://secop.nl.gob.mx/

[2] http://subasta.nl.gob.mx/

[3] http://transparencia.nl.gob.mx/site/consulta?concepto=7

[4] https://proveedores.nl.gob.mx

References

Australian Government((n.d.)), *AusTender: Annual Procurement Plan List*, https://www.tenders.gov.au/?event=public.APP.list (accessed on 07 June 2017). [6]

European Commission((n.d.)), *E-procurement*, https://ec.europa.eu/growth/single-market/public-procurement/e-procurement_fr (accessed on 15 September 2017). [8]

OECD (2013), *Implementing the OECD principles for integrity in public procurement : progress since 2008.*, OECD Publishing, Paris, http://dx.doi.org/10.1787/9789264201385-en. [2]

OECD (2015), *OECD Recommendation of the Council on Public Procurement*, https://www.oecd.org/gov/ethics/OECD-Recommendation-on-Public-Procurement.pdf (accessed on 18 May 2017). [1]

OECD (2016), *The Korean Public Procurement Service: Innovating for Effectiveness.*, OECD Publishing, Paris, http://dx.doi.org/10.1787/9789264249431-en. [10]

OECD (2016), *Towards Efficient Public Procurement in Colombia : Making the Difference*, OECD Publishing, Paris, http://dx.doi.org/10.1787/9789264252103-en. [11]

State Government of Nuevo León((n.d.)), *Sistema Electrónico de Compras Públicas (Electronic system for public procurement)*, http://secop.nl.gob.mx/ (accessed on 07 September 2017). [5]

State Government of Nuevo León((n.d.)), *Sistema Estatal de Transparencia: Licitaciones, adjudicaciones, y contratos [Transparency System of the State of Nuevo León: Tenders, awards and contracts]*, http://transparencia.nl.gob.mx/site/consulta?concepto=7 (accessed on 27 September 2017). [7]

State government of Nuevo León((n.d.)), *SECOP NL - Registro de estudios [Registry of Studies]*, http://secop.nl.gob.mx/?P=regestudios&order=lista (accessed on 27 September 2017). [9]

TI (2014), *The role of technology in reducing corruption in public procurement*, https://www.transparency.org/files/content/corruptionqas/The_role_of_technology_in_reducing_corruption_in_public_procurement_2014.pdf (accessed on 11 July 2017). [4]

Transparencia Mexicana (2012), *A New Role for Citizens in Public Procurement*, http://corruptionresearchnetwork.org/marketplace/resources/C-M%20SERIES%20-%20A%20new%20Role%20for%20Citizens%20in%20Public%20Procurement.pdf/ (accessed on 12 July 2017). [3]

Chapter 6. Ensuring the integrity of public procurement processes in Nuevo León

This chapter assesses the system for ensuring the integrity of public procurement processes in Nuevo León against the 2015 OECD Recommendation on Public Procurement and the 2017 OECD Recommendation on Public Integrity. The chapter analyses the state's existing integrity policies and legal framework to establish how effective they are at reducing the risk of corruption during the public procurement cycle. Furthermore, the chapter recommends measures to enhance integrity rules, such as a code of ethics, use of declarations and a whistle-blower programme. The chapter discusses measures to ensure accountability and control with regards to the sanctioning of suppliers. It also underlines the importance of actively engaging the private sector and civil society. Finally, the chapter looks at the experiences of other OECD countries in order to illustrate potential improvements Nuevo León could make to its integrity framework.

In OECD countries around the world, public procurement activities present a high risk of integrity violations and corruption. The main reason for this is that public procurement requires a significant level of expenditure, and the procurement cycle as a whole is quite complex. In addition, a lack of transparency, a weak governance system, and the close interaction between public officials and businesses also expose countries to integrity risks

Like other Mexican states, Nuevo León, is susceptible to such risks. While the state is currently developing initiatives and mechanisms to promote integrity in government activities and decisions, it still faces a number of challenges. These challenges include the complexities of building a coherent and comprehensive integrity system, and instilling a culture of integrity in the state's public administration.

Public procurement is particularly vulnerable to mismanagement, fraud and corruption – which can occur in all phases of the procurement cycle and at all levels of government. These issues can have a significant impact on publicly funded projects in many different sectors. This holds true in Mexico. Indeed, according to the Superior Audit Office of the Federation (Auditoría Superior de la Federación, ASF), the lack of sanction of corruption offences cost Mexico an average of USD 86 billion from 2005 to 2015. Specialists attribute these losses to deviations, underspending, waste of resources and undue payments within the government (Casar M.A, 2016[1]).

This chapter analyses Nuevo León's integrity policies, and the legal framework it applies to public procurement operations. The chapter highlights recent developments, and emphasises areas where further efforts are needed. Specifically, the chapter discusses corruption risk-mapping, disclosures and management of conflicts of interest, as well as integrity training and awareness programmes, and whistle-blower protections. It also addresses the key role of the private sector in these issues, and the importance of setting high integrity standards for all stakeholders in the procurement cycle. The chapter undertakes a discussion of how states implement anti-corruption and integrity initiatives in the public procurement sector. Finally, the chapter assesses these issues against the key principles of the OECD Recommendation on Public Procurement (OECD, 2015[2]), and the initiatives taken in the context of establishing Nuevo León's local anti-corruption system.

In Mexico, public procurement represents 5.2% of GDP and 70% of this activity is carried out at the sub-national level, as described in Figure 6.1 and Figure 6.2 Public procurement activities in Nuevo León account for nearly USD 546 million. Spending on public procurement in Nuevo León is concentrated in the areas of public safety, social development, education and health, as mentioned in Chapter 2.

Figure 6.1. General government procurement as percentage of GDP in 2007, 2009 and 2014

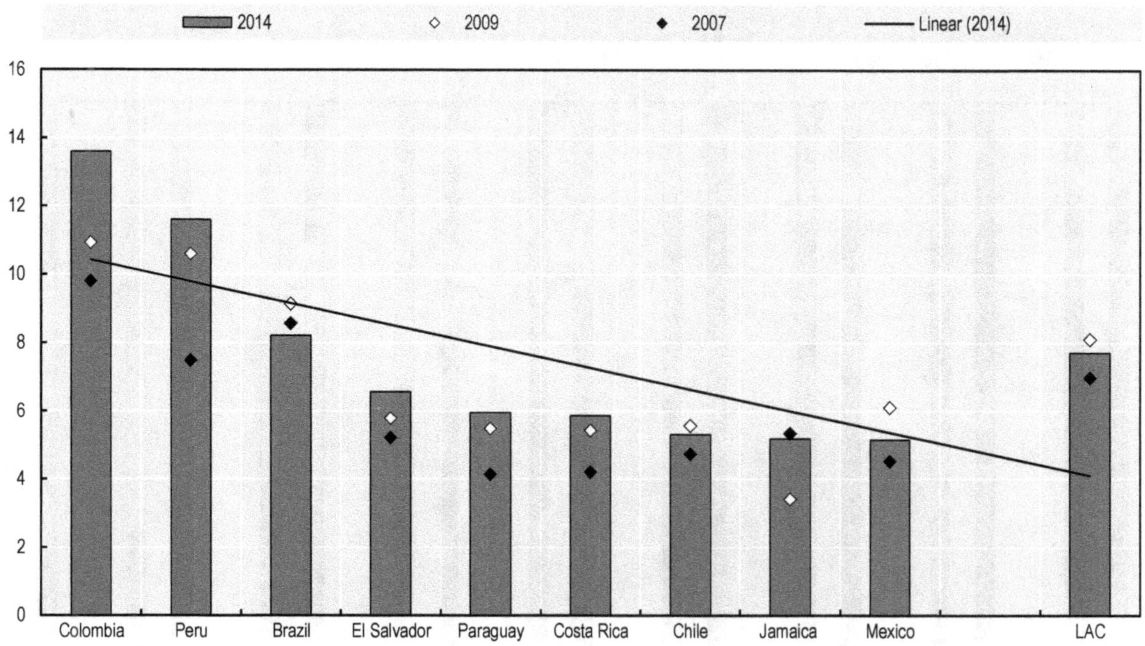

Source: IMF Government Finance Statistics (IMF GFS) database. Data for Mexico are based on the OECD National Accounts Statistics database. Data for Peru and Paraguay are recorded on a cash basis. For Costa Rica and Jamaica, the part of government procurement related to gross fixed capital formation does not include the consumption of fixed capital. Costs of goods and services financed by the general government are not included in government procurement because they are not accounted separately in the IMF Government Finance Statistics database) Data for El Salvador and Mexico refer to 2013 rather than 2014. Data for Colombia refer to 2008 rather than 2007. The Figure includes the average for Latin American countries (LAC).
Source: (OECD, 2016[3])

Figure 6.2. Share of general government procurement in the region by level of government, 2007 and 2014

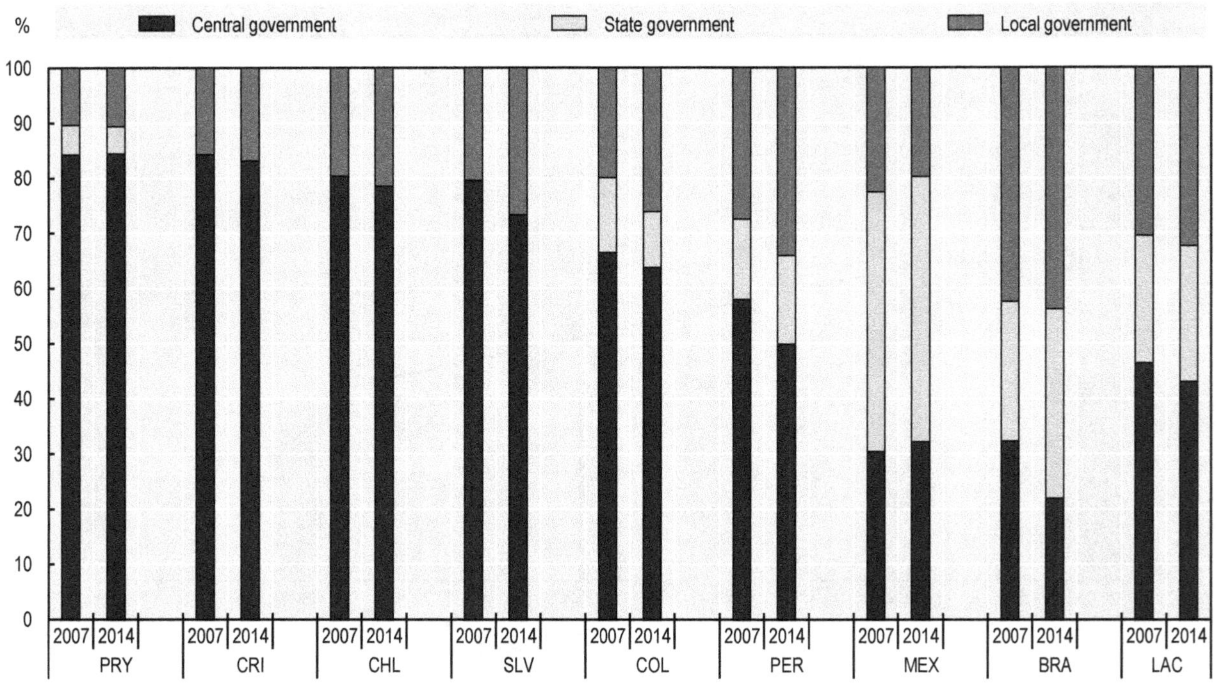

Source: (OECD, 2016[3])

Corruption and integrity breaches in public procurement have major consequences for the allocations of resources. These consequences range from economic losses due to misappropriation of public funds and the deterioration of competition, to the corrosion of citizen trust in public institutions and public officials. This lack of trust extends to officials' use of taxpayer money in the public interest. Accordingly, the OECD Recommendation on Public Procurement underscores the importance of preserving the integrity of a public procurement system (see Box 6.1).

Box 6.1. The OECD Recommendation on Public Procurement

The Council:

III. RECOMMENDS that Adherents preserve the **integrity** of the public procurement system through general standards and procurement-specific safeguards.

To this end, Adherents should:

i) Require high standards of integrity for all stakeholders in the procurement cycle. Standards embodied in integrity frameworks or codes of conduct applicable to public sector employees (such as on managing conflict of interest, disclosure of information, or other standards of professional behaviour) could be expanded (e.g. through integrity pacts).

ii) Implement general public-sector integrity tools and tailor them to the specific risks of the procurement cycle as necessary (e.g. the heightened risks involved in public-private interaction and fiduciary responsibility in public procurement).

iii) Develop integrity training programmes for the procurement workforce, both public and private, to raise awareness about integrity risks, such as corruption, fraud, collusion and discrimination; develop knowledge on ways to counter these risks; and foster a culture of integrity to prevent corruption.

iv) Develop requirements for internal controls, compliance measures and anti-corruption programmes for suppliers, including appropriate monitoring. Public procurement contracts should contain "no corruption" warranties, and measures should be implemented to verify the truthfulness of suppliers' warranties that they have not and will not engage in corruption in connection with the contract. Such programmes should also require appropriate supply-chain transparency to fight corruption in subcontracts, and integrity training requirements for supplier personnel.

Source: (OECD, 2015[4])

While integrity can be defined in different ways, the OECD Recommendation on Public Integrity (OECD, 2017[13]) considers public integrity to be "the consistent alignment of, and adherence to, shared ethical values, principles and norms for upholding and prioritising the public interest over private interests in the public sector". In the context of public procurement, maintaining the integrity of the system requires the following factors, among others:

- procurement procedures are transparent, and promote fair and equal treatment of bidders
- public resources linked to public procurement are used in accordance with intended purposes
- procurement officials' behaviour is in line with the public purpose of their organisation
- systems are in place to challenge procurement decisions, ensure accountability and promote public scrutiny (OECD, 2007[6]).

Fighting corruption is a major issue in Nuevo León. A high percentage of citizens perceive that corruption is taking place in the state; in fact, the percentage of citizens who report perceiving government corruption in Nuevo León surpassed the percentage of citizens who perceived corruption at the national level in Mexico (as shown in Figure 6.3). The high volume of expenditure on goods and services carried out by local governments in Mexico is detailed in Figure 6.2.

Figure 6.3. Perception of Corruption in Nuevo León in comparison with other Mexican States

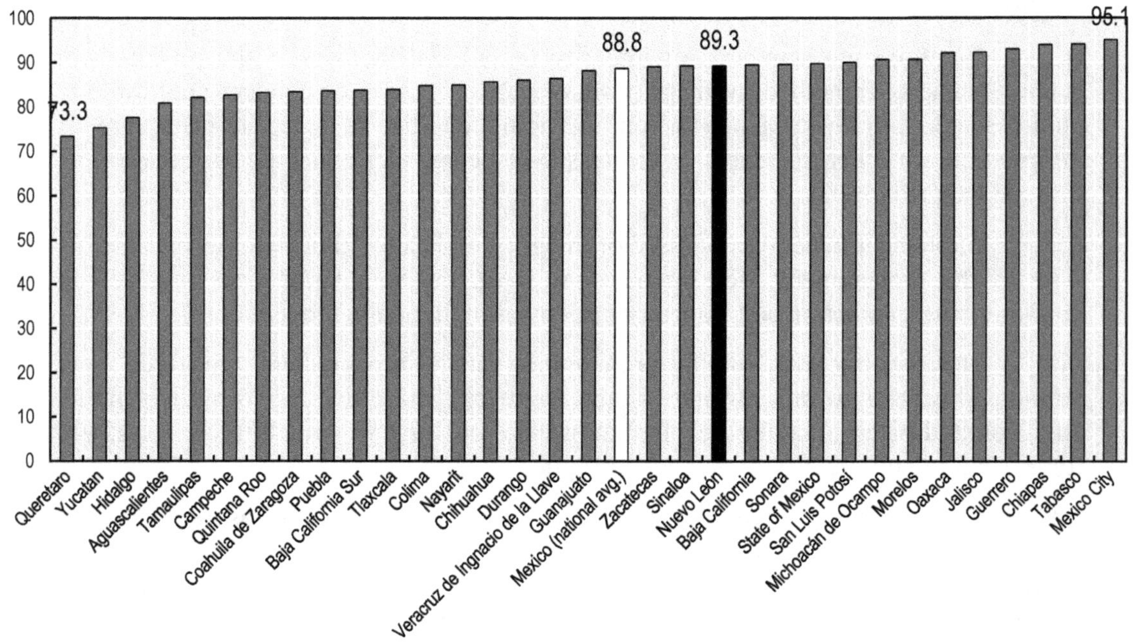

Source: (INEGI, 2015[7])

The results of the general population survey made by the National Institute of Statistic and Geography (Instituto Nacional de Estadística y Geografía, INEGI) in 2015 shows that corruption of officials and authorities in Nuevo León is by far the main problem perceived by citizens. Citizens in the state are also increasingly concerned about the integrity of government decisions (Figure 6.4).

Figure 6.4. Perception of corruption in Nuevo León by sector of activities

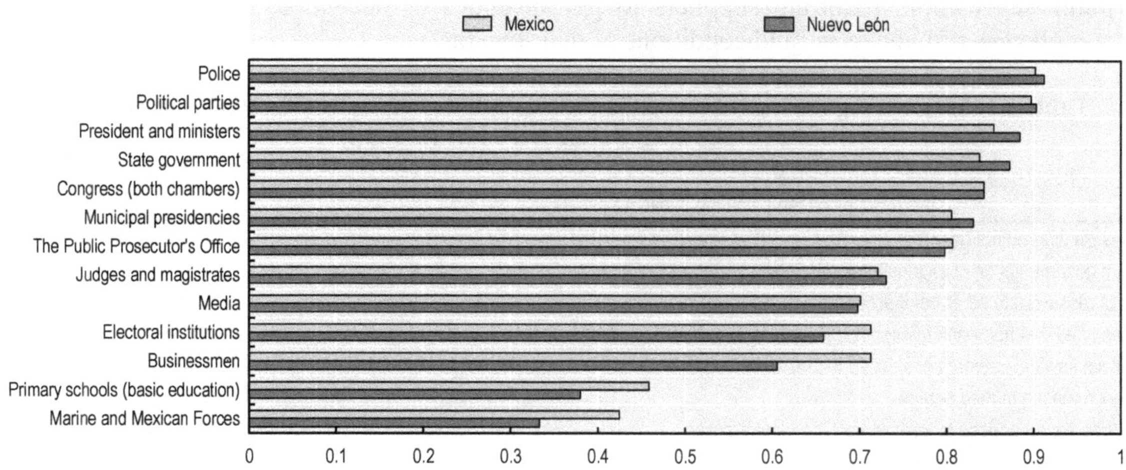

Source: (INEGI, 2015[7])

Citizen perceptions are not wrong. Corruption and integrity breaches in Nuevo León were noted in the report, *Observations to the General Public Accounts 2015*, (submitted to the Mexican Congress by the ASF in February 2017). The report states that 11.4% of the total funds transferred to the state of Nuevo León in 2015 were the subject of observations related to the proper use of resources (as detailed in Figure 6.5 and Table 6.1.

Figure 6.5. Observations made to amounts allocated to Nuevo León and other Mexican states in the Public Account

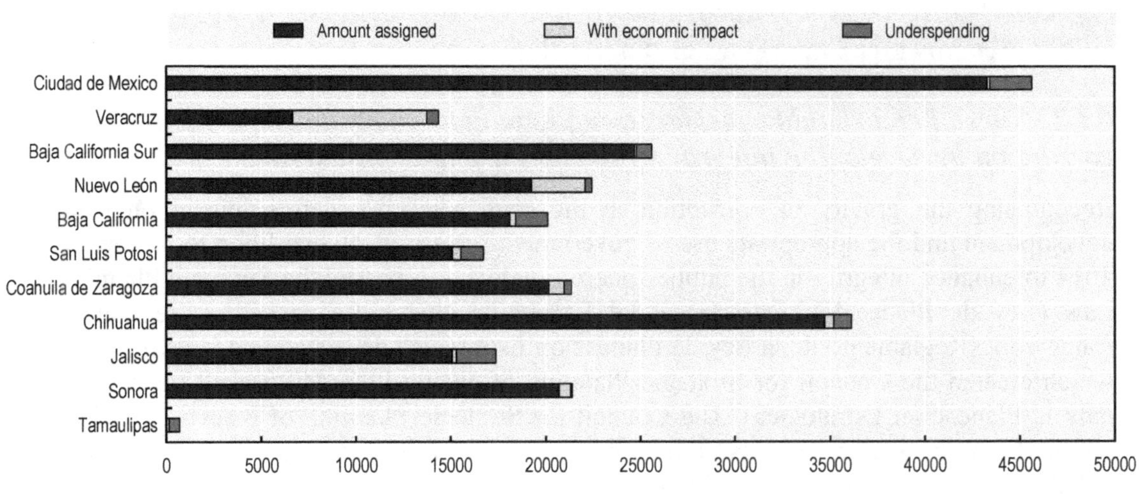

Source: Author based on the information reported in the Audit Report of Public Accounts 2015 made by the Superior Audit Institution, (Autoridad Superior de la Federación (ASF), 2015[8])

The ASF considers the main problem with public expenditure resulting from procurement to be that Mexican states use an exception set out in the Law on Procurement, Leasing and Services of the Public Sector (Ley de Adquisiciones, Arrendamientos y Servicios del Sector Público, LAASSP) to carry out their purchasing. This exception allows states to act in accordance with the parameters of the law, but to also make decisions that are not justified in terms of value for money. The exception also allows the states to make purchases without requiring suppliers to pay penalties or deductions in case of non-compliance with the terms and conditions of their contracts.

Table 6.1. Major irregularities observed in the expenditure of funds allocated to Mexican states in the 2015 Public Accounts (in mdp)

Irregularities observed during audits made	Amounts observed	%
Resources transferred not used	33 449.1	51.3
Supportive documentation of expenditures missing	7 893.7	12.1
Transfer of resources to other bank accounts	6 106.0	9.4
Resources used that not reach the specific objectives of each fund or programme	4 936.0	7.6
Undue or not justified payment of salaries to personnel	2 639.7	4.0
Undue Tax retention to third parties	2 017.8	3.1
Expenditures not authorised by the federal Coordinator entity	1 112.9	1.7
Undue payment of benefits not related to salaries	1 005.6	1.5
Other concepts	6 033.0	9.3
Total amount observed	65 193.8	100

Source: (Autoridad Superior de la Federación (ASF), 2015[8])

In this context, Nuevo León has made enhancing the integrity of the public procurement system a clear priority. The state is developing a framework to prevent, identify and sanction corrupt and unethical behaviours. This framework is described in both the State Development Plan 2016-2021 (Plan Estatal de Desarrollo del Estado de Nuevo León 2016-2021) and the Strategic Plan for the State of Nuevo León 2015-2030 (Plan Estratégico para el Estado de Nuevo León 2015-2030).

6.1. Enhancing Nuevo León's policy framework to address integrity issues in the state's public procurement processes and activities

6.1.1. Nuevo León should consider strengthening its commitment to fighting corruption by developing integrity strategies for public procurement

Recognising the gravity of corruption in the state and its negative impact on state development and the appropriate use of government resources, Nuevo León took steps in 2014 to enhance integrity in the public sphere. That year, it passed the Strategic Planning Law (Ley de Planeación Estratégica del Estado de Nuevo León) and its regulatory framework (Reglamento de la Ley de Planeación Estratégica del Estado de Nuevo León), which created the Council for Strategic Planning of Nuevo León (Consejo Nuevo León para la Planeación Estratégica). The Council for Strategic Planning of Nuevo León is a public body in which citizens, representatives from academia and the government collaborate to ensure the sustainable development of the state according to a long-term vision. The council's main objective is to elaborate and continuously update the Strategic Plan for the State of Nuevo León 2015-2030. The strategic plan was issued on 1 April 2016. It describes a strategic vision for the state, and is meant to guide the action items in the State Development Plan 2016-2021. Both the strategic plan and state development plan are meant to be utilised by Nuevo León's current and next administrations.

One of the pillars of the strategic plan is effective and transparent government (gobierno eficaz y transparente), along with other priorities like human development, sustainable development, economic development and security and justice. The effective and transparent government (gobierno eficaz y transparente) pillar has a specific section on transparency and fighting against corruption. During public consultations, efforts such as transparency and fighting corruption were among the efforts citizens most voted for as the means they thought would effectively decrease the high perception of corruption at the state level. Nuevo León's strategic plan contains an in-depth analysis of the existing situation in the state, a strategic approach going forward and areas of opportunity. The strategic plan also contains a methodology to prioritise areas of opportunity (considering feasibility and impact). By prioritising these areas, officials hope to define a set of strategic areas, initiatives and projects to work on. They also hope to define eight overarching "central themes" that will guide integrity work. One of the central themes is making the use of public resources transparent in order to fight and sanction corruption (transparentar el uso de recursos públicos, combatir y sancionar la corrupción). This strategic work is commendable, but it is incomplete, as the strategic plan does not contain any reference to *how* the state can effectively fight corruption in public procurement.

The State Development Plan 2016-2021 sets out the six governmental priorities. They are: citizen government, rebuilding the social fabric to deter poverty, mobility and transport to reduce the time and cost of transportation for the population, fighting corruption and impunity, public safety so citizens can live in peace and infrastructure for development. The State Development Plan provides a detailed and evidence-based analysis of transparency and anti-corruption issues. Each issue is linked to one of fourth topic areas under which action plans are to be developed.

Topic number three of the State Development Plan focuses on the creation and implementation of the State Anti-Corruption System (Sistema Estatal Anticorrupción). It refers to accountability, citizen participation, social audit, institutional coordination, legislative harmonisation and procurement transparency. The State Anti-Corruption System organises its strategies and guidelines according to two major objectives: 1) ensuring transparency of public sector activities, accountability and the fight against corruption; and 2) ensuring the sustainability of public finances. It is under this latter objective that the State Development Plan makes a reference to public procurement as a key priority area. The plan states that Nuevo León should seek to create the most efficient public procurement system possible based on results, and that the state should implement the electronic registration of public procurement processes (Gobierno del Estado de Nuevo León, 2016[9]). At present, Nuevo León is establishing the pillars of its Anti-Corruption Plan, based on the National Anti-Corruption System's institutional and legislative framework. This framework was approved at the federal level in May 2015 through the publication of a decree modifying several articles of the Mexican Constitution, the enactment of the General Law of the National Anti-Corruption System and seven secondary laws. Nuevo León started building its anti-corruption strategy by approving amendments to its constitution in March 2017, and by laying the foundations for the institutional framework of the local anti-corruption system. Considering that public procurement is a high-risk area for corruption and integrity breaches, and that the current legal framework does not make a precise reference to this, Nuevo León could consider developing a targeted and tailored anti-corruption strategy for procurement or an integrity regime, as countries such as Austria and Canada have done (see Box 6.2 and 6.3).

Box 6.2. The Anti-Corruption Strategy of the Austrian Federal Procurement Agency

Integrity is at the heart of the Anti-Corruption Strategy developed by the Austrian Federal Procurement Agency (BBG). The strategy is rooted in the following actions:

- set precise organisational procedures (a clear definition of roles and structures)
- integrate anti-corruption measures into the workday
- constantly re-assess and improve the strategy
- constantly raise awareness among staff
- sharpen the focus of employees on the consequences of corruption.

The strategy contains an explicit regulation of the main values and strategies that are vital to the prevention of corruption. It also includes a clear definition of grey areas (e.g. the difference between customer care and corruption), clear rules on accepting gifts and rules on additional employment. Finally, the strategy offers employees a clear view of emergency management.

Source: (OECD, 2016[10])

Box 6.3. The Integrity strategy of the government of Canada aims to ensure value for money and uphold the public interest in procurement processes

The Government of Canada upholds the core principal of being committed to open, fair and transparent contracts and property agreements at the best value for Canadians. As the government's principal contracting arm and manager of its property portfolio, Public Works and Government Services Canada (PWGSC) has implemented a number of of additional measures to further strengthen the integrity of its procurement and property transactions, as well as those it manages on behalf of its clients. PWGSC is continuously improving its procurement processes by issuing guidelines and directives to foster ethical business practices, ensure due process for suppliers and uphold the public trust in the procurement process.

In its 2015 Economic Action Plan, the Government of Canada committed to introducing a new, government-wide integrity regime for the procurement process. It did so to ensure that Canada does business with ethical suppliers internally and abroad. The new regime aims to be transparent, rigorous and act in a manner that is consistent with best practices in Canada and abroad. It also aims to support transparent competition and an ethical Canadian marketplace. The key features and rules of the regime are:

- A supplier convicted of a listed offence in Canada or abroad will remain ineligible to enter into a contract with the government for a period of ten years.
- A supplier can apply to have its ineligibility period reduced by up to five years if it addresses the causes of the conduct that led to ineligibility.
- A supplier will no longer be automatically penalized for the actions of an affiliate with which it had no involvement.
- New tools, such as independent expert third-party assessments and administrative agreements that specify required, corrective actions and ensure their effectiveness.
- The government has the ability to suspend a supplier for up to 18 months if it has been charged with of a listed offence or has admitted guilt.

Canada's integrity regime is centrally administered by PWGSC through a bilateral Memoranda of Understanding (MOU). The integrity regime consists of: ineligibility and suspension policies, directives issued to further these policies and address emerging issues, clauses used in instruments relating to contracts, and information bulletins developed to provide greater clarity and guidance to clients and stakeholders of the integrity regime. To date, five directives and ten information bulletins have been issued, all of which are available on the public integrity regime website.

Presently, 77 MOUs have been signed by federal organisations for the provision of integrity verification services, including two crown corporations. Only three federal organisations required to adopt the integrity regime have yet to sign a MOU. Revised MOUs have been drafted and distributed across departments to reflect updates made to the integrity regime in April 2016.

Canada launched a database services portal in September 2015 to implement the integrity verification, and to simplify the process for submitting an integrity verification request. To date, since the inception of the portal, a total of 148 289 integrity verifications have been conducted, with 54 139 completed since April 2016.

On 3 October 2016, the final version of the integrity verification portal was launched, with all modules operationally deployed. This enhanced version provides a centralised point of access for procurement officers to submit integrity verification requests and communicate directly with the integrity database team.

Notable statistics for the operation of the integrity verification portal include:

- Officials take action on 98.3% of requests within four hours.
- 2 491 procurement officers use the portal throughout the government.
- 40 794 searchable vendors are listed within the portal.
- Emergency verification responses are available within 30 minutes.

Source: (Public Services and Procurement Canada,(n.d.)[11])

At present, Nuevo León's integrity framework for public procurement is based on certain provisions. These provisions stem from two different legal systems, as mandated by state and federal laws and regulations (see in Table 6.2).

Table 6.2 The current regulatory framework for public procurement in Nuevo León

Legislations and regulations applicable in case of procurement made with federal resources	Legislations and regulations applicable in case of procurement made with State resources
Law on Procurement, Leases and Services of the Public Sector (Ley de Adquisiciones, Arrendamientos y Servicios del Sector Público, LAASSP);	Law on Procurement, Leases and Contracting Services of the State of Nuevo León (Ley de Adquisiciones, Arrendamientos y Contratación de Servicios del Estado de Nuevo León, LAACS);
Regulation for Procurement Leases and Services of the Public Sector (Reglamento de la Ley de Adquisiciones, Arrendamientos y Servicios del Sector Público, RLAASSP);	Regulation of the Law on Procurement, Leases and Contracting Services of the State of Nuevo León (Reglamento de la Ley de Adquisiciones, Arrendamientos y Contratación de Servicios del Estado de Nuevo León);
Law on Public Works and Related Services (Ley de Obras Públicas y Servicios relacionados con las mismas, LOPSR).	Law of Public Works for the State of Nuevo León (Ley de Obras Públicas del Estado de Nuevo León, LOPNL).

Source: Author based on information submitted by Nuevo León.

Other regulations that are also part of this complex legislative framework are the Organisational Law of the State of Nuevo León's Public Administration (Ley Orgánica de la Administración Pública para el Estado de Nuevo León) and the Regulation of the Law for Acquisitions, Leasing and Procurement of Services for the State of Nuevo León (Reglamento de la Ley de Adquisiciones, Arrendamientos y Contratación de Servicios del Estado de Nuevo León). The former establishes the institutional framework under which public procurement activities will take place. The latter establishes the rules applicable to actions and operations related to procurement and the contracting of services.

While this legislative framework includes various requirements and rules to structure and guide public procurement activities, it does not specifically address integrity and corruption risks. The Law on Procurement, Leasing and Contracting Services of the State of Nuevo León (Ley de Adquisiciones, Arrendamientos y Contratación de Servicios del Estado de Nuevo León, LAACS), for instance, ensures to some extent the integrity of the procurement process through several provisions. These provisions include: the establishment of a procurement committees (Article 16), citizen participation (Article 28), blacklisting of suppliers (Article 92), control of procurement plans and budgets, deadlines to submit bids and provisions increasing risks of collusion, clarification meetings with written and oral questions (Article 34), public meetings to present tender results with the possibility of suppliers submitting a better offer during the meeting, the possibility of bidders attending the opening meeting for bids and organisation of joint site visits for bidders when required by the tender (Article 35). Nuevo León also has other provisions referring indirectly to public procurement integrity, which have been amended as detailed in the next sections of this chapter.

In this context, developing a specific local anti-corruption plan for public procurement would help Nuevo León to reaffirm its high level of commitment to effectively fighting corruption in public procurement. A local anti-corruption plan would also help the state to recognise the specific areas and activities vulnerable to risks of corruption and integrity breaches. To accomplish these aims, the Council for Strategic Planning of Nuevo León should consider updating its strategic plan and recommending that a similar exercise be done with the State Development Plan 2016-2021. The strategic plan should be updated to effectively curb corruption and uphold integrity in public procurement in ways that are in line with the objectives of the local anti-corruption system. The plan should also identify priorities, and recognise the risks of corruption and integrity breaches in public procurement in the state. In developing this plan, the Secretariat of Administration should be named as the responsible entity for administering material and human resources. The central administration of Nuevo León could contribute to this exercise by analysing risks and identifying national priorities in coordination with the relevant authorities.

6.1.2. Creating a coherent and effective integrity framework as a mechanism to reduce corruption risks in the public procurement process

Nuevo León could benefit from enhancing integrity rules in order to set up a coherent legal framework for integrity and corruption prevention.

In advancing its integrity and anti-corruption strategy, Nuevo León needs to pay specific attention to its procurement activities and the vulnerability of its public investments. Around the world, public investment in public procurement is put at risk due to different types of malfeasance, including foreign bribery. There are, indeed, other types of conduct that have a negative impact on the integrity of public procurement. This conduct includes undue influence, the capture of investment projects by specific interests and conflicts of interests. These risks affect all stages of the procurement cycle, as they exert different kinds of pressure at all steps of the project – from the needs assessment phase to the execution and evaluation phases (see Table 6.3). Efforts to mitigate behaviours that violate the principles of integrity should be seen as the shared responsibility of the government and other involved stakeholders.

Table 6.3. Corruption risks associated with the different stages of the procurement cycle

Risks of the pre-tendering phase	Needs assessment	• Lack of adequate needs assessment • Influence of external actors on officials decisions • Informal agreement on contract
	Planning and budgeting	• Poor procurement planning • Procurement not aligned with overall investment decision-making process • Failure to budget realistically or deficiency in the budget
	Development of specifications/ requirements	• Technical specifications are tailored for a specific company • Selection criteria is not objectively defined and no established in advance • Requesting samples of goods and services that can influence • Buying information on the project specifications.
Risks of the tendering phase	Choice of procurement procedure	• Lack of procurement integrity for the use of non-competitive procedures • Abuse of non-competitive procedures on the basis of legal exceptions: contract splitting, abuse of extreme urgency, non-supported modifications
	Request for proposal/bid	• Absence of public notice for the invitation to bid • Evaluation and award criteria are not announced • Procurement information is disclose and made public
	Bid submission	• Lack of competition or cases of collusive bidding: o cover bidding o bid suppression o bid rotation o market allocation
	Bid evaluation	• Conflict of interest and corruption in the evaluation process through: • Familiarity with bidders over time • Personal interests such as gifts or future/additional employment • No effective implementation of the "four eyes-principle"
	Contract award	• Vendors fail to disclose accurate cost or pricing data in their price proposals, resulting in an increased contract price (i.e. invoice mark-ups, channel stuffing) • Conflict of interest and corruption in the approval process (i.e. no effective separation of financial, contractual and project authorities) • Lack access to records on the procedure
Risks of the post-award phase	Contract management/ performance	• Abuses of the supplier in performing the contract, in particular in relation to its quality, price and timing: • Substantial change in contract conditions to allow more time and/ or higher prices for the bidder • Product substitution or sub-standard work or service not meeting contract specifications • Theft of new assets before delivery to end-user or before being recorded • Deficient supervision from public officials and/or collusion between contractors and supervising officials • Subcontractors and partners chosen in an on-transparent way or not kept accountable
	Order and payment	• Deficient separation of financial duties and/or lack of supervision of public officials leading to: • False accounting and cost misallocation or cost migration between contracts • Late payments of invoices • False or duplicate invoicing for good and services not supplied and for interim payment in advance entitlement

Source: Based on (OECD, 2009[12])

Officials in Nuevo León need to keep in mind that integrity risks can arise during the pre-tendering phase. Risks are also sometimes associated with the procurement method used by contracting authorities (CAs). Finally, risks can arise during the post-award phase, as some authorities engage in late payment of invoices, and false or duplicate invoicing. All of these risks are possibilities, and some have been documented in Nuevo León.

The OECD Recommendation on Public Procurement promotes the use of open and competitive tendering. The OECD recommendation states that this type of tendering should be the standard method for conducting procurement, as it increases efficiencies, fights corruption, obtains fair and reasonable pricing and ensures competitive outcomes. If exceptional circumstances justify limitations to competitive tendering and validate the use of single-source procurement, such exceptions should be limited, pre-defined and should require appropriate justification when employed. These exceptions should also be subject to adequate oversight that takes into account the increased risk of corruption, including by foreign suppliers (OECD, 2015[4]).

Nuevo León employs four methods of procurement, as detailed in Chapter 2. Direct award is the most popular method, even though it increases the risk of corruption. Moreover, public procurement in Nuevo León is subject to various integrity risks, as the state uses many different methods of procurement, each subject to different rules, as described in Chapter 1 of this review.

Another integrity risk that Nuevo León faces is the complexity of its legal framework for public procurement. Indeed, like in other Mexican states, in Nuevo León, public procurement activities have to follow two distinct systems based on the origin of the financial resources. If the budgetary resources come from the federal level, contracting authorities and requesting units have to follow the federal public procurement procedures set out in the LAASSP, as detailed in Table 6.3. In addition, contracting authorities and requesting units have to use the electronic platform, CompraNet, administered by the Ministry of Public Administration (Secretaría de la Función Pública, SFP). Parastatal entities mainly use CompraNet for their purchases, as they receive federal funds and manage various programmes. However, when these financial resources come from the state, CAs have to follow the public procurement procedures developed by Nuevo León in the LACCS. In addition, they have to use the Electronic Public Procurement System (Sistema Electrónico de Compras Públicas del Estado de Nuevo León, SECOP) administered by the Secretariat of Administration of Nuevo León (Secretaria de Administracion de Nuevo León, SANL) and the Electronic Integrated Government Resources System (Sistema Integrador de Recursos Electrónicos Gubernamentables, SIREGOB). One difficulty of this arrangement is that the functionalities and objectives of each of these systems are quite different. In addition, the SIREGOB is not fully implemented yet. Another issue is that, in practise, most of the communication between public procurement officials and companies is still performed via face-to-face meetings or emails. Unfortunately, these practices increase integrity and corruption risks.

At the municipal level, the scenario is worse. Municipal authorities do not use SIREGOB or SECOP. Similar to the central administration, procurement at the municipal level is a paper-based activity. Furthermore, municipal procurement requires the presence of participants during different stages of the process. This results in a high risk of integrity violations.

An additional risk to the integrity of public procurement in Nuevo León is that providers participating in tenders are still required to register in person, though this requirement varies depending on the applicable procedure. Indeed, in the case of procurement made with state funds, registration in person is mandatory while in the case of procurement using federal funds CompraNet is used for a voluntary registration. It should be mentioned that while Nuevo León is working on finding a way to ensure that public procurement procedures are made electronically, there are still some challenges to their efforts. The reasons for this are that officials do not have full authority to make all public procurement procedures electronic, and officials are still working to link the different procurement platforms. Moreover, 35% of public investment made in Nuevo León is concentrated in areas such as health and education. These fields manage their own public procurement, and are not yet integrated into the consolidated purchases system established by the government. This arrangement opens the state up to risks, and represents a challenge for Nuevo León. The state should reform the applicable legal and regulatory mandates so that it can transition to an electronic system for public procurements across all different types of public purchasing.

Indeed, despite the fact that Nuevo León is consolidating its public procurement system, there are still 48 federal initiatives and programmes that have financial resources that need to be allocated and used properly. If the state does not follow appropriate procedures with regards to these programmes, it can be audited by the Superior Audit Office of the Federation (Autoridad Superior de la Federación (ASF), 2015[8]).

In order to prevent integrity violations and corruption, Nuevo León needs to ensure a comprehensive and effective integrity framework for staff working in public procurement. Nuevo León's public procurement workforce is composed of a total of 114 public officials. These officials work in the contracting authorities, the General Directorate for Acquisitions and General Services of the Secretariat of Administration (Dirección General de Adquisiciones y Servicios Generales, DGASG) and in 40 of the 65 parastatal entities that still carry out their own public procurement activities (as they have not yet signed a co-operation agreement with the SA). While these public officials receive ethics training, currently there is no certification mechanism to ensure they have sufficient knowledge and skills to solve ethical dilemmas and conflict of interest issues that may arise in their daily work. This situation, coupled with the current lack of skilled public officials, is concerning. Indeed, many procurement officials in the state do not use the appropriate methods for procuring goods and services – which results in a failure to stimulate competition and prevent favouritism. Indeed, interviews with public officials revealed that specific training options for officials starting new positions in public procurement are not well publicised, as detailed in Chapter 4.

In light of this, Nuevo León would benefit from strengthening its culture of integrity and instilling the values of moral conduct and integrity in its public servants. It should also set clear expectations of ethical behaviour from all actors entering into a relationship with the government. Moreover, it is important that the state adopt measures to detect wrongdoings and report them using existing channels and appropriate mechanisms (Corruptel and Corrupnet). All of these efforts will help the state build a culture of integrity where public officials, citizens and private businesses feel confident about coming forward to report breaches of integrity and wrongdoing.

6.2. Establishing effective mechanisms to enhance integrity in Nuevo León's public procurement cycle as a whole through the implementation of consistent and coherent integrity policies and stronger management of conflicts of interest

Maintaining the integrity of the public procurement system requires establishing general standards and procurement-specific safeguards for all stakeholders. This is vital, considering the fact that numerous actors participate in the system, and the procurement system grants a large number of contracts with distinct terms, conditions and values. Safeguarding integrity is a key pillar of any strategy to curb corruption in public procurement. Integrity means a consistent alignment of and adherence to shared ethical values, principles and norms for upholding and prioritising the public interest over private interests in the public sector (OECD, 2017[13]). In the context of public procurement, integrity of the system implies the following (among other factors):

- Integrity standards applicable for all public officials are enacted by the government.
- A dedicated government unit, directorate or office must be devoted to developing, updating and diffusing the government code of conduct, and may provide advice, guidance and practical examples to ensure its implementation.
- Specific standards of conduct for public officials working in public procurement should be adopted in order to mitigate the specific risks related to the complexity and characteristics of the public procurement process.
- Conflicts of interest must be properly managed to ensure that the involvement of public officials in the public procurement cycle does not improperly influence the performance of the public duties and responsibilities of these officials.
- The government sets out rules and procedure to protect whistle-blowers.

Maintaining the integrity of a public procurement system requires effective and strong co-ordination between the various actors in the procurement cycle. This co-ordination should ensure the highest standards of conduct throughout all public institutions. The current institutional framework in Nuevo León involves various actors in charge of preventing, investigating or sanctioning corruption acts – as well as solving conflict of interest issues and ethical dilemmas. Indeed, the Office of the Comptroller and Governmental Transparency (Contraloría y Transparencia Gubernamental) and its different units and directorates are responsible for promoting the best practices of internal monitoring. The comptroller and its units are also responsible for guiding the government to maintain the legality, honesty and responsibility of its public officials in the context of public procurement activities. The units of the comptroller involved in this work include the Anti-Corruption Unit (Unidad Anticorrupción), the Legal Counsel Directorate (Dirección Juridica) and the Directorate of Internal Control Bodies and Monitoring (Dirección de Órganos de Control Interno y Vigilancia). The comptroller has jurisdiction per the Organisational Law of the Public Administration of Nuevo León (Ley Orgánica de la Administración Pública para el Estado de Nuevo León) and the Internal Regulation of the Office of the Comptroller and Governmental Transparency (Reglamento Interior de la Contraloría y Transparencia Gubernamental). That said, the jurisdiction only extends to ministries and entities of the state public administration – not to municipalities. However, the comptroller may intervene at the municipal level regarding state public expenditure and federal public expenditure transfers.

Nuevo León's Anti-Corruption Unit is tasked with following up on complaints, conducting investigations and sanctioning misconduct by public officials, including by those who participate in public procurement. The Superior Audit Office of the State of Nuevo León (Auditoría Superior del Estado de Nuevo León, ASENL) also ensures the effective implementation of integrity rules. It does this by assisting the state congress in reviewing public accounts and the good management and budgetary exercises of public entities.

Another institution ensuring the integrity of public sector decisions is the Commission of Transparency and Access to Information of the State of Nuevo León (Comisión de Transparencia y Acceso a la Información del Estado de Nuevo León, CTAINL), which promotes transparency and accountability within the state government, and determines what information should be classified or considered confidential.

In addition to these entities, Nuevo León's current integrity framework also mandates that an ethics committee be created and maintained to analyse and advise on public officials' compliance with ethics rules, per the Agreement of the Ethics Code for Public Officials of the Public Administration of Nuevo León. This committee was created in 2012. Since then, the Ethics Committee has born the responsibility of providing support to the integrity system by ensuring that public officials and citizens are informed of Nuevo León's ethics rules. Its members occupy an honorary position, and its role is an advisory one. While its decisions are non-binding, its opinions and suggestions are supposed to enhance integrity within Nuevo León's public sector. It should be mentioned, however, that this committee is not currently operating. The reason for this is that most of its members resigned last year after a controversy connected to the purchase of blankets by the state of Nuevo León.

Other federal institutions such as the National Institute for Transparency, Access to Information and Protection of Data (Instituto Nacional de Transparencia, Acceso a la Información y Protección de Datos Personales, INAI) and the Ministry of Public Administration (Secretaría de la Función Pública, SFP) participate in ensuring the integrity of public procurement activities when applicable to the area of their expertise.

Other actors, such as the Central Purchasing Body of the Secretariat of Administration and the Procurement Committee are also responsible, to some extent, for ensuring the integrity of the whole procurement process. The Procurement Committee, for instance, evaluates proposals submitted by bidders in public tenders. These tenders can be requested by the 21 ministries and parastatal entities that have arrangements with the central public administration. The Central Purchasing Unit verifies whether exceptions to competitive procedures in public tendering proceed in accordance with the rules set out in Article 42 of the LAACS. It also verifies the integrity of the whole tendering process. In practice, however, as observed during the OECD fact-finding mission, this evaluation consists more of verifying if documents have been integrated into procurement files.

The recent amendments made to the Constitution of Nuevo León (Constitución Política del Estado de Nuevo León) have created two new institutions to implement Nuevo León's integrity framework to investigate and sanction breaches of integrity rules. These new institutions are the Specialised Division of Administrative Responsibility within the Tribunal of Administrative Justice (División Especializada en Materia de Responsabilidad Administrativa del Tribunal de Justicia Administrativa) and the Office of the Specialised Anti-Corruption Prosecutor (Fiscalía Especializada en Combate a la Corrupción). The specialised division will impose sanctions on public officials in cases of serious offences or corrupt conduct, and will sanction citizens if they participate in these corrupt acts. Pecuniary sanctions for damages and prejudices caused to public funds or assets of the state of Nuevo León, its municipalities or any state or municipal entity will also be imposed by this specialised division.

While corrupt acts and cases involving high-level administrative responsibilities are investigated by the Superior Audit Office of the State of Nuevo León and the internal control units, rulings will be made by the Administrative Tribunal. Other types of contraventions and administrative sanctions will be examined and solved only by the internal control units.

While it is a good thing that Nuevo León is creating new institutions aimed at halting corruption, the state needs to give these institutions the authority to do their jobs. The specialised division will intervene alongside the internal control units in matters where other authorities have imposed administrative sanctions. However, the specialised division cannot begin operations until it receives the appropriate disciplinary powers. In addition, fitting operational procedures and mechanisms still need to be approved (such as reforms to secondary legislation following the creation of the State Anti-Corruption System). In the case of the Office of the Specialised Anti-Corruption Prosecutor, Nuevo León's constitutional reform mandates that it will be vested with financial, technical, budgetary, management and decision-making autonomy to investigate and prosecute corrupt acts. That said, the appointment of the head of this office requires the full implementation of the local anti-corruption system.

Nuevo León needs to effectively co-ordinate this new institutional arrangement with aspects of the current public procurement governance structure so as to ensure integrity in the whole procurement process. In the context of these constitutional amendments, Nuevo León will need to ensure coherence of all new public actors in charge of preventive, investigatory and punitive functions. The state must enforce consistency in order to strengthen the integrity system and make sure that the allocation of financial resources through public procurement is not distorted. The integrity framework that results from the Local Anti-Corruption Law and other secondary laws may also change this current framework.

6.2.1. Nuevo León should consider developing a code of ethics for public procurement officials to guide their conduct during the whole public procurement cycle, as well as providing practical guidelines to public procurement officials and suppliers

The current integrity framework in Nuevo León is composed of a series of laws, regulations and policies. The framework sets the standards of conduct that public officials should follow as they do their jobs and interact with citizens and the private sector (see Table 6.4).

Table 6.4. Integrity framework setting the standard of conduct for public officials in the public administration of Nuevo León

Legal provisions	Descriptions
Constitution of Nuevo León which most recent version is dated as of 14 April 2017.	Article 105 and ss sets out that the responsibility regime of public officials will be established by the Law of responsibilities and mentions who are covered under the scope of these articles in case of misconduct. These provisions lay out the pillars of the integrity system, establish the administrative disciplinary framework and create the institutional arrangement of the new local anti-corruption system.
State Law on Anti-Corruption (Ley del Sistema Local de Anticorrupción de Nuevo León, LACS of Nuevo León) enacted the 6 July 2017	In addition to create the local anti-corruption system, this law sets out in its article 5 the values of the public service and provides that the public sector entities are obliged to create and maintain structural and normative conditions allowing the appropriate management of the whole government and the ethical and accountable behaviour of all public servants.
General Law on Administrative Responsibilities (Ley General de Responsabilidades Administrativas, LGRA) which will enter into force following the precisions of the transition provisions	Articles 26 to 42 set out among other things the obligation to submit a declaration of conflict of interest as well as fiscal and assets declarations that will be contained in the National Digital Platform. Articles related to other aspects than the conflict of interest declaration will not apply in Nuevo León as they are regulated in the LRSPEMNL. This law contains a definition of what constitutes a conflict of interest situation. The third transitory provision mentions that this law will guide public official's behaviour working at the federal level and in the states until the Co-ordinator Committee of the National Anti-Corruption System (Sistema Nacional Anticorrupción, NACS) issue the guidelines, criteria and other resolutions to implement the new anti-corruption system.
Law of Responsibilities of Public Servants at state and municipal level of the State of Nuevo León (Ley de Responsabilidades del Estado y Municipios de Nuevo León, LRSPEMNL) enacted the 29 January 1997 and amended in various occasions.	Articles 7, 11 and 50 and Fraction XXIII of this law set out the minimum rules to prevent corruption and to sanction administrative faults committed by public officials. Article 50 sets out prohibited conflict of interest situations in the context of the exercise of public servants duties, such as prohibited activities, recusal, gifts and the misuse of insider information, undue influence and prohibition of use of public funds for political purposes, as well as applicable sanctions in cases of integrity breaches.. It does not contain, however, clear rules on what constitutes a conflict of interest situation. It prohibits public procurement officials from contracting with any person that has been prohibited from holding a job, position or commission in the public administration (Article 50, Fraction XI); intervening in any situation that may create any personal or business-related conflict of interest (Article 50, Fraction XIII); refraining from acting or failing to act as to not comply with any of the obligations related to the public service (Article 50, Fraction XXII); contracting with any person who performs a public function, or with any company in which such a person participates (Article 50, fraction XXIII); using public funds for political purposes (Article 50, Fraction XXXIV); inhibiting whistle-blowing or the filing of a complaint (Article 50, Fraction XXVI); and contracting without obtaining the documentation required to prove banking, accounting and financial resources of providers (Article 50, Fraction XXVII). Article 51 and ss set out the disciplinary sanction regime. Other situations that could lead to an integrity breach are regulated in Articles 112 -124 and 131-135, and contain rules on disclosure of assets, gifts disclosure and subsequent forfeiture to the internal control units.
Organic Law of the Public Administration of the State of Nuevo León (Ley orgánica de la administración del Estado de Nuevo León) which most recent version dated as of 8 April 2016	Article 33 fraction XVIII describes one of the functions of the Office of the Comptroller and Governmental Transparency and sets out the principles that should guide officials when delivering service to the whole community.
Code of Ethics (Código de ética) enacted in accordance with article 140 of the LRSPMNL in August 2016.	This code contains three articles. Article 1 of the code refers to seven principles and integrity rules that should guide their conduct. It also sets out that its dissemination will be responsibility of the Office of the Comptroller. These ethics standards are the following: Say no to corruption; service, respect and empathy; austerity and sustainability; innovation and efficiency; inclusion, and transparency.
Law to promote report of corrupt acts of public officials (Ley para incentivar la denuncia de actos de corrupción de servidores públicos), enacted 30 June 2013	Article 2 defines what constitutes a corrupt act and refers to contraventions of Article 50 of the LRPSMNL) with the purpose of obtaining an undue advantage for the public official and/or a third party. It also defines who is considered a public servant for the purpose of its application. Article 9 imposes the obligation to report an act of corruption to the superior or to the Office of the Comptroller and provides that failure to comply with this obligation constitutes an administrative fault. It also contains a series of protection measures that could be implemented to protect the public servant or the citizen who reports misconducts or corrupt acts

As detailed in Table 6.4, this framework also includes the Ethics Code for Public Officials of the Public Administration (Código de Ética de Servidores Públicos de la Administración Pública). The code of ethics was adopted in August 2016, and was developed in a consultative way, as per Article 140 of the LRSPEMNL and the LAACS. It sets out seven ethics standards public officials should comply with in their daily work. Principle one (say no to corruption), principle three (austerity and sustainability) and principle four (innovation and efficiency) refer to behaviours that public officials should exhibit when managing funds or state assets. It does not contain rules on how to solve ethical dilemmas and conflicts of interest that may arise in their daily work. Its scope covers all individuals do work and are paid with public resources, as long as they are engaged in the exercise of public service activities. As such, the ethics code does not include suppliers and consultants whose behaviour could also impact public sector integrity.

This integrity framework provides sanctions that may consist of warnings, suspensions, removals or disqualifications. Sanctions are detailed in the LRSPEMNL. Pecuniary sanctions can also be imposed based on the economic gains and prejudices caused. Administrative responsibility arising from corrupt practices is also regulated under these rules, and any breaches resulting from illicit enrichment are to be sanctioned under the Criminal Code of Nuevo León. These sanctions can range from three months to fourteen years of imprisonment, as well as fines. According to constitutional reforms, superiors are considered liable in cases of serious administrative contraventions or corrupt acts where nepotism or collusion also exist. Further amendments are required to establish which corrupt acts should be investigated and sanctioned by the new institutional framework. Further amendments are also required to determine the actions and omissions that constitute serious and non-serious offences, as well as the mechanism to challenge the decision classifying an action or omission as a non-serious offence.

According to the Constitution of Nuevo León, state and municipal entities should have internal control or monitoring units. These units should operate with a broad mandate consisting of preventing, redressing and investigating facts, actions and omissions that could be considered corrupt – or upon which an administrative sanction could be imposed. However, most parastatal agencies in Nuevo León still lack internal control units. In addition, solid coordination mechanisms between ministries, agencies and the state comptroller to aid in the control and monitoring tasks by allowing for better communication channels between government entities and agencies have not been established.

As for mechanisms that enhance integrity by ensuring appropriate management of conflict of interest issues, the constitutional reforms regarding the establishment of an anti-corruption system establish that public officials should submit two declarations in addition to the assets declaration already required under the LRSPEMNL. They are: the conflict of interest declaration and the fiscal declaration. Failure to submit the assets declaration may be sanctioned by an administrative pecuniary sanction (a fine). That said, the law does not make reference to sanctions resulting from a failure to submit the other two declarations. In addition to the rules mentioned above, specific provisions contained in public procurement laws complement the legal framework (Table 6.5). There are some overlaps between the legal framework and these provisions, which can create confusion for public officials. This overlap could be resolved through a complete integration of the national and state anti-corruption systems.

Table 6.5. Integrity provisions under the public procurement laws applied in Nuevo León

Legal provisions	Descriptions
Law on Procurement, Leases and Services of the Public Sector (Ley de Adquisiciones, Arrendamientos y Servicios del Sector Público, LAASSP);	The LAAPS in its various provisions (Articles 24, 28, 31 (fraction XII) and 37 (factions I to X), sets out the rules that public officials and providers should follow when participating in public procurement process, such as recusing themselves from not being part of the public procurement procedure, submitting an integrity declaration under oath under which participants commit to conduct themselves in an honest manner during the whole procurement process, not contracting with a provider in case of conflict of interests arising from a variety of situations (incompatibility of certain activities; acting as an expert; when blacklisted, etc.), using insider information, etc. It also sets out the appropriate sanctions in its Articles 97 and 101.
Law on Public Works and Related Services (Ley de Obras Públicas y Servicios relacionados con las mismas, LOPSR)	According to the public works legislation a contract cannot be awarded if public official participating in the procedures is placed in a conflict of interest situation based on a family and business related interests. This law also provides that social witness should avoid participating in public works tenders.
Law on Public Works of the State and Municipalities of Nuevo León (Ley de Obras Públicas para el Estado y Municipios de Nuevo León, LOPNL)	LOPNL provides that public works should be executed based on transparency, economy, impartiality, efficiency, efficacy and honesty criteria as to have the best options in terms on price, quality, financing and opportunity (Article 6), establishes that participants in the tender process should submit an integrity declaration under oath mentioning that they are in compliance with the provisions of Article 44 requiring that contracts are not signed if a public officials who is part of the procurement process is a public official. It also prohibits ministries, entities and municipalities to accept proposals or contract with individuals or legal entities in which their public officials are shareholders, administrators, managers or legal representative or entrepreneurs, and those in which these officials intervening in anyway in the contract award have a private, family related or business interest (Article 44). The non-disclosure of a conflict of interest situation to a superior is considered a contravention of the LRSPEMNL and public officials can be sanctioned administratively.
Law on Procurement, Leases and Contracting Services of the State of Nuevo León (Ley de Adquisiciones, Arrendamientos y Contratación de Servicios del Estado De Nuevo León, LAACS);	Article 37 of this law prohibits CAs to receive proposals and award contracts if public officials, participating at any stage of the public procurement process, or their superiors, including the head of the contracting or administrative unit, have personal, family or business interests or a family member of the public official (up to the fourth degree, by affinity or in-law), a third party with whom they have professional, work or business relations; or partners or companies in which they were part during the two years prior to the date the procurement procedure could receive a potential benefit (Article 37 fraction I). Article 97 of this law provides that conflict of interest arising between a public procurement official and a contractor will be considered a serious offence. Moreover, article 101 fraction II of the law establishes that public officials who do maintain a conflict of interest with providers and do not recuse themselves from participating in the whole procurement process commit a contravention and are liable to sanctions imposed under the LRSPEMNL

As detailed in Table 6.5, the LAASSP refers to principles in Articles 24-26 that should guide decisions related to the use of federal funds for procurement processes (including procurements undergone by the state of Nuevo León using federal funds). In contrast, the state law of Nuevo León for procurement, leases and contracting services (LAACS) using state and municipal funds sets out only five ethical principles and excludes the requirement for decisions related to the planning and use of public funds to be taken in an impartial manner.

No specific code of conduct for public procurement officials is a cure-all. Even codes of conduct with specific restrictions and prohibitions cannot ensure with total certainty that officials fulfil their duties and that the government achieves its commitment to greater transparency, accountability and the highest standards of ethical conduct. However, there are some actions governments can take to make their codes of conduct more effective than others. Interviews with public officials in Nuevo León demonstrated that the current ethics code is perceived as a type of regulation. Indeed, officials said they viewed the ethics code as a formal declaration of ethical priorities and a duty-related document for public officials' behaviour and performance. In spite of this, they did not systematically integrate the ethics code into their day-to-day work. Indeed, public procurement officials mentioned that their priority was to comply with the law, rather than systematically think about how to prevent, for instance, conflicts of interest from arising.

In light of the above, Nuevo León should adopt standards based on the code of ethics for public procurement officials. In particular, the state should establish specific restrictions and prohibitions to ensure that officials' private interests are not improperly furthered. These standards of conducts will guide public procurement officials' behaviour, which should be in line with the public purpose of their organisation.

Most common integrity issues involve conflict-of-interest situations. These situations are most often related to: personal, family or business interests and activities; gifts and hospitalities; disclosures of confidential information; and future employment. Because of this, Nuevo León must address these issues in addition to its other efforts (such as asset declaration requirements, whistle-blowing procedures and protection measures for whistle-blowers). A model Nuevo León could look to is the Protocol for Interactions Between Procurement Officials and Suppliers enacted in 2015 by the Federal Government of Mexico. Another model is the Code of Conduct for Procurement issued by the Government Canada. These protocols are described in Boxes 6.4 and 6.5.

Box 6.4. Mexican ethics code and rules of integrity – provisions related to public procurement

According to Mexico's Ministry of the Interior (Secretaría de Gobernación, SEGOB), the ethics code and rules of integrity for public procurements include the following.

"Public contracts, licenses, permits, authorisations and concessions:

The public servant who participates in public contracting or in the granting and providing of extensions to licenses, permits, authorisations and concessions, on the grounds of their employment, position, commission or function or through subordinates, needs to behave with transparency, impartiality and legality, orients his or her decisions towards the needs and interests of the society, and guarantee the best conditions for the state.

The following behaviours violate this rule, among others:

A. Omit to declare, in accordance with the applicable provisions, the possible conflicts of interest as well as particular business and commercial links with persons or organisations registered in the Single Registry of Contractors for the Federal Public Administration.

B. Fail to apply the principle of equal competition that should prevail among participants in the public procurement processes.

C. Formulate requirements differently from those strictly necessary for the fulfilment of the public service, causing excessive and unnecessary expenses.

D. Establish conditions in the invitations or calls for tenders which confer advantages or provide a differential treatment to certain bidders.

E. Favour certain bidders by considering that they meet the requirements or rules foreseen in the invitations or calls for tender when they do not, simulating the fulfilment of them or contributing to their temporary fulfilment.

F. Help suppliers to fulfil the requirements foreseen in the requests for quotes.

G. Provide undue information about individuals involved in the public procurement processes.

H. Be partial in the selection, designation, contracting and, as the case may be, removal or termination of the contract, in the framework of public procurement processes.

I. Influence decisions of other public servants in order for one participant to benefit from the public procurement processes or from the granting of licenses, permits, authorizations and concessions.

J. Avoid imposing sanctions on bidders, suppliers and contractors who violate applicable legal provisions.

K. Sending e-mails to bidders, suppliers, contractors or concessionaires through personal e-mail accounts or accounts which are distinct from the institutional e-mail.

L. Meet with bidders, suppliers, contractors and concessionaires outside the official buildings, except for the proceedings related to on-site visits.

M. Request unsubstantiated requirements for the granting and providing of extensions to licenses, permits, authorizations and concessions.

N. Give inequitable or preferential treatment to any person or organisation in the framework of granting and extending licenses, permits, authorisations and concessions.

O. Receive or request any type of compensation, offering, treat or gift in the framework of granting and providing extensions to licenses, permits, authorizations and concessions.

P. Fail to observe the protocol of action in matters of public contracting and providing extensions to licenses, permits, authorisations, concessions and their extensions.

Q. To be a direct beneficiary or through relatives up to the fourth degree of government contracts related to the agency or entity that directs or to which are directed the services."

Source: (Secretaría de Gobernación, 2015[14])

Box 6.5. Code of Conduct for Procurement in Canada

The Code of Conduct for Procurement in Canada provides all those involved in the public procurement process – public servants and vendors alike – with a clear statement of mutual expectations to ensure a common basic understanding.

The code reflects the policy of the Government of Canada, and is framed by the principles set out in the Financial Administration Act and the Federal Accountability Act. It consolidates the federal government's measures on conflict of interest and anti-corruption, as well as other legislative and policy requirements relating specifically to procurement. This code is intended to summarize existing laws by providing a single point of reference to key responsibilities and obligations for both public servants and vendors. In addition, the code describes vendor complaints and procedural safeguards.

Source: (Public Works and Government Services Canada, 2016[15])

As set out in the OECD Recommendation on Public Procurement, integrity standards should go beyond minimum requirements. They should prioritise public interests and encourage high standards of conduct, good governance and adherence to public service values. In addition, integrity standards should foster an open culture that facilitates and incentivizes learning in the service of a cleaner public administration. Accordingly, the proposed code of conduct for public procurement officials should be concise, flexible and written in clear language. Such a code can effectively promote integrity and ensure that public procurement officials and their institutions are accountable in case of contraventions.

Ensuring integrity in the public sector requires more than a sound integrity framework; it requires that public sector actors actively behave in an ethical manner. Therefore, in addition to adopting a sound integrity framework, Nuevo León should work to create a common understanding among officials of ethical rules and a common dedication to thinking and acting with integrity during day-to-day activities. To achieve this objective, Nuevo León should disseminate ethical rules via different tools, such as an awareness campaign or trainings of procurement officials, clients and suppliers. Moreover, the state could consider developing a practical manual or guidelines detailing and providing examples of where ethical values and public-sector principles could be put in jeopardy – and the appropriate steps officials are expected to take in these situations. Australia could serve as a model for Mexico in this respect (see Box 6.6). The measures proposed above could serve as a reminder to public officials participating in the public procurement process of how to behave when confronted with different situations (e.g. receiving a gift or invitation).

Box 6.6. Ethics, probity and accountability in procurement in Queensland, Australia

The following excerpt from the Ethics and Probity and Accountability in Procurement manual describe how procurement officials in Australia should act in situations where they risk committing unethical behaviour. The example below details what officials should do when they receive an invitation to seminar from a supplier:

> *"Attendance by a procurement officer at a public seminar offered by a potential supplier is unlikely to create a conflict of interest. However, the officer must not discuss confidential matters relating to the tender process, and must not use the tender process to obtain a discount on any registration fee. Officers directly involved in the tender process should inform the tender management team as well as their own manager, and gain approval for their attendance at the seminar, which should be fully documented."*

Source: (Commonwealth Government, 2006[25])

Adopting an awareness campaign, training and practical guidelines in addition to other initiatives for providing public procurement officials with the appropriate skills could help ensure that Nuevo León's integrity strategy is perceived by public officials as a mechanism for enhancing the reputation of the public sector – rather than a burden and a sanctioning tool. To be successful, superiors and management should be engaged in disseminating these campaign and training instruments across all public sector entities, including the existing parastatals entities. Superiors and management should also motivate by example. They should show their personnel that they embrace ethics, values and integrity standards in their daily activities. Management should also encourage consultation in cases of doubt. This means that improper conduct will be monitored and sanctioned, as well as relevant data published, so that management can clearly demonstrate that ethics standards apply to everyone. As such, consequences will be applied to offenders, regardless of their positions or performance within the government. While sending a clear message of zero tolerance against corruption in public procurement activities is important, Nuevo León also needs to create an environment where public officials and their superiors are able to solve integrity issues and be accountable for them.

6.2.2. Adopting an effective and balanced approach to forming an integrated framework for integrity management

Nuevo León should consider adopting a clear definition of conflict of interest so as to effectively manage conflicts of interest in public procurement and ensure the use of public funds in an efficient manner

Ensuring that conflicts of interest are identified and managed adequately is among the first steps states must take towards safeguarding integrity and transparency in public sector activities. Conflicts of interest should be understood not as inherent acts of corruption, but as normal situations that have the potential to result in corruption if not properly prevented and managed. If conflicts of interest occur in the context of public procurement, they can have important implications. One of the most significant is that conflicts of interest can jeopardize certain fundamental principles of public procurement, like transparency, fair competition and equal treatment of bidders. Therefore, governments need to set out coherent and consistent frameworks with clear definitions of conflicts of interest to enable objective and effective identification and management of these situations. Governments also need to create efficient internal systems to prevent and effectively solve conflicts of interest that arise, while upholding the principles listed above.

In its Guidelines for Managing Conflict of Interest in the Public Service, the OECD provides a definition of conflict of interest. This definition makes a distinction between actual, apparent and potential conflict-of-interest situations. The OECD defines a conflict of interest as a conflict between the public duty and private interests of a public official, in which the public official has private-capacity interests that could improperly influence the performance of his or her official duties and responsibilities (OECD, 2005[16]). An actual conflict of interest is a direct conflict between a public official's current functions and his or her private interests. An apparent conflict of interest occurs when a public official's private interests could improperly influence the performance of his or her duties, but this is not, in fact, the case. A potential conflict of interest encompasses, on the other hand, a situation in which a public official has private interests which could create a conflict of interest if the official becomes involved in the future.

In public procurement, implementing appropriate measures to prevent apparent and potential conflicts of interest is as important as implementing measures to manage actual conflicts of interest. One of the reasons for this is the close nature of interactions between the public and private sector in public procurement. Indeed, officials in Nuevo León stated in interviews that sometimes, potential bidders are former public officials. In other cases, newly hired public officials have experience in the private sector (for instance in engineering and architecture). This practice, of working with actors who are closely linked to the sector in which procurement will occur, is known as a "revolving door", and is not sanctioned by state law. "Revolving door" practices increase the risk of integrity breaches and opportunities for conflicts of interest. Therefore, a clear legal framework for all public officials, and especially for those involved in public procurement activities, is required to ensure that their decisions are not influenced by personal preferences, past experiences or pressure from family, friends or past and future associates. The state of Nuevo León has addressed conflicts of interest in Article 50, Fractions XIII and XIV of the LRSPMNL.

OECD countries have adopted different approaches to managing conflicts of interest based on factors like their political systems and cultures. That said, two major approaches can be identified: the descriptive and the prescriptive approach. The descriptive approach defines conflicts of interest in general terms, and issues specific rules and procedures to indicate what it is expected in these situations. The prescriptive approach defines a range of specific situations that are considered incompatible with public office or in conflict with the public interest and official duties. This approach is based on enforceable rules and standards of conduct set out in law and regulations, but is also based on fundamental public service principles (OECD, 2016[17]).

Conflict of interest rules in Nuevo León are embedded in different laws and regulations which vary in terms of scope and mechanisms (see Table 6.5). The LRSPEMNL contains rules on managing conflicts of interest, including in the context of public procurement and public works processes. For example, the LRSPEMNL states that public officials should disclose a conflict of interest in writing to their superior when it arises. It also states that officials should recuse themselves from being a part of any procedure or decision if they have a personal, family-related or business interest that could influence the procedure or decision.

This law sets out rules regarding gifts at the municipal level, and mechanisms to forfeit these gifts based on their nature. That said, information gathered during the OECD fact-finding mission to Nuevo León implied that these rules have not been implemented, as gifts are not systematically disclosed and forfeited in the state. Indeed, despite the rules, public officials in Nuevo León do not seem to understand that receipt of gifts of any nature has the potential to place them in a situation of conflict of interest. Officials mentioned during interviews that receiving gifts is considered normal. Sometimes, individuals offer gifts secretly and give them to public officials personally, rather than the official occupying a specific position within the public sector. That said, the public officials who receive gifts are sometimes later called upon to exercise a duty or function that could advance the giver's private interests. While according to the law, there is an obligation to report and forfeit gifts, the registry to which the LRSPENNL refers has not been implemented. Currently, the government is encouraging the donation of gifts to public organisations, but only during Christmas, the period of the year when the number of gifts increases. The LRSPENNL also contains post-employment rules, but they are weak. These rules cannot effectively avoid undue influence and "capture" of decision-making processes.

Nuevo León has, adopted a prescriptive approach to addressing conflicts of interest. Nuevo León's conflict of interest rules makes reference to: 1) situations affecting the legal capacity of the contractor or public officials entering into a contract; and 2) special relationships between parties interested in a selection process and public officials affecting equal treatment. It must be said, however, that none of the existing laws provide a definition of what constitutes a conflict of interest. In addition, these laws do not clearly refer to situations that could lead to a potential or apparent conflict of interest.

A basic definition of conflict of interest is crucial. Such a definition would help public officials to determine whether they can execute their duties and functions in situations where there appears to be a conflict of interest, but this is not or may not be the case. If Nuevo León adopts a definition of conflict of interest, it should label the situation above an "apparent conflict of interest" – which could be as serious as having an actual conflict. The reason for this is the potential for doubts to arise about the official's integrity and the integrity of the official's organisation (OECD, 2005[16]). Because potential or apparent conflicts of interest are not listed in Nuevo León's regulations, detection and enforcement of these types of conflicts is difficult. Whichever approach Nuevo León adopts in its framework for the management of conflicts of interest, it is important that the state clearly defines conflict of interest in its legislative framework (and especially in its procurement legislation). The definitions Canada and New Zealand use could serve as models for Nuevo León (see Box 6.7).

Box 6.7. Definition of conflict of interest adopted by OECD member countries

Canada

Canada's Conflict of Interest Act (S.C. 2006, co., sq.) states that "a public office holder is in a conflict of interest when he or she exercises an official power, duty or function that provides an opportunity to further his or her private interests or those of his or her relatives or friends or to improperly further another person's private interests" (Article 4). Furthermore, in Article 5, the act also specifies the general duty expected of public servants. "Every public office holder shall arrange his or her private affairs in a manner that will prevent the public office holder from being in a conflict of interest." While the Conflict of Interest Act is primarily aimed at elected and other senior officials, the Treasury Board Code of Values and Ethics applies this definition and similar responsibilities to every public servant in government.

New Zealand:

In New Zealand, the definition of conflict of interest is tailored to targeted groups, such as public servants, ministers or board members of crown companies. Nevertheless, these definitions contain common features. For example, they all cover actual and perceived conflicts of interest, as well as direct and indirect conflicts. In addition to the general definitions developed for the targeted groups outlined here, supplemental documents also list possible types of situations where conflicts of interest arise, together with concrete practical examples.

For public servants:

"Conflicts of interest are defined as, … any financial or other interest or undertaking that could directly or indirectly compromise the performance of their duties, or the standing of their department in its relationships with the public, clients, or ministers. This would include any situation where actions taken in an official capacity could be seen to influence or be influenced by an individual's private interests (e.g. company directorships, shareholdings, offers of outside employment). […] A potential area of conflict exists for public servants who may have to deal directly with members of Parliament who have approached the department in a private capacity" (Code of Conduct).

For ministers: "Conflicts of interest can arise because of the influence and power they wield – both in the individual performance of their portfolio responsibilities and as members of Cabinet. Ministers must conduct themselves at all times in the knowledge that their role is a public one; appearances and propriety can be as important as actual conflict of interest in establishing what is acceptable behaviour. A conflict of interest may be pecuniary (that is, arising from the Minister's direct financial interests) or non-pecuniary (concerning, for example, a member of the Minister's family) that may be either direct or indirect" (Cabinet Manual).

For board members of crown companies, a conflict of interest is defined as a situation in which a board member is "party to, or will or may derive a material financial benefit from" a transaction involving his or her company (The Companies Act 1993, Part VIII, Sections 138 and 139).

Sources: (Treasury Board Code of Values and Ethics in Canada, 2006[18]) (OECD, 2004[19])

In addition, Nuevo León could also consider issuing guidelines to assist public officials to determine how to manage a conflict of interest properly when it arises. Canada uses guidelines that could serve as a model for the state (see Box 6.8). In addition, guidelines issued at the federal level in Mexico could be more strenuously applied in Nuevo León. These guidelines were released by the SFP. They are supposed to serve as a reference for all members of the civil service – including employees of federal, state and municipal governments. The guidelines are called Guide to identify and prevent behaviours that may constitute a conflict of interest for public servants (Guía para identificar y prevenir conductas que puedan constituir conflicto de interés de los servidores públicos) and the aim to identify and prevent conduct that could constitute a conflict of interest.

Box 6.8. Considerations to take into account to solve an apparent conflict of interest in Canada

The following is an excerpt from Values Alive: A Discussion Guide to the "Values and Ethics Code for the Public Sector that describes for public servants at all levels the values and ethical practices that guide direction, decision making and behaviour within the Government of Canada.

Integrity in action: An example of an ethical dilemma

Situation

Hélène is a public servant in an agency that provides counselling and federal government financial assistance to senior citizens. She has been in her position for many years, and along with having great expertise, Hélène loves her job. She takes pride in providing her clients the best service possible, and she is always careful to be impartial in her dealings. As a result, Hélène has developed a solid professional reputation and excellent relationships with her clients. Hélène was saddened to hear of the death of one of her clients, Mr. Beaulieu, but was very surprised several months later when she was informed that Mr. Beaulieu had left her his retired racehorse in his will. They had often discussed their mutual love of horses, but she had no idea that Mr. Beaulieu was going to do this, and she would have never asked him for anything. Not knowing what else to do, Hélène immediately reported the matter to her agency's conflict of interest office to seek advice.

Possible steps for resolution

Seeking help from her organisation on this decision was certainly a helpful first step. The analysis to follow could include questions around the nature of the gift and whether it could be considered "minor". Also, if Hélène accepted the gift, would it compromise her integrity or the integrity of her agency? Would it appear to do so? Any appropriate solution should take the answers to these questions into consideration.

Things to think about

This is an example of how sometimes, by doing nothing more than being excellent at their jobs, public servants find themselves in a conflict of interest. A conflict of interest does not imply that there was any wrongdoing, but simply that the situation presents competing interests, or in this case, the appearance of competing interests. Under the Public Sector Code, it is as important to avoid apparent conflicts of interest as it is to avoid real or potential conflicts of interest.

In the actual case upon which this scenario is based, the Federal Court of Appeal upheld the department's instruction to the employee to return the legacy. It was not because the employee had committed misconduct, but rather, the acceptance of the legacy and the appearance of a conflict of interest could erode the public's confidence and trust that the decisions made by public servants in such sensitive areas are based on the highest standards of impartiality and integrity.

Source: (Government of Canada,(n.d.)[20])

Nuevo León needs to provide its public officials with training on how to handle conflicts of interest. This training should be available to all public officials, but should focus on those working in public procurement. The training should create a common understanding of what constitutes a conflict of interest, and how this situation could arise. Officials should learn through this training that conflicts of interest can occur not only through relationships, but also if officials hold certain assets or certain positions, receive gifts, and more.

6.2.3. Maximising the use of the three declarations as prevention tools to ensure the integrity of the public procurement process

Nuevo León should consider using disclosure of assets and interests as a mechanism to prevent conflicts of interest and integrity breaches in the public procurement cycle

Disclosure of assets is a mechanism to preserve and enhance the integrity of the procurement process by making information about assets publically available in order to effectively manage conflicts of interest. These disclosures hold public officials more accountable for their actions. The public availability of this information, in particular, enables involved citizens to serve as a control mechanism. Nevertheless, disclosures of assets sometimes raise concern with regards to public officials' privacy. Therefore, it is important to strike the right balance. In some countries, the nature of the position the official holds and his or her seniority are taken into account. Moreover, if only seen as an administrative formality, this disclosure cannot be used as a mechanism to prevent and properly manage conflicts of interest.

OECD countries have applied a tailored approach to disclosing public procurement officials' private interests and making them publicly available (see Figure 6.6). (OECD, 2017[13]).

Figure 6.6. Level of disclosure and public availability of private interests of public procurement officials in comparison to civil servants

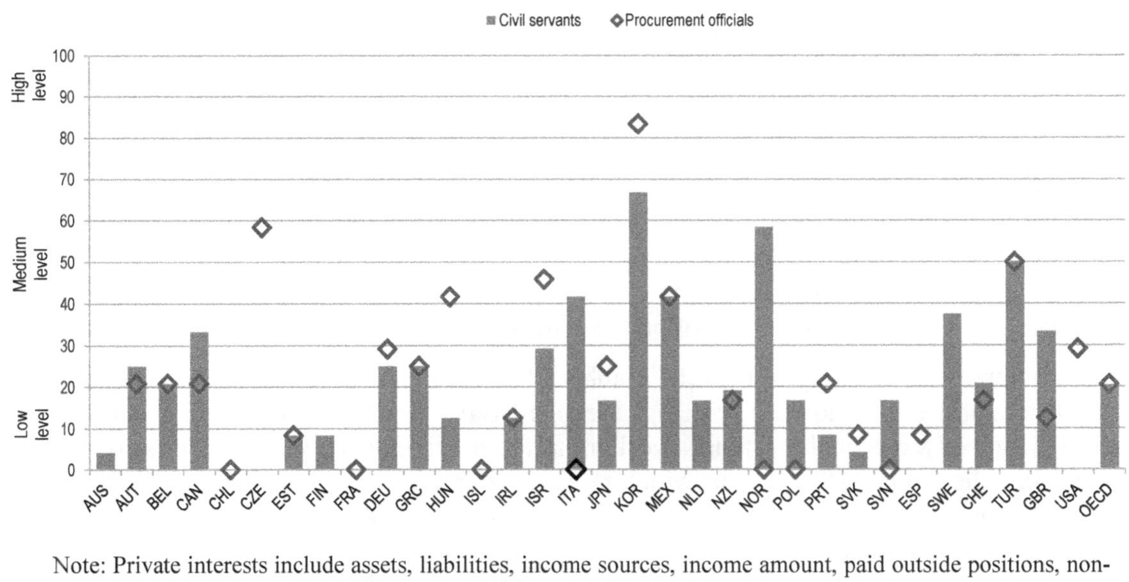

Note: Private interests include assets, liabilities, income sources, income amount, paid outside positions, non-paid outside positions, gifts and previous employments.

Source: (OECD, 2014[21])

Public officials in Nuevo León working in different government and parastatal organisations should make a declaration of their assets, per Article 50, Fraction XVIII; Article 112, Article 116 and Article 121, Fractions I, II and III of the LRSPEMNL. As such, the following officials working within the public sector administration should disclose their assets: high-ranked officials (from governor, ministers, heads of agencies, deputy ministries, presidents of corporation, directors, deputy directors, heads of administrative units, co-ordinators, and chiefs of departments). Per the law, these officials and officials who handle, collect, manage and safeguard funds and assets should disclose their assets at three different times.

First, public officials should submit a declaration of assets 30 working days after occupying their position of office. Second, on an annual basis, these officials should declare their assets in October (as long as the official started his or her position one year before the date of this declaration and continued to work in the same office the following year and subsequent ones). Third, officials should submit a declaration of assets 15 working days after they leave their positions. The annual declaration should also contain a disclosure of authorised gifts received.

Compliance with these obligations is the responsibility of the Legal Affairs Directorate of the Office of the Comptroller for Government Transparency. This directorate publishes the list of those who have complied with this obligation in the *Official Journal of the State* (*Periódico Oficial del Estado*). It should be mentioned that one of the main challenges this directorate is currently facing is that it does not have enough personnel to guarantee effective compliance with this obligation. Because of this, the directorate does not know the total number of public officials who should submit this declaration.

The content of the asset declaration includes references to information on family members, but does not make reference to disclosures of business associates, former employers, acquaintances or friends. This is a problem, as disclosures of these contacts could also be useful to implementing the appropriate measures to prevent conflicts of interest from arising. Furthermore, such disclosures could help effectively manage conflicts of interest that arise in the day-to-day activities of public servants working in sensitive areas, such as procurement. This information would be part of the declaration of interests that will become mandatory once Nuevo León's General Law of Administrative Responsibilities is implemented as a part of its local anti-corruption system.

The asset declaration is submitted through a digital platform named Declaranet. The information disclosed by public officials is contained in a registry that is not available to the public unless the public official has given his or her authorisation. This information can also be released to the public per a judiciary resolution. Currently, Nuevo León does not publicly disclose these forms, and it is not possible to consult the contents of these disclosures. Therefore their main purpose, which is to properly manage conflicts of interests and ensure accountability of public officials, cannot be accomplished.

While there is no certainty of the total number of public officials in compliance with this disclosure obligation, the main challenge the legal affairs directorate faces is to ensure the compliance of those public officials working in the procurement sector (and in sensitive areas like the public safety sector, which procures goods and services directly). Because of this, Nuevo León should view reforms to its disclosure rules as an opportunity. The state could consider adopting a strategy to ensure that the 140 public officials who compose the public procurement workforce comply with disclosure obligations. To achieve this objective, the legal affairs directorate could sign a memorandum of understanding with the Secretariat of Administration in order to obtain the names and positions of those public officials working in the public procurement area who have not yet submit their declarations. By doing this, the legal affairs directorate could ensure their compliance with their obligations, and accountability for their actions when participating in public procurement activities.

Nuevo León needs to continue working to ensure that public officials understand that assets and interest declarations are tools that, used correctly, can prevent and manage conflicts of interest that arise. The prevention function of these tools needs to be reinforced by additional mechanisms. One technique could be raising awareness among public servants so that they understand 1) what constitutes a conflict of interest; and 2) how to manage conflicts of interest when they arise.

6.2.4. Enhancing the whistle-blower programme to strengthen Nuevo León's integrity system and get value for money from procurement activities

Nuevo León should improve its internal reporting and whistle-blowing system in order to safeguard the public interest and ensure efficiency in public procurement activities by reinforcing the mechanisms that protect anonymity and prevent reprisals

Protecting whistle-blowers is an effective way to help governments detect misuse of public funds, and discover waste, fraud and other forms of corruption. Protecting whistle-blowers is also key to fostering integrity in the public sector and promoting a culture of public accountability and integrity in government activities like public procurement. Whistle-blower protections enable the determent and detection of wrongdoing, as public officials have access to up-to-date information concerning practices in their workplaces, and are usually the first to recognise wrongdoings (UNODC, 2015[22]). In addition, these protections can also support an open organisational culture. In such a culture, employees are aware of how to report corruption, and they have confidence that when they report problems, they will be afforded effective protection against retaliation.

To facilitate whistle-blowing in the public sector, some countries have adopted incentive measures, including monetary rewards or compensation, and follow-up mechanisms. While some countries also have penalties for retaliation against whistle-blowers, there are others that provide legal protection to whistle-blowers through provisions found in one or more laws. Laws providing these protections include anti-corruption, competition, public service and employment laws, as well as criminal codes. Regardless of whether a state regulates these protections via one or more laws, an effective whistle-blower protection system depends on clear and effective communication. Indeed, informing both employers and employees about their rights, responsibilities and the resources available to them is crucial to creating an environment of trust, professionalism and collegiality that supports the principles of integrity in both the workplace and society.

Unlike the legislative framework at the federal level (where whistle-blower protections are set out in several laws), Nuevo León has a distinct whistle-blower protection law. This law, the Law to Promote Report of Corrupt Conducts of Public Officials of Nuevo León (Ley para Incentivar la Denuncia de Actos de Corrupción de Servidores Públicos del Estado de Nuevo León, LIDACSP), was enacted 29 June 2013. According to this law and the Agreement under which the Anti-Corruption Unit of the Executive Power was created (Acuerdo por el que se crea la Unidad Anticorrupción del Poder Ejecutivo del

Estado de Nuevo León, AUAPENL), the Anti-Corruption Unit that depends on the Office of the Comptroller for Government Transparency is responsible for the law's implementation. This means that the Anti-Corruption Unit determines the terms and references of the protection programme, receiving and following up on the disclosure of corrupt conduct. It also grants economic rewards if conditions are met and received, and handles complaints of reprisals. Finally, the unit determines if reports are based on accurate, true and legally obtained information.

Nuevo León's Strategic Plan 2015-2030 mandates that all ministries and parastatal entities establish appropriate procedures to raise awareness among public officials and citizens about the mechanisms contained in this law. However, interviews with public officials showed that there are currently no internal processes within institutions to promote disclosures. Interviews also revealed that the state does not conduct awareness-raising campaigns (such as trainings, newsletters or information sessions) regarding the existing reporting channels and procedures for disclosures. Nuevo León could, therefore, consider using internal processes and the other methods listed above to raise awareness among public officials, potential providers and citizens. Finally, the state could make good use of electronic platforms and websites to promote disclosures.

The LIDACSP contains clear definitions. It streamlines and sets out procedures and mechanisms to: 1) facilitate and promote the reporting of corrupt conduct by public officials from the central and parastatal public administration of the state of Nuevo León (which can be investigated and sanctioned administratively or criminally); and 2) protect public officials or persons who witness or report this misconduct – as well as any person related to them – from retaliation and any other intimidation. As delineated by the LIDACSP, the Protection Programme and other mechanisms and exceptional measures ensure the personal integrity and anonymity of those who report misconduct. These mechanisms also protect wrongly accused individuals from administrative and criminal sanctions in cases of false and vexatious testimonies. This law imposes on managers of whistle-blowers to provide a report on the alleged reprisal actions within a deadline of 5 days after which the alleged facts will be presumed true. However, the law does not contain specific provisions referring to corrupt behaviours related to public procurement processes.

Corruption as an act is defined in a very broad manner under this law. The definition includes actions or omissions contravening Article 50 of the LRSPEMNL and giving a personal, unfair advantage to a public official or a third party. It also includes conduct that promises to provide these unfair advantages. Thus, the definition covers not only fraud, bribery or any other corruption acts, but also breaches of the ethics framework and conflict of interest rules. Technically, the law also opens the door to providing a protective mechanism to legal persons who report a corrupt act. The reason for this is that the law mentions that "any person" can be subject to the provisions. This statement refers to then, natural or legal persons.

The scope of the law covers all conduct of those who carry out functions in the public administration of Nuevo León, including those from municipalities and trusts established by the state. Moreover, per this law, through the legislative and judiciary, the autonomous bodies and municipalities can also determine that their public officials be subject to this law. Non-compliance with the provisions of the law is sanctioned under the LRSPEMNL.

The law sets out three different channels to ensure effective reporting of misconduct and corrupt acts by public officials. Reports and complaints can be made anonymously or officially through Corruptel, a telephone line (070), and Corrupnet, a website to which anyone can log on to and report misconduct by filling out a form. Reports and complaints can also be made in person. As mentioned during OECD interviews with public officials, all of these three channels generate a tracking number per complaint. This allows whistle-blowers to follow up on their reports in person or by phone. This tracking number also serves to protect their identities, and to ensure anonymity.

One of the major challenges Nuevo León is currently facing as it tries to guarantee anonymity and protection of whistle-blower information is that the Corruptel service is not under the jurisdiction of the Anti-Corruption Unit. In addition, while phone operators are trained, they do not sign a confidentiality agreement. Therefore, Nuevo León should consider reorganising the service. The state could assign some personnel to the Anti-Corruption Unit who will be exclusively dedicated to receiving and acting on these kinds of calls.

In addition to the three channels mentioned above, suppliers can also submit complaints using a link on the public procurement for public works portal. Unfortunately, interviews conducted during the OECD fact-finding mission revealed that the link does not seem to have been well disseminated among public officials and bidders.

When reports of misconduct are submitted directly to the Anti-Corruption Unit, whistle-blowers or witnesses can still refuse to reveal their identities. In this case, the Anti-Corruption Unit will assess the information it receives and determine the appropriate actions for the reported case. Misconduct or corrupt acts can also be reported to the Anti-Corruption Unit by internal control units in the context of verifications. Corruption can also be reported by the organisation in which it has taken place, as long as the report is submitted directly to the superior of a public official. In this case, if the whistle-blower is a public official, he or she can report any wrongdoing or misbehaviour to his or her superior without fear of retaliation. The reason for this is that the law imposes criminal and administrative sanctions on the superior if he or she retaliates. If the whistle-blower is a citizen, he or she will receive legal assistance to protect his or her rights. In addition, precautionary measures can be adopted to protect the whistle-blower further.

Public officials, citizens and private firms can also report misconduct directly to the Public Prosecutor, who will transfer the case to the Anti-Corruption Unit for its determination. The Public Prosecutor can also apply, if necessary, administrative sanctions, per the LRSPEMNL. According to information obtained in interviews, it appears that only two hundred misconduct reports were submitted to the Public Prosecutor and then redirected to the Anti-Corruption Unit.

The personal information of whistle-blowers is considered confidential per the Transparency and Access to Public Information Law of the State of Nuevo León (Ley de Transparencia y Acceso a la Información Pública del Estado de Nuevo León, CTAINL). Personal information cannot be disclosed in any subsequent administrative or judicial procedure unless a legal provision expressly mentions it, or an order to unseal this information is issued by the concerned judicial authority. Despite these safeguards, very few whistle-blower complaints have been received by the state – compared to the high level of perceived corruption in Nuevo León. Indeed, as detailed in Table 6.6, the Anti-Corruption Unit received a total of 2 759 complaints related to corruptions acts between October 2011 to June 2017.

Table 6.6. Volume of complaints received annually since 2011

Year	Complaints received	Result in administrative sanctions	Result in criminal complaint
2011	649	0	0
2012	678	38	18
2013	373	64	3
2014	361	42	4
2015	269	23	13
2016	342	44	83
2017	87	0	15

Source: Information provided by the Anti-corruption Unit, 6 June 2017.

According to the Anti-Corruption Unit, the volume of complaints related to public procurement activities represents only 5% of the complaints received that then result in administrative sanctions or criminal procedures. This total is very low compared to the volume of complaints received on a yearly basis that result in an administrative sanction or a criminal procedure.

During interviews, former providers and potential bidders mentioned that they felt that there were two reasons why public procurement complaints did not result in sanctions. The first was that most shareholders have a lack of knowledge of the existing procedures to report misconduct. The second reason was that providers and bidders felt there were potential costs to reporting irregularities. Providers mentioned that they felt there was a high risk of not being invited to participate in a procurement process again if they reported corruption. Given these issues, Nuevo León should establish effective mechanisms to reiterate and assure providers that their anonymity will be protected if they decide to report any irregularities during the procurement process. Indeed, whistle-blowers need to be informed that the law provides some mechanisms to guarantee them effective protection in terms of their identities and other factors. Whistle-blowers need to know that the Anti-Corruption Unit holds a registry of those who are authorised to consult the file containing all information related to reported misconduct. They also need to know that, as a current practise, only few employees of the Anti-Corruption Unit have access to their information. Finally, if anyone contravenes the procedures in place to protect whistle-blowers, those individuals could be considered administratively, civilly and criminally liable.

The Protection Programme of whistle-blowers and witnesses of corrupt acts operates in cases of administrative misconduct. The programme works to avoid reprisal actions and to protect whistle-blower and witness identities, assets and labour rights. It also works to protect the personal integrity of whistle-blowers, as well as those of their spouses, common law ascendants or descendants until the first degree, relatives. Whistle-blowers receive this protection for a minimum of three months and it can be challenged through an administrative and contentious trial. The protection can also be renewed or modified after a review of the facts of the case. In addition, it is subject to compliance oversight, with specific requirements. If no longer required, a decision for removing this protective measure must be issued. The law provides administrative, civil and criminal sanctions in cases of breaches of the obligations imposed in relation to protective measures. However, the law also provides that these measures should be determined by both the Anti-Corruption Unit and the applicable heads of ministries or bodies within the government. Therefore, there is a high risk of anonymity being breached. This risk in turn affects future reports.

Finally, the law states that whistle-blowers may receive economic compensation, provided they comply with a few requisites. First, they must provide truthful, sufficient and relevant information that proves corrupt misconduct was committed by a public official. Second, whistle-blowers must disclose their identities if they are contacted by the authorities investigating the accusations. The monetary compensation ranges from MEX 5 000 to MEX 20 000, and is subject to budgetary availability. It is also subject to the terms and conditions of the agreement issued by the comptroller, which are published in the *Official State Journal*. As structured, the monetary compensation is not an effective tool to protect integrity, as the amount does not guarantee financial support for whistle-blowers. For instance, these funds may not be sufficient to cover the legal expenses a whistle-blower could incur, and the funds are subject to a waiver of the whistle-blower's anonymity right. Moreover, Nuevo León's whistle-blower protection mechanisms require that no breaches of the measures protecting whistle-blower identities occur. This means that the personnel overseeing the process must be well-trained. In addition, strong mechanisms must be in place to control any leak of information.

6.2.5. Ensuring integrity of public procurement officials and of the whole public procurement process through awareness-raising activities and trainings

Nuevo León should make efforts to provide trainings specifically on public procurement integrity in order to enhance the integrity of the whole public procurement process and the workforce

Ethical training provides practical guidance on ethical behaviour in situations where official rules contradict practises or do not provide clear answers on how to behave in sensitive situations. Ethical training is especially important in contexts with high levels of corruption, where many ill-defined situations have not yet been addressed by formal rules. While lectures appear appropriate for training on integrity rules, interactive and tailor-made practical methods may be more useful for trainings on values and ethical conduct in risk situations. Public procurement officials can also receive specialised training in order to make them accountable for their behaviour.

Public procurement is recognised as an important government activity in Nuevo León. That said, in interviews with the OECD, public officials in the state mentioned that the state's procurement workforce is composed of a very low number of public officials with a deep knowledge of public procurement methods. Furthermore, many public procurement officials need to learn more or receive updated training on public procurement procedures. In the case of newly recruited personnel, these officials need enhanced training because they have very little experience in the field. Many also do not have in-depth knowledge of how government institutions and regulations work.

Nuevo León has developed a training programme called the Culture of Legality and the Fight against Corruption. The programme is mandatory for all public officials, and is offered on an annual basis. This programme covers the following topics: rule of law, a culture of legality, introduction to the National Anti-Corruption System (Sistema Nacional Anticorrupción, SNA), the legal framework, principles and the structural framework of the SNA, sanctions for serious offenses and administrative faults, procedural processes, the national digital platform and system of assets evolution, Section 50 of the LRSPEMNL, new powers of the Superior Audit Office of the State of Nuevo León, the LIDACSP, and the ethics code.

The heads of Nuevo León's public-sector entities designate which public officials attend this training. In order to attend, officials need to: 1) pass examinations; 2) develop projects identifying corruption risk areas, transparency issues and more; and 3) provide an action plan based on quantitative and qualitative analyses that identify responsible persons, deadlines, expected results and recommendations. Assistance to all training classes is monitored, and memorandums are sent to all heads of public entities confirming the participation of public officials. The reason for this is that public entities have ethics training objectives, and need to provide a statistical report on the progress they have made towards their objectives. When entities reach 100% of their training objectives, certificates attesting to the participation of their public officials are issued. Subsequently, these officials are certified as Agents of Change (Agentes de Cambio).

Currently, Nuevo León disseminates integrity rules among public officials working in various public entities. These entities include the Office of the Comptroller General, where public officials certified as Agents of Change are training. They also include the Directorate of Control and Audits of the Parastatal Sector (Dirección de Control y Auditoria del Sector Paraestatal), and the Directorate of Internal and Monitoring Control Bodies (Dirección de Órganos de Control y Vigilancia). However, these training sessions do not focus on how to solve ethical dilemmas or properly manage conflicts of interest in daily work, or, more precisely, in the context of public procurement activities. Nuevo León could consider looking at trainings in France and Germany, if it decides to update its integrity trainings. In these countries, the objectives of trainings are to raise awareness, to develop knowledge and to increase the commitment of public officials to integrity. In so doing, both France and Germany aim to foster a culture of integrity in public organisations (see Box 6.9).

Box 6.9. Specialised training for public procurement in France

The Central Service of Corruption Prevention, an inter-ministerial body attached to the French Ministry of Justice, has developed training materials for public procurement to help officials identify irregularities and corruption in procurement. Below is a case study from these training materials that illustrates the challenges faced by various actors at different steps of the procedure. The example also highlights the difficulty of gathering evidence on irregularities and corruption.

Issue at stake

Following an open invitation to bid, an unsuccessful bidder complains to the mayor of a commune accusing the bidding panel of irregularities because his bid was lower than that submitted by the winning bidder. How should the mayor deal with the problem?

Stage one: Checking compliance with public procurement procedures

The firm making the complaint is well known and is not considered "litigious". The mayor therefore gives the claim his attention, and requests that the internal audit service check the conditions of the award of contract. In particular, the mayor asks that the audit service check whether the procedure complied with the regulations, as the lowest bidder is not necessarily the best bidder. The mayor also asks the internal audit service to make sure that tender notices were published in the official journal. The mayor learns from the report prepared by the bidding committee that although the procedure followed regulations, the bid by the firm in question had been revised upwards by the technical services responsible for comparing the offers. Apparently, the firm lodging the complaint had omitted certain cost headings which were added on to its initial bid.

Stage two: Replying to the losing bidder

The mayor lets the losing bidder know exactly why its bid was unsuccessful. However, by return post, he receives a letter pointing out that no one had informed the company of the change made to its bid. In fact, the change to the bid was unjustified, given that the expenditure that had purportedly been omitted had been included in the bid under another heading.

Stage three: Suspicions

The internal audit service confirms the unsuccessful bidder's claim and points out that nothing in the report helps to establish any grounds for the change made by the technical service. It also points out that it would be difficult for an official with any experience, however little, not to see that the expenses had been accounted for under another heading. The mayor now requests that the audit service find out whether the technical services were in the habit of making such changes, whether they have already processed bids from the winning bidder and if contracts have been awarded frequently to the winning bidder in this case. He also requests that the audit service check the background of the technical service officials involved in the case. Do they have experience? Have they been trained? Do they have links with the successful contractor? Could they have had links with the contractor in their previous posts? What do their partners and children do? Examination of the personnel files of the officials, and the shares of the company which won the contract fail to yield anything conclusive. The only links between the officials or their families and the successful bidder are indirect.

Stage four: Handing the case over to authorities of the Ministry of Justice

Having suspicions, but no proof, the mayor hands over information so that investigations can begin. The investigators now have to find proof that a criminal offence (favouritism, corruption, undue advantage, etc.) has been committed. These investigators will exercise their powers to examine bank accounts, conduct hearings and surveillance, etc. The case has now moved out of the domain of public procurement regulations and into the domain of criminal proceedings.

Conclusion

Unable to gather any evidence, and with no authority to conduct an in-depth investigation or question the parties concerned, the mayor makes the only decision that is within his power – he decides to reorganise internally and change the duties of the two members of staff who are involved in the case. However, he must proceed cautiously when giving the reasons for his decision so as to avoid exposing innocent people to public condemnation or himself to accusations of defamation while the criminal investigation is in progress.

The mayor also decides that, going forward, the reports made to the bidding committee by technical services should give fuller explanations of calculations and any changes technical services make to the bids. The mayor also mandates that technical services inform bidders systematically of any changes.

Source: (OECD, 2007[6])

As confirmed during interviews with public officials in Nuevo León, there is no specialised training for public procurement officials in the state. This is not the case in Canada, where employees who work in public procurement or material management can obtain a professional designation through a government-wide certification programme (see Box 6.10). Nuevo León should consider establishing a professional training programme for public procurement officials. This programme should be part of a broader effort to recognise public procurement as a strategic profession, rather than an administrative one. This is vital, as public procurement can play a key role in preventing mismanagement of resources, waste of public funds and potential corruption (as detailed in Chapter 4).

Box 6.10. Certification programme for federal government procurement and managerial communities in Canada

In today's rapidly changing environment, the Government of Canada's Procurement and Materiel Management Communities has evolved. Officials working for the organisation need to possess specific knowledge and skills that align with the office's strategic advisory role. In an environment where accountability is foremost, it is essential that practitioners demonstrate that they possess the advanced skills and knowledge required to function effectively and efficiently.

The Procurement Materiel Management and Real Property (PMMRP) Communities Management Office (CMO) provides strategic direction and central leadership for the collaborative development and implementation of strategies, programmes and initiatives to support capacity building, community development and the professional recognition of the federal government's Procurement, Materiel Management and Real Property Communities.

One of the most notable achievements to date is the national and international recognition of the federal government's first ever Certification Programme for Procurement and Materiel Management specialists. Through this programme, practitioners in procurement and materiel management can acquire a professional designation through their own certification programme.

Certification provides professional recognition for the community, and offers a professional designation to formally acknowledge a practitioner's level of achievement. A procurement specialist can acquire certification as a Certified Federal Specialist in Procurement (CFSP), Level I and II. Those in materiel management can acquire certification as a Certified Federal Specialists in Materiel Management (CFSMM), Level I. Both designations are based on the Federal Government Procurement and Materiel Management Communities Competency Suite. A competency describes an employee's proficiency in a particular job function in terms of knowledge, skills and abilities. Each competency has a definition, a proficiency level and behavioural indicator statements.

Level II (Procurement only) requirements are similar to those of Level I in terms of experience and training. For the knowledge requirement, candidates must pass a case study exam.

Source: (Public Service and Procurement Canada,(n.d.)[23])

In order to build a professional team of public procurement officials, Nuevo León could use the information contained in the Registry of Public Officials who Intervene in Contracts to be Executed with Federal Funds (Registro de Servidores Públicos que Intervienen en Procedimientos de Contrataciones Públicas, Licencias y Permisos con Recursos Federales, RUSPEF). This registry currently administered by the Office of the Comptroller, could be used by the state for the purposes of identifying officials who could benefit from further training and knowledge. Nuevo León has begun uploading a list of the names of officials from 16 of the 33 ministries and entities who intervene in contracts using federal funds. The state began uploading the list onto a registry available on the Office of the Comptroller's website, but, now, officials plan to upload the list to the RUSPEF portal. The Office of the Comptroller General has already published two lists since the beginning of this year. These lists could be very useful as to ensuring in the future that these public officials are duly trained and receive opportunities to update their knowledge in the future.

Nuevo León could consider developing specific training programmes on integrity in public procurement. The content of these programmes must be regularly revised and updated, due to the relatively weak internal controls in Nuevo León's public procurement process, and the gaps observed in the capacities and knowledge of the public procurement workforce. To disseminate its content and ensure that all public officials meet high professional standards of knowledge, practical implementation and integrity, Nuevo León could consider implementing these trainings using e-learning mechanisms. Doing so will make this information accessible to all public officials who participate in the public procurement process.

Public officials could also be asked, after completing these trainings to fill out a survey. The survey could ask officials what they learned, what was missing in the training sessions and whether some improvements are required. Internal control public officials and auditors could also be included in these learning programmes, so as to ensure consistency in the implementation of integrity policies and rules in public procurement activities. Nuevo León faces the challenge of having sufficient financial resources to provide appropriate training to its public officials and to newly recruited public procurement personnel. Thus, e-learning is good choice, as it is less costly than in-person trainings. Nuevo León could implement e-learning programmes for its public procurement officials by signing agreements with some of the universities in the state. Procurement officials have co-operated on trainings with universities in the past. And, OECD interviews showed that there was no resistance from the personnel working on public procurement to this arrangement.

Nuevo León could benefit from implementing anti-corruption programmes for suppliers as an additional mechanism to enhance integrity of public procurement activities

Private sector engagement is critical to effectively countering corruption. Corruption in public procurement consists of more than bribing public officials. Public procurement contracts should contain "no-corruption" warranties, and should be implemented to verify the truthfulness of suppliers' warranties that they have not and will not engage in corruption in connection with contracts. Such programmes should also require appropriate supply-chain transparency to fight corruption in subcontracts, and integrity training requirements for supplier personnel.

Implementing an anti-corruption programme is not a one-time event; it needs to be followed up on through regular periodic evaluation (monitoring). This monitoring ensures that strengths and weaknesses are properly identified, and that the programme is improved. The result of this is that the programme remains effective and up-to-date.

In Nuevo León, suppliers should declare a statement made under oath indicating that they are not do not have any of the conflicts set out in Section 37 of the LAACS. Suppliers should make these statements at the time of submitting their proposals, either through the SECOP or in person. Furthermore, bidders are obliged to submit an integrity statement declaring their commitment to conducting themselves honestly in the various stages of the procurement process. This integrity statement should also state suppliers will refrain from engaging in behaviours that violate the laws directly, or through a third party. Similar to the legal framework for acquisitions and contracts of providers and contractors, the LOPNL also has a provision requiring participants in the call for tenders of public works or services to submit a written declaration under oath. This declaration states that participants in calls for tender are not in violation of the provisions of Article 44 of this law.

Public procurement contracts contain "no-corruption" warranties according to LAACS. That said, during interviews with the OECD, public officials mentioned concerns about the truthfulness of suppliers' warranties. These warranties are supposed to guarantee that suppliers have not and will not engage in corrupt activities in connection with the contract. But the warranties are not verified. In addition, the process is seen as administrative and conducted as such, rather than implemented with a strategic vision.

To be effective, anti-corruption programmes for suppliers require that participants in public procurement processes implement internal procedures. These procedures ensure that corruption and integrity breaches are well understood by employees. They also guarantee that sanctions are properly imposed and communicated to any potential contractors or subcontractors the supplier works with. The requirements are meant to ensure that suppliers for future works comply with current rules, and that they avoid conflicts of interest situation and any irregularities that could result in corrupt acts. These requirements call for a strong collaboration between the private sector and the public sector. Therefore, the public sector should also provide integrity training to the private sector. In so doing, officials can ensure the engagement of private sector actors in efforts to maintain the integrity of the whole public procurement cycle.

As mentioned during interviews, Nuevo León has not yet implemented specific integrity trainings for supplier personnel. This is important, if the state wishes to foster supplier commitment to fighting corruption in contracts and subcontracts. Therefore, a first initiative Nuevo León could consider in its integrity work in this area could be introducing participants to the applicable legal framework and the potential sanctions in cases of breach. This introduction should also include an explanation on the rationale behind decisions taken in the past against corrupt acts, including the actions taken by the Legal Affairs Directorate and the internal control units.

Moreover, mechanisms should be implemented in the context of an anti-corruption programme to detect bid-rigging. If the state has already undertaken such measures, the state should also implement an assessment of whether their design effectively reduces the risk of bid-rigging in the procurement process. In addition to these mechanisms, initiatives seeking to ensure civil society and private sector engagement in preventing integrity breaches and corruption acts should be implemented. Integrity pacts, as described later in the chapter, could be useful tools.

6.3. Reviewing and adopting policies and tools for conducting an evaluation of suppliers so as to reduce public procurement's vulnerability to corruption

6.3.1. Nuevo León should consider strengthening the public procurement mechanisms it has in place so as to ensure that decisions are made based on what is most beneficial to the public interest

Efficiency in public procurement processes could enhance integrity frameworks and reduce vulnerability to corruption. When funds are better accounted for and used for the intended purposes, the risk of corruption is diminished. The main purpose of bid evaluation is to determine the best bid according to evaluation and selection methodology specified in the solicitation document. The best bid is chosen from among all bids submitted before the bid closing time on a specified date. Therefore, bid evaluation is a sensitive step in the whole public procurement cycle. Of particular concern is whether the economic, social and environmental criteria (e.g. favouring bidders from economically disadvantaged areas, using environmental-friendly materials, etc.) are applied.

To ensure the satisfaction of the requirements of contracting authorities, procurement decisions should be made based on up-to-date information. This information should include potential and actual performance and bidders or contractors, as well as information on their integrity. Contracting authorities also need information on bidders and contractors regarding their past procurement performance (in terms of the delivery of goods and services and the execution of contracts). Finally, contracting authorities need information on the recent performance of current bidders. In a few countries, this information is also filtered and integrated at the government-wide level. These countries use statistical report analysing tools to detect patterns in procurement. The results of these analyses are made available to policy makers and the public at large to ensure best value for money.

As detailed in Chapter 2, Nuevo León needs to rethink its procurement process. The state's current process for procurement is based on paperwork, and not all procurement activities are done using information and communication technologies. Indeed, public officials in Nuevo León state that information accessible through the SECOP, for instance, is documented on paper and then uploaded to the platform as a PDF. The current process for reviewing technical and financial requirements, compliance with current legislation, contracts, inspection and payment are not exchanged online.

Moreover, while e- procurement activities could be accessible online, it is important that purchases are adequately planned to ensure the best value for money, and that budgets are properly allocated to each entity. The state is currently centralising its procurement activities into under the Secretariat of Administration, which does the majority of purchases for public sector entities and ministries of the central administration. Exceptions to this are the Secretariat of Public Security, the Attorney General's Office and parastatal entities with no agreement with the SA. While this centralisation appears to be a good option for increasing the efficiency of public procurement in the state, there are still high risks of integrity breaches and corruption. Indeed, not all entities and parastatals entities have integrated their procurement into the centralised system. It is currently used only to buy goods such as paper, toilet paper and ink for printers, and to contract services such as cleaning services.

Information gathered during the OECD's two fact-finding missions showed that there is no real purchase planning or effective monitoring of public sector entities' expenditures in Nuevo León. This opens the door to different integrity breaches. It also prevents the state from achieving better value for money. In addition, purchases are not made based on market analyses, even though that is a requirement under Nuevo León's procurement legal framework (with the exception of direct awards).

As confirmed during the OECD's fact-findings missions, at present, the evaluation criteria used to procure goods in Nuevo León is not based on market analyses but on a binary methodology, as detailed in Chapter 2. This methodology is not adequate for all kinds of purchases. Without market analyses, public procurement officials cannot really understand how the supply market works. They also cannot have an idea of the direction the market is going in, or of competition and the key suppliers in the market. Without some analysis of the marketplace, the state will not be able to adequately plan its future purchases. Accordingly, this feature needs to be included in the state's public procurement strategy.

An additional consideration to effectively evaluate providers is to have them properly registered in the registry of suppliers, and to ensure the information in this registry is duly uploaded to the SECOP or the interactive platform for public works. As previously detailed, this registration is still paper-based. This process can have an impact on the accuracy of information, as it is not systematically uploaded and updated. Procurement is carried out electronically only when purchases are made with federal funds. In these cases, providers only interact with public officials. However, their registration in the providers list is still done in person.

As not all purchase orders or requests are made throughout the Secretariat of Administration, they are not negotiated by experts working in this secretariat, but rather directly by requesting units. These units do not necessarily have the strongest expertise and knowledge of the market. This in turn may impact government capacity to negotiate the best price for goods and services. To adequately evaluate suppliers and achieve greater value for money, Nuevo León must rethink its annual purchasing programme for the central government and parastatal entities. The purchasing programme should be strategically planned and make available for consultation. The government should also utilise a more user-friendly format, and synchronise and standardise the use of technologies for all stages of public procurement. It can do this by using an electronic platform with various applications that allows citizens, participants and public officials to have access to complete information. It may also make sense for the state to sign framework agreements where appropriate and feasible.

Certain other measures could also increase efficiency. E-catalogues to list available products and services that can be viewed and bought in an electronic format, dynamic purchasing, e-auctions, joint procurements and contracts with options that guarantee supplier performance are some examples. Nuevo León needs to view the whole procurement process as a strategic exercise, not a check in the box. The state needs to completely move from a paperwork registration to an e-procurement method. As stated above, it should also adopt enhanced electronic tools, such as electronic catalogues, which are strong tools for avoiding corruption and mismanagement and waste of public funds.

Finally, in order to accurately determine the best value of bids, a logical systematic evaluation procedure covering all aspects of the evaluation process should be followed. To accomplish this, Nuevo León should mandate that procurement public officials create and use a checklist of requirements. Officials can then consult the checklist throughout the evaluation of each bid.

6.4. Ensuring accountability and monitoring with regards to sanctions imposed on suppliers in cases of integrity breach

6.4.1. Nuevo León should consider improving the functionalities of its current webpage for blacklisted suppliers, and ensuring that this information is published in a timely fashion through the SECOP. Nuevo León can also make this information accessible through different links so that different actors can access it

In Nuevo León, private sector procurement participants can be sanctioned with fines and disqualifications if they contravene the provisions of the LAACS and the LOPNL. These contraventions can be linked to non-compliance with the regulatory framework, as well as integrity breaches. According to Article 92 of the LAACS, sanctions are imposed by the Office of the Comptroller and Governmental Transparency or by the internal control unit, depending on the individual and entity involved. These sanctions may be imposed for a period of three months to five years. Sanctions can range from a warning to disqualification to a fine, depending on the seriousness of the misconduct and the existence of fraud. In other situations, disqualification can be accompanied by a sanctions agreement in the contract, or reparatory measures for damages caused to public institutions. In the case of public works, which are regulated by the LOPNL, sanctions are established by the Office of the Comptroller, but imposed by the secretariat or contracting authority. Suppliers and participants can solicit their re-integration to the list of suppliers.

The Legal Counsel of the Office of the Comptroller (Director Jurídico) needs to be informed of these proceedings, as it is responsible for the registry of suppliers sanctioned and disqualified. Sanctions are published through the SECOP, and by the Central Purchasing Body on the website of the corresponding secretariat, entity or administrative unit.

Article 98 of the LAACS refer to minor offences, which are sanctioned with fines from 50-500 times the daily general minimum wage in place in the metropolitan economic municipality of Monterrey at the time of the contravention. For serious offences, Article 97 of the LAACS establishes sanctions that can reach 100-1000 the daily general minimum wage in the area standing in force daily in Monterrey. As well, serious offences are sanctioned with a fine and disqualification of the supplier. Sanctions imposed on providers and published on the SECOP mention the sanction imposed, but users cannot access information on the resolution issued by the Office of the Comptroller General. This is too bad, as this information could help future providers know and understand the rationale behind the decision to impose sanctions. In the case of sanctions applicable to breaches of the LOPNL, sanctions are imposed by the contracting ministries or entities. These sanctions can range from 50-100 times the daily general minimal wage to a maximum of 200-500 times the daily general minimal wage. Currently, there is no local registry that makes information on these sanctions publicly available.

The list of blacklisted suppliers is accessible through the website of the government of Nuevo León where information on tenders is published. For each supplier, the following information is mentioned: name, company registration number, type of breach or infringement, duration of the sanction, date of the publication of the blacklisting, which government organisation imposed the sanction and the reason for the sanction. The information disclosed should be complete, and is expected to allow officials to identify potential areas of risks and organisations that may need to adopt corrective measures.

While the list of blacklisted suppliers is very accessible, the list of suppliers sanctioned is very short due to incomplete information. This constitutes a real challenge for public officials selecting the bidders and those monitoring the public procurement process. In the case of public works, there is no possibility of consulting which private firm has been sanctioned, as there is no public registry available for consultation.

To facilitate the access to the list of sanctioned suppliers, Nuevo León could consider adding a search engine to the page. If the state does this, it can also add filters in the future as to facilitate access to information. Nuevo León could also consider adding the ability to download documents containing resolutions sanctioning private firms. This type of functionality would help public officials working at the internal control units, as well as those at the Directorate of the Office of the Comptroller, to more easily determine the fines to be imposed and the length of disqualification.

Because public procurement is subject to different rules depending on the source of funds allocated, public officials need to consult CompraNet in order to confirm whether providers have been blacklisted. This represents an additional task that public officials need to execute to ensure the integrity of the public procurement process. Public officials need to verify providers on two lists before awarding a contract – the one published on CompraNet and the one published on the SECOP. This can be challenging for officials, as the SECOP registry is not updated systematically. Nuevo León should resolve these issues, but continue to require that officials check blacklisting registries before awarding contracts. Moreover, Nuevo León should consider implementing a similar initiative for public works activities as well as make efforts to forward system interconnection between CompraNet and SECOP.

6.5. Actively engaging the private sector and civil society to enhance transparency and ensure accountability of all actors in the public procurement cycle

Public procurement depends on the partnership that must exist between the government and the private sector to create the public procurement marketplace. In this marketplace, the government is the buyer and the private sector is the supplier of needed goods, works or services. Accordingly, transparency is required to allow governments and citizens to engage in a mutually responsive way, thus rendering the public procurement system more accountable. In this sense, low levels of transparency and accountability in the public procurement system can compromise the effective use of public resources and funds. Integrity breaches, on the other hand, require active engagement and efforts from the government, the private sector and civil society, due to their complexity.

Civil society and citizens can play an oversight and monitoring role in public procurement. By serving as a kind of direct social control on government activities, civil society and citizen can further increase transparency in government activities and restore public trust in the system.

Ensuring transparency requires that public procurement entities provide adequate and timely access to relevant information in each phase of the public procurement cycle. In doing so, these entities must disclose information in a way that promotes competition. Public procurement entities must have clear policies, requirements and justifications for determining what information should be made publicly available or considered confidential. This information should be accessible for free throughout the centralised online portal; the information webpage should also operate under open data standards. Suppliers should provide appropriate transparency in subcontracting relationships and make this information publicly available. The OECD recommends that information be freely accessible to all stakeholders, including potential domestic and foreign suppliers, civil society and the general public. By doing this, officials can ensure open access to public procurement information and the visibility of the flow of public funds from the beginning of the budgeting process to the end of the public procurement cycle (OECD, 2015[2]).

6.5.1. Promoting transparency of public procurement activities throughout the use of IT technologies

Nuevo León should consider enhancing the functionalities of its different digital platforms in order to make procurement information more accessible and useable by all stakeholders, and to ensure accountability

The Directorate of Government Transparency and Quality of the Office of the Comptroller General (Dirección de Transparencia Gubernamental y Calidad) is the main body in charge of designing transparency and integrity policies. One of its main functions is to formulate, co-ordinate, supervise and assess policies regarding access to information and transparency. It is also tasked with ensuring accountability and integrity of governmental decisions. Other functions of this directorate involve coordination with all ministries and entities of the public administration to modernise monitoring and follow-up systems so that they verify and audit processes within the public service. As such, the directorate works to: strengthen prevention and accountable programmes; design programmes and actions to promote legality and transparency in public management; enhance accountability; promote access to all information generated by the government; guarantee access to public information to anybody; and issue and supervise the implementation of policies and guidelines by ministries, entities and tribunals in order to ensure their compliance with the transparency law. This directorate is also responsible for reviewing and jointly coordinating with ministries that receive requests, claims, reports, suggestions and recommendations submitted by citizens. The directorate helps these ministries do follow up and establish programmes to comply with the commitments set out in the Code of Ethics. These commitments include promoting ethical values that should be observed in the service of citizens. Finally, the directorate promotes policies and programmes on e-governance that allow strong transparency of the public function, and facilitate relationships with citizens (Article 33 of the Organisational Law).

As seen in previous chapters of this review, public procurement processes are mainly administered by the SA. It carries out procurement processes of goods and services for the 21 entities of the central administration and 24 parastatal entities with which it has signed co-operation agreements. Public works procurement is made through the Ministry of Infrastructure (Secretaría de Infraestructura) or by the procurement division of specific parastatals organisations, like Water and Drainage, the Institute for Education and Sports, and the State Highway Network (Agua y Drenaje, ICIFED and the Red Estatal de Autopistas, REA). The Directorate of Government Transparency and Quality of the Office of the Comptroller General should coordinate with these entities in order to ensure that information uploaded onto the different platforms is recorded systematically and using the appropriate format. The Office of the Deputy Ministry of Technologies administers a database. As such, it facilitates the publication of information and the creation of users accounts for suppliers and negotiators on the public procurement portals.

As mentioned in Chapter 2, Nuevo León can use four available procurement methods as set out in its current legislative framework, but it mainly practises direct awards. If the state continues this practice, it will need as much up-to-date information as possible to be effective. As observed in previous sections, public procurement officials are in need of further specialization, and could benefit from having access to detailed guidelines and manuals. These resources should be available for their consultation. In addition, citizens and participants should have access to this information, so they can observe the whole process. This information is available online but it is not easily accessible, as it does not have a user-friendly search engine.

The SGNL is attempting to centralise the process for carrying out public procurement. A large portion of public procurement still occurs in a decentralised manner, through the two non-integrated digital platforms, the SIREGOB and SECOP. The scope and content of procurement processes vary on these platforms, and different actors intervene depending on the method used for public procurement. As mentioned in Chapter 5, while the platforms synchronise automatically, there is no validation of this synchronisation. This points to an additional weakness of the procurement process.

When bids are opened in a hearing they are also transmitted via Facebook (bidders with incomplete information are disqualified immediately). Subsequently, contracting authorities answer technical questions and give a technical assessment. This assessment is then evaluated by the Acquisitions Committee which has the power of approval. None of this information is accessible on the government webpage or the SECOP – which is supposed to gather all information related to public procurement.

The registry of suppliers and list of blacklisted suppliers are also available in an electronic format on the central government's general website. The Directorate of Government Transparency and Quality of the Office of the Comptroller is responsible for the registry and list. In the case of the list of blacklisted suppliers, users are re-directed to SECOP. As information is mainly entered manually in these various electronic databases, there is a high risk of errors and delays in accessing information. Nuevo León should, therefore, urgently consider enhancing its current platforms so as to give to all actors access to the information they need. Information available on these electronic databases should encompass all categories of goods, services and public works, though this is not currently the case. As it overhauls its electronic databases, Nuevo León could also improve the second version of the SECOP. If it does so, it should ensure that existing functionalities are upgraded so as to allow the entry of relevant data that could help not only public officials, but also providers. If both officials and providers gain access to these data, they will be better positioned to make informed decisions. Officials will then be able better able to participate in the public procurement process and choose the best offer for the state.

Nuevo León could also consider, for instance, developing a series of additional resources that describe how state procurement processes work. The resources could be made available on the central government website or the SECOP, and could be targeted at citizens and suppliers. This information could also be useful to ensuring a common understanding of the whole integrity process among newly recruited personnel. This tool could take on the form of a question and answer document (Q&A), which would help suppliers in the procurement process. It could also support business associations and their advisors to understand public procurement regulations and processes. Currently, the only opportunity suppliers have to raise questions and ask for clarification is during clarification meetings. This Q&A could be put together and uploaded to the SECOP. It could be accompanied by guides and manuals on specific topics, so as to enable suppliers and authorities to do the best job possible (especially those external and international suppliers who may not be familiar with local practices or law). This online information should be free and accessible with no registration requirements. Colombia uses a system like this; even videos on Colombia's electronic procurement system have been developed to show providers how the system works.

6.5.2. Increasing civil society participation in public procurement activities

Nuevo León should consider enhancing transparency mechanisms so as to ensure civil society participation in public procurement processes and engagement in fighting corruption

Citizen and civil society oversight of public procurement is essential. First, these two groups can play a role in terms of scrutiny and monitoring. Second, their involvement can further increase transparency of government activities, and, as such, restore public trust in government, to some extent. Indeed, legal and regulatory frameworks in Nuevo León could be used to establish the obligation or opportunity for the government to consult with the public during the procurement planning process (e.g. prior to large-scale or environmentally or socially sensitive procurements). In some countries, citizens are – under clearly specified conditions and subject to signing a statement of confidentiality – permitted or encouraged to act as observers in procurement proceedings. Nuevo León could consider permitting citizens to be officially involved in the monitoring of procurement performance and contract completion (e.g. through the application of innovative techniques, such as geo-tagging, or in the context of social audits) (OECD, 2016[24]).

Nuevo León has launched various initiatives to ensure transparency and civil society participation in public procurement processes. Its legal framework is composed of two different regimes and contains some rules allowing citizen participation during the procurement process. Indeed, the LAACS contains a provision that is similar to one at the federal level that allows citizens to participate in all stages of public tendering above a certain threshold as a way to promote public scrutiny. Citizens may also participate in cases determined by the Acquisitions Committee (Comité de Adquisiciones), due to the impact of the contract on the ministerial, entity or administrative unit's programmes. Unlikely the LAACS, the LOPNL does not contain any reference to social witnesses.

Information provided during the OECD fact-finding missions showed that there are currently only 13 social witnesses of the public procurement process registered with the state (out of the 21 who received training). Their names are currently available on line through the website promoted by the Directorate of Transparency of the Office of the Comptroller General. According to public officials, the low number of citizens interested in acting as social witnesses is due to the lack of information available to the public about this programme. In addition, the public has little information about the monitoring of the programme's results or the fact that social witness' reports are made public. Another problem is that social witnesses work as volunteers. Their work also requires a sound understanding of the whole public procurement process, which can deter citizens from volunteering. While testimonies of social witnesses are published online within 10 days of their participation in a procurement process, the number of irregularities detected and the corrective measures implemented is not made available to the public. This has an impact on the perception of the actual contribution these witnesses make to improving public procurement processes. Therefore, Nuevo León could consider setting a strategy to engage more citizens to enrol as social witnesses. One component of the strategy could be, for instance, issuing a certificate to social witnesses. Another could be giving them compensation for their service, such as transportation cards.

In addition to regulated initiatives to ensure civil society's participation in public procurement, Nuevo León is currently implementing a transparency portal. Via this portal, citizens can consult all public work contracts from 1999 to present – including information on awarded companies, but not catalogues of unit prices. The state is implementing this portal through the Commission of Transparency and Access to Information of the State of Nuevo León (Comisión de Transparencia y Acceso a la Información del Estado de Nuevo León, CTAINL), the National Institute for Transparency, Access to Information and Protection of Data (Instituto Nacional de Transparencia, Acceso a la Información y Protección de Datos, INAI) and three other non-governmental organisations. This website will allow citizens and firms to have access to information on awards. That said, as currently structured the portal does not provide information on offers submitted during tendering processes of previous years. An additional problem is that this information is not linked to the SIREGOB or SECOP. If citizens want to monitor the whole public procurement cycle, they need to consult each database independently. This poses a problem, as they use different formats and citizens will need to download information in order to have a full view of the public procurement process.

In 2016, Nuevo León created the State Registry of Contractors (Registro Estatal de Contratistas, REC) with the purpose of making information about construction firms accessible to those participating in the bidding process. The state also worked to classify contractors within the registry in an effort to ensure better proposals for the state in public works processes. This new registry is accessible on line. Users can also access it by consulting the website directly, which provides information on pre-tendering bases, observations made by providers, the request for tenders, the economic and technical requirements and awarded contracts for public works. The online registration facilitates bidder participation in public works, and the state must respond within 30 days, per the current legislation. That said, the information contained under this registry is not currently accessible to the public for consultation. In this regard, Nuevo León should consider making this information accessible to all, as this registry has been used to compile and store legal and financial information on suppliers, the field of activity in terms of categories of goods and services they can supply, their performance in public contracts and sanctions imposed in cases of integrity breaches.

Information available online for procurement in public works is currently accessible for consultation. Suppliers, citizens and civil society organizations consulting the website can also ask to obtain information on the latest publications of public procurement in public works.

Other initiatives have also been implemented to allow citizens to oversee public expenditures in their localities. One example is the programme, Works in Sight of All, which allows citizens to learn in detail about public works projects executed in their communities. Via this programme, citizens can gain access to public transmissions of tenders and decisions through social media platforms, such as Facebook.

In addition to these government initiatives whose purpose is to give citizens, civil society organisations and firms access to data on public procurement processes, citizens and civil society organisations have developed initiatives of their own. These initiatives aim to improve public management, to create a culture of legality, to increase transparency and to fight corruption in Nuevo León. Some examples of these initiatives are: Gober ¿Cómo Vamos?; Alcalde, ¿Cómo Vamos?; Hagámoslo Bien; and Haz Corto con la Corrupción. The purpose of Haz Corto con la Corrupción is to fight corruption and restore trust in public government decisions.

While the government is making efforts to ensure citizens and civil society groups have open access to information and data, there are still some challenges. Because many of the government's initiatives are recent, citizens have not yet become a true part of the process. It also seems that while these initiatives aim at effectively allowing citizens and civil society organisations to fulfil an oversight role, citizens are not allowed to truly participate in public procurement decision-making or monitoring.

Mechanisms ensuring an open and regular dialogue between the government, suppliers, business associations and citizens are vital. These mechanisms can help reinforce a mutual understanding of the factors influencing the procurement market. They can also help citizens and shareholders to not only monitor the procurement process, but propose ideas for how the government could enhance transparency, impartiality and improve the public procurement cycle. At present, the main problem private firms seem to be facing is that they do not receive information on public tenders and other important decisions related to public procurement in time. This means that, on many occasions, they cannot even be a part of the procurement process.

To ensure dissemination of integrity rules and allow citizens and the private sector to effectively oversee and monitor public procurement activities, Nuevo León could consider using integrity pacts. Integrity pacts extend integrity standards that are applicable to public officials to private sector actors. This occurs in the context of major public procurement projects that require the active involvement of civil society groups. For a reference of existing examples of integrity pacts in countries around the world, see Table 6.7.

Table 6.7. Examples of the use of integrity pacts in various countries

Countries	Objective of these integrity pacts
Germany	An Integrity Pact has been implemented for the construction of the Schönefeld International Airport in Berlin, a project worth € 2.4 billion
India	Integrity Pacts are an essential part of the Draft National Anti-corruption Strategy. The Central Vigilance Commission (CVC) issued the Directive 008/CRD/013, which refers to the implementation of integrity pacts as "standards operating procedures" in procurement contracts of any major government department.
Indonesia	Integrity Pacts have been adopted and applied to local government contracts in up to 20 districts
Italy	Integrity Pacts have been introduced mainly at municipal level in the Milan City Council.
Korea	The Korean pact model emphasises the protection of whistle-blowers and the creation of an ombudsman system to carry out independent external monitoring
Mexico	Transparencia Mexicana has implemented integrity pacts in over 100 contracts, worth approximately USD $30 billion in total
United Kingdom	Integrity Pacts have been adopted and implemented with particular focus on the defence sector.

Source: (OECD, 2016[9])

6.6. Proposals for action

Nuevo León has made notable efforts to increase the integrity and transparency of its public-sector activities. Despite many efforts directed at providing an institutional, legal and regulatory framework to prevent corruption and properly manage conflicts of interest, citizen trust of government institutions and activities remains low. At the same time, public perception of government corruption is high in the state, as reported by various civil society organisations.

Nuevo León has issued various initiatives to comply with its commitment to fighting corruption and promoting integrity in the public sector. There is still work to be done, however. Nuevo León should enhance the measures it has in place and implement new ones. These efforts could include: dedicated and tailored measures against corruption; similar measures to manage conflicts of interest in public procurement activities, reporting of integrity breaches and corruption behaviours; measures to build a coherent and efficient institutional and normative public procurement framework; and capacity-building and awareness-raising initiatives.

In that regard, in order to enhance integrity in its public procurement system, Nuevo León should undertake the actions below.

Enhancing the policy framework to address integrity issues in public procurement processes and activities in Nuevo León.

- Nuevo León should consider strengthening its commitment to fighting corruption by developing integrity strategies for public procurement
- Nuevo León could benefit from enhancing integrity rules in order to set up a coherent legal framework for integrity and corruption prevention.

Establishing effective mechanisms to enhance integrity in the public procurement cycle in Nuevo León through the implementation of a consistent and coherent integrity system and stronger management of the conflict of interest system.

- Nuevo León should consider developing a code of ethics for public procurement officials to guide their conduct during the whole public procurement cycle, as well as providing practical guidelines to public procurement officials and suppliers.
- Nuevo León should consider adopting a clear definition of conflict of interest so as to effectively manage conflicts of interest in public procurement and ensure the use of public funds in an efficient manner.
- Nuevo León should consider using disclosure of assets and interests as a mechanism to prevent conflicts of interest and integrity breaches in the public procurement cycle.
- Nuevo León should improve its internal reporting and whistle-blowing system in order to safeguard the public interest and ensure efficiency in public procurement activities by reinforcing the mechanisms that protect anonymity and prevent reprisals.
- Nuevo León should make efforts to provide trainings specifically on public procurement integrity in order to enhance the integrity of the whole public procurement process and the workforce.
- Nuevo León could benefit from implementing anti-corruption programmes for suppliers as an additional mechanism to enhance integrity of public procurement activities.

Reviewing and adopting policies and tools for conducting an evaluation of suppliers so as to reduce the vulnerability of its public procurement activities to corruption.

- Nuevo León should consider strengthening the public procurement mechanisms it has in place so as to ensure that decisions are made based on what is most beneficial to the public interest.

Ensuring accountability and monitoring with regards to sanctions imposed on suppliers in cases of integrity breaches.

- Nuevo León should consider improving the functionalities of its current webpage for blacklisted suppliers, and ensuring that this information is published in a timely fashion through the SECOP. Nuevo León can also make this information accessible through different links so that different actors can access it.

Actively engaging the private sector and civil society so as to enhance transparency and ensure accountability of all actors in the public procurement cycle.

- Nuevo León should consider enhancing the functionalities of its different digital platforms in order to make procurement information more accessible and useable by all stakeholders, and to ensure accountability.
- Nuevo León should consider enhancing transparency mechanisms so as to ensure civil society participation in public procurement processes and engagement in fighting corruption.

References

Autoridad Superior de la Federación (ASF) (2015), *Informes de auditoría de la Cuenta Pública 2015*, http://www.asf.gob.mx/Trans/Informes/IR2015i/Documentos/InformeGeneral/ig2015.pdf. [8]

Casar M.A (2016), *México: Anatomía de la corrupción*, CIDE-IMCO Publishing, México, http://imco.org.mx/wpcontent/uploads/2015/05/2015_Libro_completo_Anatomia_corrupcion.pdf (accessed on 06 June 2017). [1]

Commonwealth Government (2006), "Ethics and Probity and Accountability in Procurement", *Financial Management Guidance* , No. 14, http://www.hpw.qld.gov.au/SiteCollectionDocuments/ProcurementGuideEthicsProbityAccountability.pdf. [25]

Gobierno del Estado de Nuevo León (2016), *Plan Estatal de Desarrollo 2016.2021.* [9]

Government of Canada((n.d.)), *Values Alive: A Discussion Guide to the "Values and Ethics Code for the Public Sector*, https://www.canada.ca/en/treasury-board-secretariat/services/values-ethics/code/values-alive-discussion-guide.html#Toc11 (accessed on 22 June 2017). [20]

INEGI (2015), "Encuesta Nacional de Calidad e Impacto Gubernamental.". [7]

OECD (2004), *Managing Conflict of Interest in the Public Service: OECD Guidelines and Country Experiences*, OECD Publishing, Paris, http://dx.doi.org/10.1787/9789264104938-en.. [19]

OECD (2005), *Managing a conflict of interest. A toolkit*, OECD Publishing, http://www.oecd-ilibrary.org/docserver/download/4205121e.pdf?expires=1497846763&id=id&accname=ocid84004878&checksum=555045C69B60BBCA87297D7DFB1BF5D9 (accessed on 06 June 2017). [16]

OECD (2007), *Integrity in Public Procurement: Good Practice from A to Z*, OECD Publishing, Paris, http://dx.doi.org/10.1787/9789264027510-en. [6]

OECD (2009), *OECD Principles for Integrity in Public Procurement*, OECD Publishing, Paris http://dx.doi.org/10.1787/9789264056527-en. [12]

OECD (2014), "Survey on Managing Conflict of Interest in the Executive Branch and Whistleblower Protection". [21]

OECD (2015), *OECD Recommendation of the Council on Public Procurement*, https://www.oecd.org/gov/ethics/OECD-Recommendation-on-Public-Procurement.pdf (accessed on 18 May 2017). [2]

OECD (2015), *Recommendation of the Council on Public Procurement*, http://www.oecd.org/gov/public-procurement/recommendation/ (accessed on 11 September 2017). [4]

OECD (2016), *Government at a Glance: Latin America and the Caribbean 2017*, OECD Publishing, Paris, http://dx.doi.org/10.1787/9789264265554-en. [3]

OECD (2016), *Towards Efficient Public Procurement in Colombia: Making the Difference*, OECD Publishing, Paris, http://dx.doi.org/10.1787/9789264252103-en. [17]

OECD (2016), "METHODOLOGY FOR ASSESSING PROCUREMENT SYSTEMS (MAPS)", http://www.oecd.org/gov/public-procurement/Methodology-Assessment-Procurement-System-Revised-Draft-July-2016.pdf. [24]

OECD (2016), *Preventing Corruption in Public Procurement*, OECD, http://www.oecd.org/gov/ethics/Corruption-in-Public-Procurement-Brochure.pdf, [10]

OECD (2017), *OECD Recommendation of the Council on Public Integrity*, http://www.oecd.org/gov/ethics/Recommendation-Public-Integrity.pdf. [13]

Public Service and Procurement Canada (n.d.), *Certification Program for the Federal Government procurement and materiel management community*, https://www.tpsgc-pwgsc.gc.ca/ongc-cgsb/certification/index-eng.html (accessed on 19 June 2017). [23]

Public Services and Procurement Canada (n.d.), *Canada Integrity Regime in Public Procurement*, https://www.tpsgc-pwgsc.gc.ca/ci-if/rpri-irr-eng.html (accessed on 15 June 2007). [11]

Public Works and Government Services Canada (2016), *Code of Conduct for Procurement*, http://www.tpsgc-pwgsc.ca/app-acq/cndt-cndct/contexte-context.htm. [15]

Secretaría de Gobernación (2015), *Ethics Codes and Rules of Integrity*, http://www.dof.gob.mx/nota_detalle.php?codigo=5404568&fecha=20/08/2015. [14]

Treasury Board Code of Values and Ethics in Canada (2006), *Conflict of Interest Act*, http://dx.doi.org/www.tbssct.gc.ca/pol/index-eng.aspx?|=V;. [18]

UNODC (2015), *Resource Guide on Good Practices in the Protection of Reporting Persons*, United Nations, Vienna. [22]

Chapter 7. Fostering effective risk management and internal controls in Nuevo León

This chapter assesses how Nuevo León fosters risk management and internal control in its procurement processes against international models and better practices. It provides an overview of the strengths and weaknesses of the internal control environment and the framework for risk assessment, treatment and monitoring. It also looks at how these aspects could be strengthened to align with international standards and good OECD country practices in the areas reflected in the OECD Recommendation of the Council on Public Procurement.

A government's procurement activities are particularly at risk of waste, mismanagement, fraud and corruption. This is due to a number of factors, including the large number and value of transactions a government undertakes and the close interactions between the public and private sectors. Risk management and internal control activities help an entity to address these risks and support an accountable and ethical public procurement system.

The federal government of Mexico has undertaken several initiatives to implement a consistent and effective internal control system across the country. The Secretariat of Public Function of the federal government of Mexico developed the General Standard for Internal Control (*Norma General de Control Interno*) in 2006. The Standard was revised for application at state levels. The revision resulted in the General Standards of Internal Control Model for States (*Modelo de Normas Generales de Control Interno para los Estados),* which was implemented by the State Government of Nuevo León (SGNL) in 2013.

The General Standards of Internal Control Model for States is based on five elements (or standards) set by the Committee of Sponsoring Organizations of the Treadway Commission (COSO)'s Internal Control Integrated Framework. These include:

- the control environment;
- risk evaluation and administration;
- control activities;
- information and communication; and
- oversight and continuous improvement of internal control (COSO, 2013[1]).

To implement the general standards, the SGNL established the Single Internal Control System (*Sistema Único de Control Interno*), which aimed to implement internal control mechanisms in July 2013. The Office of the Comptroller and Government Transparency (*Contraloría y Transparencia Gubernamental*) (hereafter, the Comptroller's Office) has been devoting efforts to strengthen the structure and the functioning of the internal control units. The Anticorruption Plan of the SGNL (*Plan Anticorrpción del Poder Ejecutivo del Estado de Nuevo León*), published in January 2017, reaffirmed the SGNL's commitment to having a sound implementation of the Single Internal Control System.

This chapter assesses the State Government of Nuevo León (SGNL)'s internal control and risk management frameworks in public procurement activities against the OECD *Recommendation of the Council on Public Procurement* (hereafter referred to as the Recommendation) and international good practices. In particular, it will assess the SGNL's internal control and risk management frameworks against the principles of the Recommendation outlined in Box 7.1.

Box 7.1. OECD Recommendation of the Council on Public Procurement

The Council:

XI. Recommends that Adherents **integrate risk management strategies** for mapping, detection and mitigation throughout the public procurement cycle. To this end, Adherents should:

i. **Develop risk assessment tools to identify and address threats to the proper function of the public procurement system.** Where possible, tools should be developed to identify risks of all sorts - including potential mistakes in the performance of administrative tasks and deliberate transgressions - and bring them to the attention of relevant personnel, providing an intervention point where prevention or mitigation is possible.

ii. **Publicise risk management strategies**, for instance, systems of red flags or whistle-blower programmes, and raise awareness and knowledge of the procurement workforce and other stakeholders about the risk management strategies, their implementation plans and measures set up to deal with the identified risks.

XII. Recommends that Adherents apply **oversight and control mechanisms to support accountability** throughout the public procurement cycle, including appropriate complaint and sanctions process. To this end, Adherents should:

(…)

iv. **Ensure that internal controls (including financial controls, internal audit and management controls),** and external controls and audits are **coordinated, sufficiently resourced and integrated** to ensure:

1) the monitoring of the performance of the public procurement system;
2) the reliable reporting and compliance with laws and regulations as well as clear channels for reporting credible suspicions of breaches of those laws and regulations to the competent authorities, without fear of reprisals;
3) the consistent application of procurement laws, regulations and policies;
4) a reduction of duplication and adequate oversight in accordance with national choices; and
5) independent ex-post assessment and, where appropriate, reporting to relevant oversight bodies.

Source: (OECD, 2015[2])

As outlined in the Recommendation, an internal control framework should include risk management strategies and internal controls. A solid internal control framework is the cornerstone of an organisation's defence against various integrity and efficiency risks that are present in public procurement processes. An effective internal control framework includes policies, structures, procedures, and processes that enable an organisation to identify and appropriately respond to risks. Internal controls constitute checks and balances that are the responsibility of management and are carried out by staff on a daily basis. Internal controls include a wide range of processes seeking to ensure that employees and managers exercise their duties within the parameters established by the entity.

An effective internal control framework should ultimately help the organisation comply with its mandate and relevant legislation, safeguard an organisation's assets, and facilitate internal and external reporting. In public procurement, particularly, sound functioning of an internal control framework helps ensure that public resources are spent in an efficient and effective way.

This chapter provides an overview of the SGNL's internal control framework and structures as they relate to public procurement activities. Furthermore, the chapter identifies strengths and weaknesses of the SGNL's internal control framework, and provides proposals for action.

7.1. Nuevo León's internal control framework, structures and environment

In Nuevo León, the Comptroller's Office (*Contraloría y Transparencia Gubernamental*) is the main state-level entity responsible for strengthening the coordination with the internal control and oversight bodies of the agencies and entities of the state public administration. In particular, the Directorate of Internal Control and Oversight Bodies (*Dirección Órganos de Control Interno y Vigilancia*) coordinates, reviews and evaluates internal control activities of the internal control units. In particular, the Comptroller's Office is responsible for:

- establishing and issuing rules that regulate instruments and procedures of internal control of the agencies and entities of the SGNL;
- monitoring compliance of the agencies and entities of the SGNL to the legal provisions on financial and public resources management; and
- establishing programmes aimed at fulfilling the commitments contained in the Code of Ethics of public servants of the SGNL, in order to promote ethical values.

The Central Procurement Body (Unidad Centralizada de Compras, UCC), under the Secretariat of Administration (Secretaría de Administración, SA) is in charge of procuring goods and services for the 21 central agencies and 24 (of 65) parastatal entities in Nuevo León. Previously, the Secretariat of Administration carried out purchasing activities only for the central agencies (*gobierno central*). With the new regulations, in force as of April 2016, it also does this for the parastatal entities that have signed a cooperation agreement with the UCC.

The UCC is involved in the entire procurement process, from defining needs and selecting suppliers to ensuring the delivery of goods and services. However, as described in Table 7.1, the unit that requires the procurement is responsible for defining its needs. Furthermore, once a contract is awarded, each unit is involved in managing the contracts. In this sense, internal control of not only the UCC, but also each unit is crucial to ensuring efficient and effective public procurement. Accordingly, the risks that each entity faces (according to its responsibilities) need to be adequately identified and properly managed.

Table 7.1. Responsible authorities during pre-tendering, tendering and post-tender phases for procurement of goods and services[1]

Pre-tendering phase				
Procurement planning	**Definition of requirements**	**Market research**	**Determination of estimated value or reference value**	**Development of tender documents**
Requiring unit	Centralised Procurement Unit (UCC)	UCC - Directorate of Procurement or Directorate of Maintenance and General Services[2]	UCC - Directorate of Procurement or Directorate of Maintenance and General Services[3]	UCC - Directorate of Procurement or Directorate of Maintenance and General Services
Tendering phase				
Tender notice	**Clarification about tender documents**	**Modification of tender documents**	**Integration of tender documents**	**Tendering**
UCC - Directorate of Tenders	UCC - Directorate of Tenders	UCC - Directorate of Procurement or Directorate of Maintenance and General Services	UCC - Directorate of Tenders	UCC - Directorate of Tenders Procurement Committee Requiring Unit Procurement Committee of the State Public Administration

Post-tendering			
Signing of the contract	**Subcontracting**	**Additions and reductions**	**Extension of the agreed period**
UCC - Directorate of Procurement or Directorate of Maintenance and General Services Winning bidder Requiring Unit			

Source: (Information provided by the SGNL.)

Note 1: The roles of these "authorities" (administrative units) change, according to whether the requisition is made by a central government agency or a decentralized agency (parastatal).

Note 2: Decentralised (parastatal) entities conduct their own market research.

Note 3: For parastatal entities, the requiring unit is also involved at this stage.

The UCC is also responsible for preparing and submitting an annual report of results of corresponding progress of the annual programme of procurement to the Procurement Committee, the State Treasury or Municipal Treasury, as appropriate, and the Comptroller or internal control unit.

7.1.1. Nuevo León could ensure that its internal control environment is a supportive foundation for its internal control system

The Comptroller's Office is responsible for the oversight of public works in Nuevo León, as well as the procurement of goods and services in the state. The Office of Control and Audit of Public Works carries out reviews, audits, verifications, monitoring actions and expert reports. It does this work in order to ensure that public works, procurements and related services are carried out according to the planning, programme, budget, and agreed-upon specifications mandated by the internal control bodies of the agencies and entities of the state public administration. In addition to checking for compliance with state laws and regulations, the office is also responsible for verifying the procurement process from the approval, award, contracting and payment of advances to termination and delivery. However, it remains the responsibility of the requesting entity to ensure the procurement is well executed. These directorates have some resource limitations, particularly relating to staff and the professionalisation of staff.

In 2007, the Executive Power of the State of Nuevo León issued an *Agreement for the Functional Coordination of the Internal Control Bodies.* This agreement outlines that: the Comptroller's Office shall functionally coordinate the internal control and monitoring system between the entities and the Comptroller's Office, and shall carry out public inspection and evaluation; and that entities that have established their own internal control body should coordinate and plan their activities with the Comptroller's Office, to avoid duplication.

The coordination is carried out through the Annual Audit and Internal Control Programme (*Programa Anual de Auditoría y Control Interno,* PAACI), which is prepared in accordance with the 2007 agreement and the associated guidelines. The audit programme includes audits titles, associated timelines and areas responsible.

The Internal Control Normative Provisions sent by the Comptroller's Office to the state public administration units and entities are in effect through a letter dated 3 July 2013. These provisions are based on the Internal Control Framework issued at the federal level. According to the Normative Provisions, the Single Internal Control System comprises the set of processes and mechanisms that are applied in an entity in the stages of planning, organising, implementing, directing, and monitoring their management processes, to give certainty to the decision-making process and to achieve their objectives in an environment of integrity, quality, continuous improvement, efficiency and compliance with the law (Nuevo León, 2013[3]).

The purposes of the Single Internal Control System, with respect to the achievement of the objectives of the units or entities, are outlined in the Table 7.2.

Table 7.2. Purposes of Nuevo León's Single Internal Control System

	Purpose
1	Promote efficiency, effectiveness and economy in operations, programs, projects and quality of services provided to society
2	Have mechanisms to monitor the progress in the achievement of the objectives and targets and to identify and manage the risks that may block
3	Measure effectiveness in meeting institutional objectives and prevent deviations in the achievement of the same
4	Maintain adequate management of public resources and promote efficiency, economy and transparency
5	Generate the financial statements and other accounting information and Accordance with the themes established in The General Law on Government Accounting and the guidelines issued by The National Council for Accounting Harmonisation
6	Encourage compliance with laws, regulations and other provisions that govern the operation of the entities
7	Safeguard, preserve and maintain public resources to ensure integrity, transparency and availability for the purposes they are intended
8	Strengthen substantive and supportive processes for achievement of objectives; As well as those used for the application of resources or those prone to possible acts of corruption, to prevent or correct deviations or omissions that affect compliance

Source: (Nuevo León, 2013, pp. 2–3[3])

The Normative Provisions outline specific standards on: the control environment; risk assessment and administration; control activities; information and communication; and continuous improvement of internal control.

7.1.2. Nuevo León could consider making better use of its Internal Control reporting function for identifying gaps, issues and risks and reporting on them to management

Each entity's Internal Control Unit is responsible for reporting to the Directorate of Internal Control and Oversight Bodies (*La Dirección de Órganos de Control Interno y Vigilancia*) within the Comptroller's Office every two months on whether the entity has complied with relevant laws, norms and requirements—including those related to procurement. As at May 2017, 11 entities had internal control units. For those entities without an Internal Control Unit, including the UCC, this responsibility is given to an Internal Control contact—a person who has another full-time job, but takes responsibility for completing the reporting template every two months. If an entity has not met requirements, they need to provide an explanation. This type of reporting can assist with the consistent application of procurement laws, regulations, and policies across the government. However, although the Office of Internal Control and Oversight Bodies indicated that they try to follow up on these cases, they have limited resources for doing so and there is no process for collating this information to identify trends or report on it to management.

A government should also have a system for reliable reporting on compliance with laws and regulations as well as clear channels for reporting credible suspicions of breaches of those laws and regulations to the competent authorities, without fear of reprisals (whistle-blowing and complaint mechanisms are discussed in Chapter 6).

7.1.3. Nuevo León could ensure that clear objectives are established at the outset of a procurement activity

Before determining risks and internal controls, it is vital that an entity establishes clear objectives for the entity as a whole, for individual programme and for specific activities. For a procurement activity, it should be clear why the purchase is being made, what objective it will support, how value for money will be ascertained and what the key requirements and merit criteria for the procurement will be. Where there is no clear objective, internal control activities and risk management cannot be effectively implemented. It is possible to have a controlled activity with a risk management process in place that does not achieve a valuable or desired outcome.

As discussed in Chapter 2, the SGNL's yearly planning for public procurement is still quite fragmented and there is some flexibility within budgets to make purchases that were not initially planned, as long as the total spending does not exceed the budget. Clearer objectives and a more controlled and robust planning and monitoring system would assist with ensuring the integrity of procurement activities.

7.1.4. Nuevo León could ensure that its tone at the top, human resources policies, and defined roles and responsibilities for internal control support its internal control system

Once clear objectives are established and have been effectively communicated to relevant staff, management should consider the elements of its control environment. The control environment is the foundation for all other components of internal control. According to the INTOSAI's *Guidelines for Internal Control Standards*, elements of the control environment are:

- the personal integrity and ethical values of management and staff, including a supportive attitude towards internal control throughout the organisation;
- commitment to competence;
- the "tone at the top" (i.e., management's philosophy and operating style);
- organisational structure; and
- human resource policies and practices (INTOSAI, 2010, p. 17[4])

Embedding a culture of personal integrity and an ethical "tone at the top" should be an ongoing part of an organisation's operations. It requires the commitment of management and staff, the positive reinforcement of ethical actions and attitudes and also, the censure of unethical behaviours.

One of the priorities of the Nuevo León government, as outlined in the 2016–2021 State Plan, is "combatting corruption". A culture of integrity and an ethical "tone at the top" is vital for combatting corruption. As discussed in Chapters 4 and 6, Nuevo León has taken some action to promote a culture of integrity through training courses, the implementation of a commencement "honesty test" and the introduction of a code of ethics.

The Executive Coordination of the State Public Administration (*Coordinación Ejecutiva de la Administración Pública del Estado*) requires that public servants sign the Code of Ethics, stating they understand it and commit to comply with it. Signing the Code of Ethics is part of the hiring process.

The Comptroller's Office has also carried out training sessions for internal comptrollers, with the first one conducted in March 2016 on performance of internal control units in the state public administration (attended by 135 officials). In April 2016, another training session was organised on enhancing transparency and prevention of corruption through internal control units (attended by 127 officials); and in May 2016, a session was presented on internal control and risk management. As discussed in Chapter 6, procurement officials have received only general training and would benefit from more specific training on public procurement integrity.

These types of training sessions can help staff understand the roles and responsibilities for internal control. This should be communicated more broadly as well, as everyone in an entity bears some responsibility for internal control and risk management. Managers are directly responsible for all activities, including designing, implementing, and monitoring the internal control system. Internal auditors examine and contribute to the ongoing effectiveness of the internal control system through their audits and recommendations; however, auditors should not have the primary responsibility for the internal control system—this system needs be owned and implemented by management. Staff also share in the responsibility—implementing internal controls and reporting issues, emerging risks and irregularities as they occur.

7.2. Risk management

7.2.1. Nuevo León could integrate risk management strategies for the assessment, treatment and monitoring of risk throughout the public procurement cycle

As previously mentioned, public procurement is particularly susceptible to risks of waste, mismanagement, fraud, and corruption. Further, there is a risk that the failure to achieve procurement outcomes or the delayed delivery of goods and services could hinder the performance of an entity's functions and could result in an entity not fulfilling its mandate.

After establishing clear objectives and setting a firm control environment foundation, the risks that may hinder the achievement of objectives and outcomes need to be identified. Nuevo León indicated that it considers this a vital element of planning process, which aligns with good governance practices among OECD member countries. Better practice also provides that risk management should be considered an integral part of the institutional management framework rather than managed in isolation. Risk management should permeate the organisation's culture and activities in such a way that it becomes the business of everyone within the organisation. Thus, all the officials that participate at any stage of public procurement—from the entity that requires the procurement to the UCC and Comptroller's Office—should take responsibility for risk management.

While the SGNL's *Internal Control Normative Provisions* (2013) state that the internal control system should "have mechanisms [...] to identify and manage the risks that may block [objectives]" and the SGNL Anticorruption Plan reaffirms the importance of risk management, the SGNL has not established specific risk management activities in its public procurement processes (Nuevo León, 2013[3]).

7.2.2. Nuevo León could develop risk assessment tools and methodologies to identify, assess and treat risks to the proper function of the public procurement system

As part of a risk management strategy, risk assessments help entities to understand risk exposure and allow public organisations to make cost-effective, risk-based decisions about control activities. This includes identifying risk factors (e.g. why would corruption occur in these specific areas of the procurement activity?). The evaluation of the probability that the identified risks might occur and the potential impact of the materialisation of these risks is also essential to prioritise responses and allocate adequate resources.

The output of the risk assessment is the identification of inherent and residual risks, which form the basis of the risk treatment action plan. Finally, considering that the risk environment is constantly evolving the risk management strategy should be monitored and refined on an ongoing basis to ensure the risk treatments remain effective.

Risk management is key to understanding risk exposure and allowing public organisations to reach informed risk management decisions. COSO defines entity risk management as "a process effected by an entity's board of directors, management and other personnel, applied in strategy setting and across the entity, designed to identify potential events that may affect the entity and manage risk to be within its risk [tolerance], to provide reasonable assurance regarding the achievement of entity objectives" (COSO, 2004[5]). This broad definition may also be applied in the public sector, where the concept of operational risk management would encompass the systems, processes, procedures, and culture that facilitate the identification, assessment, evaluation, and treatment of risk in order to help public sector organisations successfully pursue their strategies and performance objectives (OECD, 2013[6]).

Risk assessment is a three-step process that starts with risk identification and is followed by risk analysis (or 'mapping'), which involves developing an understanding of each risk, its consequences, the likelihood of those consequences occurring, and the risk's severity. The third step is risk evaluation, which involves determining the tolerability of each risk and whether the risk should be accepted or treated. Risk treatment is the process of adjusting existing internal controls or developing and implementing new controls to bring a risk's severity to a tolerable level (Figure 7.1).

Figure 7.1. Risk management cycle according to International Standards (ISO 31000:2009)

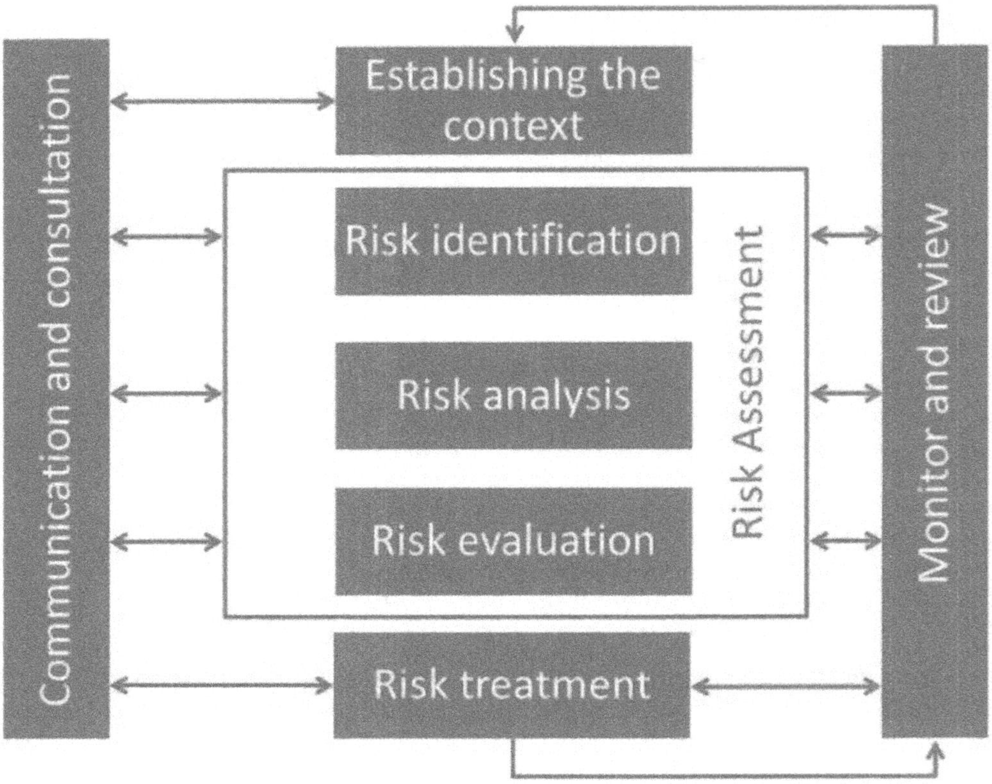

Source: Adapted from (ISO, 2009[7]).

Nuevo León should develop risk assessment tools and methodologies to identify, assess and treat risks to the effective and ethical achievement of public procurement objectives. Identifying risks and bringing them to the attention of relevant personnel provides an opportunity for intervention, where prevention or treatment is possible.

The case study in Box 7.2 provides an example of how to integrate risk assessment into a tendering process. In this example, the entity is focusing on risks to health and safety, but a similar approach could be applied when looking at risks of waste, mismanagement, fraud and corruption.

Box 7.2. Case Study: Standardised pre-contracting risk assessment in the Australian Federal Government

An Australian Government federal entity used a wide range of contractors on a regular basis, for example, for IT support, corporate services, professional advice, publicity and promotion, and alterations. The role of the entity involved significant public access to their facilities. The agency needed to be able to effectively manage high levels of risk without assigning unnecessary resources.

The entity revised its business processes to require a risk assessment before entering into any contracts. The level of risk was determined by a standard risk survey template. For example, the template assessed whether the work of the contractor might pose a risk to the safety of members of the public, the degree of financial risk and so on. The level of risk then informed decisions on:

- which contract form to use, from a set of standard contracts maintained by the entity;
- how the contract would be managed and by whom;
- the transition-in measures necessary, for example, determining the type of briefing the incoming contractors should receive on the task, the entity's environment and on issues such as workplace health, safety and security;
- the monitoring and management processes necessary; and
- how the contract was to be evaluated and the process completed.

Determining these issues at the planning stage also allowed the entity to plan their resource requirements for managing the contract.

Source: Adapted from *Developing and Managing Contracts: Getting the right outcome, achieving value for money* (ANAO, 2012, p. 19[8]).

7.2.3. Nuevo León could raise awareness and knowledge among its workforce and other relevant stakeholders about its risk management strategies

Communication and consultation, monitoring, and reviewing should be continuous elements of the risk management cycle. Communication and consultation with internal and external stakeholders is a key step towards securing their input into the process and giving them ownership of the outputs of risk management.

It is also important to understand stakeholders' concerns about risk and risk management, so that their involvement can be planned and their views taken into account in determining risk criteria (OECD, 2013[6]) . Clear communication of how risks should be identified, assessed and treated will assist staff in addressing risks through the procurement process.

7.2.4. Nuevo León could integrate the regular monitoring, reviewing and reporting of risks into its procurement processes

Monitoring and reviewing supports the identification of new risks and the reassessment of existing ones when there are changes in the organisation's objectives or in its internal and external environment. This involves scanning for possible new risks and learning lessons about risks and controls from the analysis of successes and failures (OECD, 2013[6]).

Timely reporting assists management to intervene, where necessary to prevent or address risks.

When identifying and monitoring risks, it is useful to be aware of particular red flags that may indicate corruption or fraud in a procurement process. The Chartered Institute of Public Finance and Accountancy has come up with a list of red flags that should be considered, as outlined in Box 7.3.

Box 7.3. Chartered Institute of Public Finance and Accountancy Red Flags for Procurement Activities

- Physical losses of goods
- Unusual relationship with suppliers
- Manipulation of data
- Photocopied documents
- Incomplete management/audit trail
- IT controls of audit logs disabled
- Budget overspends
- IT login outside working hours
- Unusual invoices (e.g. format, numbers, address, phone)
- Vague description of goods/services to be supplied
- Duplicate/photocopy invoice
- High number of failed IT logins
- Round sum amounts invoiced
- Favoured customer treatment
- Sequential invoice numbers over an extended period of time
- Interest/ownership in external organisation
- Non-declaration of interest/gifts/hospitality
- Lack of supporting records
- No process identifying risks (e.g. a risk register)
- Unusual increases/decreases in amounts

Source: (OECD, 2015, p. 152[9])

In order to support and facilitate the implementation of the OECD *Recommendation of the Council on Public Procurement*, the OECD has developed an online Public Procurement toolbox, which includes a section on how to identify risks or 'red flags' in a procurement process, as outlined in Box 7.4.

Box 7.4. OECD Procurement Risk Checklist

In order to support and facilitate the implementation of the OECD *Recommendation of the Council on Public Procurement*, the OECD has developed the Public Procurement Toolbox. While referring to 12 integrated principles of the Recommendation, it provides public officials with tools for successfully implementing procurement activities, as well as country-specific examples that showcase how to tackle procurement challenges in complex environments.

A designated tool, "Indicators of procurement risk", is provided by the Toolbox with regard to the risk management principle. It is designed specifically for procuring entities and can be implemented at all stages of the procurement process. It serves as a guide to identify potential corruption risks, and to flag what type of risks procurement practitioners might face.

Depending on the procurement stage and the complexity of the procurement, it is ultimately each procuring authority's responsibility to identify potential risks and 'red flags' and to manage these risks through treatments or internal controls. The following are a number of "red flags" that could help identify corruption and fraud risks in a tendering process:

1. Pre-tendering phase

- **Planning and budgeting**: Lack of an annual procurement plan aligned with strategic objectives; cost estimates inconsistent with market rates; or government unable to oversee units in charge of purchase.
- **Definition of requirements**: No clear conditions regarding technical requirements; limitations imposed on foreign participants; unclear selection and award criteria; tender requirements drafted by a biased service provider; inappropriate care taken on the anonymity of suppliers or bidders; or selection of unqualified providers due to fraudulent quality assurance certificates.
- **Choice of procedure**: Lack of strategy for non-competitive tenders; misuse of exception procedures; or inconsistent timeframes.

2. Tendering phase

- **Invitation to tender**: Lack of public notice; invitation advertised on a limited basis; non-public information disclosed; insufficient information included in public notice; or unsealed or opened bid envelopes.
- **Evaluation and analysis of bids**: Limited number of bids; similarities between bids; delayed bid evaluation; or vested interests among the evaluation committee members.
- **Award**: Lack of lists of firms excluded from procurement; rigged selection criteria; lack of submitted certificates; or lack of access to records on procedure.

3. Post-award phase

- **Contract management**: Modifications in contract conditions; product or service not meeting contract requirements; lack of penalty clauses; or lack of due reporting of contract changes.

- **Order payment**: Lack of internal or external audit activities; financial inconsistencies between contracts; late payments and invoices; or invoicing for unsupplied goods or services.

Source: (OECD, 2017[10]).

7.3. Internal control activities

One fundamental way risks are mitigated and treated is through the implementation of internal controls. Internal controls are implemented by an entity's management and personnel and continuously adapted and refined to address changes to the entity's environment and risks. Internal control activities are designed to address risks that may affect the achievement of the entity's objectives and to provide reasonable assurance that the entity's: operations are ethical, economical, efficient and effective; accountability and transparency obligations are met; activities and actions are compliant with applicable laws and regulations; and resources are safeguarded against loss, misuse, corruption and damage (INTOSAI, 2010[4]).

7.3.1. Nuevo León could strengthen, standardise and integrate its Internal Control activities to ensure that reasonable assurance is provided over the integrity of the procurement process

According to INTOSAI's *Guidelines for Internal Control Standards*, internal control activities should occur throughout at entity, at all levels and in all functions. They include a range of detective and preventive control activities as diverse as:

- authorisation and approval procedures;
- segregation of duties (authorising, processing, recording, and reviewing);
- verifications;
- reconciliations;
- reviews of operating performance;
- reviews of operations, processes, and activities; and
- supervision (assigning, reviewing, and approving) (INTOSAI, 2004).

For example, authorising and executing procurement transactions should only be done by persons acting within the scope of their authority. Authorisation is the principal means of ensuring that only valid transactions and events are initiated as intended by management. Authorisation procedures, which should be documented and clearly communicated to managers and employees, should include the specific conditions and terms under which authorisations are to be made. Conforming to the terms of an authorisation means that employees act in accordance with directives and within the limitations established by management or legislation (INTOSAI, 2010[4]).

7.3.2. Nuevo León could review its procurement system to ensure that each internal control serves a purpose—with its benefits outweighing its costs—and that the overall system is controlled, ethical and efficient

Internal control activities for procurement should be designed to provide reasonable assurance to management that risks are being addressed and that the goal of the activity (for which the procurement is required) is being achieved. Internal controls should not attempt to provide absolute assurance—as this would constrict activities to a point of severe inefficiency.

'Reasonable assurance' is a term often used in audit and internal control environments. It means a satisfactory level of confidence, given due consideration of costs, benefits and risks. Determining how much assurance is reasonable requires judgment. In exercising this judgment, managers should identify the risks inherent in their operations and the levels of risk they are willing to tolerate under various circumstances. Reasonable assurance accepts that there is some uncertainty and that full confidence is limited by the following realities: human judgment in decision-making can be faulty; breakdowns can occur because of simple mistakes; controls can be circumvented by collusion of two or more people; and management can choose to override the internal control system (INTOSAI, 2010[4]).

In setting internal controls, management should consider the costs of each control—e.g., monetary costs, time costs, and opportunity costs. Management needs to weigh the potential benefit of each control against the potential cost and ensure that benefits will outweigh costs. If this is not the case, management should consider alternate methods of control that will achieve the same desired outcome. Management should monitor internal control systems and adapt them, where necessary, to ensure that internal controls are pitched at the right level to be effective and provide reasonable assurance while not overburdening systems and staff with controls to such a point that quality, timeliness and responsiveness are affected. A system out of balance can lead to staff circumventing burdensome control processes, which defeats the purpose and can expose an entity to additional risks.

Internal controls also provide reasonable assurance to the public and key stakeholders that government transactions are being undertaken in a transparent, ethical and fair manner. As mentioned, procurement is a government activity that is particularly vulnerable to fraud and corruption. The government needs to put levels of control in place to ensure that public funds are being spent appropriately, that value for money is being achieved, that regulations and laws are complied with and that suppliers and tenderers are treated fairly and without favouritism. This is a matter of reputation and credibility. There are two sides to this. On the one hand, internal controls increase confidence in government and promote fair and consistent treatment of key stakeholders. On the other hand, internal controls that are out of balance or have too many layers of bureaucracy can lead to lethargic administrative processes that reduce the credibility of government.

During OECD fact-finding missions, staff indicated that a culture has developed in the SGNL where staff purchase items (such as ink for the printers) with their own personal funds, without prior authorisation, and then seek, and receive, reimbursement. This culture appears to have developed as a result of an inefficient and cumbersome purchasing system. For example if staff purchase their own airline tickets for work travel and then receive reimbursement, with little to no control over the cost of the ticket, there is no assurance that value for money was achieved or that the expense was made in alignment with public procurement law.

Another fundamental internal control is segregation of duties. It is a basic principle that no single individual or team should control all key stages of a procurement activity. Duties should be assigned to a number of individuals to ensure that effective checks and balances exist and to reduce the risk of fraud and corruption. At some stages of the procurement cycle, the SGNL has quite a few players involved. On the one hand, segregation of duties is a beneficial control. However, taken out of balance—where too many players are involved—this control can create new problems and introduce new risks.

It was raised during fact-finding missions that the SGNL's complex multi-faceted procurement system sometimes results in suppliers not being paid for up to six months. This is an example of internal controls having unintended negative consequences. Having suppliers left unpaid for 6 months is an untenable situation. A government with a bad reputation in the marketplace—whether from corrupt practices or from being an inefficient organisation that does not pay its bills on time—is not a government that can achieve the best results for taxpayers. Suppliers who are not paid on time will be hesitant to engage with the government again, and where there is reduced supply, costs can increase.

7.3.3. Nuevo León could ensure the internal control system is monitored and that there are clear means for adapting and refining procedures to respond to changes in objectives, risks and circumstances

Internal control activities are a vital element of a functioning and ethical public service, but internal controls out of balance can lead to additional risks, costs and inefficiencies. A balanced internal control system, coupled with a culture of integrity promotes good governance and is essential to securing public trust.

Further, internal control should be a dynamic process that is refined and adapted as risks and environments change. An internal control system is more effective when it is monitored and has clear means for responding to changes in objectives, risks and circumstances.

7.4. Proposals for action

In order to develop effective internal control mechanisms and risk management in public procurement and to help combat corruption, the following actions could be undertaken by the State Government of Nuevo León.

1. **Nuevo León's internal control framework, structures and environment**
   a. Nuevo León could ensure that its Internal Control environment is a supportive foundation for its internal control system
   b. Nuevo León could consider making better use of its Internal Control reporting function for identifying gaps, issues and risks and reporting on them to management.
   c. Nuevo León could ensure that clear objectives are established at the outset of a procurement activity.
   d. Nuevo León could ensure that its tone at the top, human resources policies, and defined roles and responsibilities for internal control support its internal control system.
2. **Risk Management**
   a. Nuevo León could integrate risk management strategies for the assessment, treatment and monitoring of risk throughout the public procurement cycle
   b. Nuevo León could develop risk assessment tools and methodologies to identify, assess and treat risks to the proper function of the public procurement system.
   c. Nuevo León could raise awareness and knowledge among its workforce and other relevant stakeholders about its risk management strategies.

   d. Nuevo León could integrate the regular monitoring, reviewing and reporting of risks into its procurement processes.

3. **Internal control activities**
   a. Nuevo León could strengthen, standardise and integrate its Internal Control activities to ensure that reasonable assurance is provided over the integrity of the procurement process
   b. Nuevo León could review its procurement system to ensure that each internal control serves a purpose—with its benefits outweighing its costs—and that the overall system is controlled, ethical and efficient
   c. Nuevo León could ensure the internal control system is monitored and that there are clear means for adapting and refining procedures to respond to changes in objectives, risks and circumstances.

References

ANAO (2012), "Developing and Managing Contracts: Getting the right outcome, achieving value for money". [8]

COSO (2004), *COSO Enterprise Risk Management -- Integrated Framework*, http://www.aicpastore.com/AST/Main/CPA2BIZ_Primary/InternalControls/COSO/PRDOVR~PC-990015/PC-990015.jsp (accessed on 01 August 2017). [5]

COSO (2013), "Internal Control - Integrated Framework", https://www.coso.org/Pages/ic.aspx (accessed on 11 September 2017). [1]

Gobierno del Estado de Nuevo León (2013), "Nuevo León's Internal Control Normative Provisions", http://oecdshare.oecd.org/gov/sites/govshare/psi/integrity/Shared%20Documents/Nuevo%20Leon%20Integrity%20Review/Questionnaire%20integrity%20Review/13.%20Anexo%2013.%20Disposiciones%20Normativas%20Control%20Interno%20en%20APENL.pdf (accessed on 13 November 2017). [3]

INTOSAI (2010), "Guidelines for Internal Control Standards for the Public Sector", *INTOSAI Guidance for Good Governance*, No. GOV 9100, http://www.issai.org/en_us/site-issai/issai-framework/intosai-gov.htm (accessed on 01 August 2017). [4]

ISO (2009), *ISO 31000-2009 Risk Management*, https://www.iso.org/iso-31000-risk-management.html. [7]

OECD (2013), "Strengthening integrity in the Italian public sector", in *OECD Integrity Review of Italy: Reinforcing Public Sector Integrity, Restoring Trust for Sustainable Growth*, OECD Publishing, Paris, http://dx.doi.org/10.1787/9789264193819-4-en. [6]

OECD (2015), *Recommendation of the Council on Public Procurement*, http://www.oecd.org/gov/public-procurement/recommendation/ (accessed on 11 September 2017). [2]

OECD (2015), *Effective Delivery of Large Infrastructure Projects: The Case of the New International Airport of Mexico City*, OECD Publishing, Paris, http://dx.doi.org/10.1787/9789264248335-en. [9]

OECD (2017), *Public Procurement Toolbox*, http://www.oecd.org/governance/procurement/toolbox/ (accessed on 11 September 2017). [10]

Chapter 8. Encouraging participation in the dispute resolution system in Nuevo León

This chapter examines the courses of action that suppliers in Nuevo León can take to challenge procurement decisions during the procurement procedure and contract execution. The chapter also discusses how effective these two distinct processes are currently, and whether they have affected public procurement procedures. Furthermore, it highlights some of the strengths and weaknesses of the system, and discusses which steps Nuevo León needs to take to improve system functions. The chapter also highlights relevant experiences in other OECD countries that could prove useful to the State Government of Nuevo León (SGNL).

In the state of Nuevo León, there is a clear separation between procedures for the procurement of goods and services and procedures for the procurement of public works. There is also a clear separation between procedures concerning complaints that arise during the tendering process, and procedures concerning issues that come up during the execution of contracts. Limited information is available regarding the number of challenges to procurement decisions that take place. However, during the OECD fact-finding mission to Nuevo León, civil society members and suppliers revealed that the number of challenges is very low – given the lack of trust in the actual system. Nuevo León is not an isolated case; the same problem can be found in Mexico City (OECD, 2017[1]). Furthermore, stakeholders raised concerns during the fact-finding mission about the integrity of the system. Criticism was specifically directed at the tendering process, with claims of corruption occurring at different stages. Some stakeholders also alleged that public funds are regularly diverted to companies, individuals and groups due to favouritism among procurement officials.

To be effective, a remedies system must be well designed, capable of offering protection, accessible to suppliers, uncomplicated, inexpensive and efficient in processing cases. Any stakeholder, including unsuccessful tenderers, who believe that the public procurement process has been conducted in violation of relevant laws must have access to effective review and remedy mechanisms. These mechanisms build confidence in the system among businesses. They also increase the overall fairness, lawfulness and transparency of the procurement procedure. In this respect, the 2015 OECD Recommendation of the Council on Public Procurement encourages countries to "handle complaints in a fair, timely and transparent way through the establishment of effective courses of action for challenging procurement decisions to correct defects, prevent wrong-doing and build confidence of bidders, including foreign competitors, in the integrity and fairness of the public procurement system. Additional key aspects of an effective complaints system are dedicated and independent review and adequate redress" (OECD, 2015[2]). Furthermore, the OECD promotes accountability in public procurement by emphasising that states must apply oversight and control mechanisms to support accountability throughout the public procurement cycle. This includes appropriate complaint and sanctions processes (see Box 8.1).

Box 8.1. OECD Recommendation of the Council on Public Procurement

The Council:

XII. **RECOMMENDS** that Adherents apply oversight and control mechanisms to support **accountability** throughout the public procurement cycle, including appropriate complaint and sanctions processes.

To this end, Adherents should:

i) Establish clear lines for oversight of the public procurement cycle to ensure that the chains of responsibility are clear, that oversight mechanisms are in place and that the delegated levels of authority for approval of spending and approval of key procurement milestones are well defined. Rules for justifying and approving exceptions to procurement procedures should be comprehensive and clear, such as in cases of limiting competition.

ii) Develop a system of effective and enforceable sanctions for government and private-sector procurement participants in proportion to the degree of wrong-doing to provide adequate deterrence without creating undue fear of consequences or risk aversion in the procurement workforce or supplier community.

iii) Handle complaints in a fair, timely and transparent way through the establishment of effective courses of action for challenging procurement decisions to correct defects, prevent wrong-doing and build confidence of bidders, including foreign competitors, in the integrity and fairness of the public procurement system. Additional key aspects of an effective complaints system are dedicated and independent review and adequate redress.

iv) Ensure that internal controls (including financial controls, internal audit and management controls), and external controls and audits are coordinated, sufficiently resourced and integrated to ensure:

1. the monitoring of the performance of the public procurement system;
2. the reliable reporting and compliance with laws and regulations, as well as clear channels for reporting credible suspicions of breaches of those laws and regulations to the competent authorities, without fear of reprisals;
3. the consistent application of procurement laws, regulations and policies;
4. a reduction of duplication and adequate oversight in accordance with national choices; and
5. independent ex-post assessment and, where appropriate, reporting to relevant oversight bodies.

Source: (OECD, 2015[2])

The structure of Nuevo León's supervisory system is similar to what can be found in other states in Mexico. Despite having a moderately strong supervisory and control culture, a remedies framework has not been implemented. The system as whole is quite complicated from a supplier's perspective. For example, the remedies process is different depending on whether the source of the funding for a project is federal or state. In addition, the process for goods and services is not the same as for public works. The Secretariat of Administration (SA) is responsible for handling complaints regarding goods and services procurement, with the involvement of the Office of the Comptroller and Government Transparency (Contraloría y Transparencia Gubernamental). However, for public works, the comptroller receives the complaints. The process for conciliation and arbitration during the execution of contracts is normally predetermined in the contract, (see Table 8.1). Clauses specifying the arbitration and conciliation process may be included in contracts for public works. The procedure stated in the Law of Alternative Methods for the resolution of Conflicts of the State of Nuevo León is accessible for both parties in case of goods, services and public works.

Table 8.1. Mechanisms to solve disputes during the tendering process, and resolution processes during the execution of the contract

Phases	Activity	Goods and services	Public works
Tendering	Complaints	Submit to the unit issuing the decisions which is then submitted to the management of the Secretariat of Administration	Complaints should be presented to the Comptroller or to the corresponding municipal comptroller. They can also appeal to the Administrative Contentious Court the decision of the Comptroller.
Execution of contract	Conciliation and arbitration	Parties may agree to use a dispute resolution mechanism to resolve disputes concerning the interpretation or implementation of contracts or (and) can resort to arbitration based on the Alternative Methods for Conflict Resolution Act of Nuevo León (Ley de Métodos Alternos para la Solución de Conflictos del Estado de Nuevo León, LMASCENL	Arbitration clause may only be agreed in contracts with respect to those disputes that the Secretariat and the Comptroller jointly determine, by means of general rules.

Source: Information provided by the state of Nuevo León.

The approach of this chapter is to assess two distinct mechanisms Nuevo León uses to resolve complaints raised during the tendering stage and the post-tendering stage of public procurement. With regards to the tendering stage, the chapter aims to assess to what extent remedies are in place that allow economic operators to request the enforcement of public procurement regulations. The chapter also looks at the rights of economic operators under these regulations in cases where contracting authorities, either intentionally or unintentionally, fail to comply with the legal framework for public procurement. For the post tendering stage, the chapter assesses the processes in place for mediation and conciliation during the execution of contracts. Finally, the chapter looks at the arbitration process that normally follows if parties are unable to reach a settlement.

While Nuevo León has some measures in place to resolve procurement disputes, several issues inhibit the functioning of the system. The central problem is that the state's public procurement process is fragmented. In addition, when officials make mistakes or violate procedure, these mistakes generally go unreported. This should be of great concern to the state of Nuevo León. It begs the question – how are issues resolved if not through official processes? How can the state of Nuevo León improve its procurement system or its remedies processes if no one complains, and the system is never tested? To put the situation in context, a lack of complaints is not the norm in Latin America. Two recent reviews carried out by the OECD in Colombia and Peru found that, in both countries, public procurement complaints per year numbered in the hundreds (OECD, 2016[3]) (OECD, 2017[4]).

The aim of the remedies system in the state of Nuevo León should be to allow irregularities to be challenged and corrected as soon as they occur during the procurement procedure. It is an important part of any public procurement framework that suppliers have an instrument that is accessible to them to enforce procurement rules. However, they can only do this when adequate courses of action are available to them. To be effective, a remedies system must be well designed, clear and capable of offering protection in an accessible, uncomplicated, inexpensive and speedy manner. Box 8.2 shows some core requirements for an effective remedies system.

Box 8.2. Requirements for an effective remedies system

It is important for suppliers to have remedies available to them to enforce procurement rules. If suppliers have remedies, they can be motivated to monitor procurement procedures and require that procurement rules be followed so that their chances of being awarded a contract are not unlawfully diminished. Thus, remedies both enhance the lawfulness of procedures and encourage competition.

In order for remedies to be effective, they must be:

- clear and straightforward (i.e. understandable and easy to use);
- available to all economic operators wishing to participate in a specific contract award procedure without discrimination, in particular on the grounds of nationality;
- effective in preventing or correcting instances of unlawfulness on the part of suppliers or public authorities.

Source: (OECD, 2016[3])

8.1. The functioning of the review and remedy system

8.1.1. The process for handling non-conformities during the tendering process

Nuevo León needs to make its mechanism for remedies more effective for goods and services by ensuring anonymity and impartiality throughout the process

According to Nuevo León's public procurement legislation, there is a mechanism in place to challenge procurement decisions made during the tendering process for goods and services. Participants may submit complaints or disagreements within 30 working days after the winning bidder of a procurement procedure has been announced. Once that time has passed, the right to submit a complaint is over. The authority who receives the complaint must forward it the following day to their oversight authority in order for the authority to decide whether to revoke, modify or confirm the result of a purchasing process. Within three days of receiving a complaint from the oversight body, the Secretariat of Administration (SA) has to accept or discard the appeal (see Figure 8.1). If the SA accepts the appeal, it will inform the requesting unit and the party that has raised an objection. They are both then given five working days to provide further evidence. The procurement procedure will only be suspended if there are obvious irregularities that jeopardize the attainment of the purposes of the acquisition, lease or service. The Secretariat of Administration must review grievances, weigh evidence and resolve the complaint within 45 working days. If the SA is unable to resolve the complaint on time, the original decision will be considered confirmed. That said, following this procedure, the party that has appealed the procurement decision can take the case before a competent court. The decisions of the SA and court with regards to challenges and appeals are published on the electronic procurement platform.

Figure 8.1. The process for challenging non-conformities of goods and services

Non-conformity - complaint	• Supplier - bidder
Receives and forwards the complaint	• The Requesting Unit
Reviews the complaint - decision	• Secretariat of Administration
Receive an appeal of SA decision	• Court

Source: Information provided by the state of Nuevo León

The number of challenges to procurement processes reported every year in Nuevo León is unclear. The data provided seems to suggest that the state has faced two reported challenges since 2015. This figure is rather low for such a large state. Based on these figures and on interviews with officials during the OECD fact-finding mission, it is apparent that the process has not really been tested. The culture discourages reporting of non-conformities. This culture of silence is a roadblock for the state. If it hopes to improve its procurement system, stakeholders will have to feel comfortable expressing their grievances. In addition, if bidders and suppliers are concerned about being blacklisted if they complain, the procurement system will become less effective. This fear of reprisal prevents the state from achieving real value for money in its purchases. The problem of non-reporting of complaints is not exclusive to procurement. The culture within the public sector in Nuevo León seems to regard complaints as a failure of the system. Hence, more controls might be needed to prevent any further complaints from being reported. Furthermore, the repercussions of complaints can be substantial for public employees who make the mistakes that lead to violations of legislation or breach of protocols. When this happens, staff are can be reprimanded or even charged. The punitive quality of the system gives staff less incentive to encourage reporting of complaints. There is a need for greater understanding within the public sector that a complaint does not necessarily signal a failure of the system or of officials. Complaints should be considered normal, as bidders often want to see things go differently. If a bidder is willing to take the necessary steps to challenge the system through a complaint process, the bidder should be able to do so. Public officials should try to view complaints as an opportunity. By addressing the complaint in a structured and fair manner, officials can strengthen the system from within.

It is important to have a clear definition of the legal and structural basis of the remedies system. Remedies are legal actions that allow economic operators to request the enforcement of public procurement regulations and their rights under those regulations in cases where contracting authorities, either intentionally or unintentionally, have failed to comply with the legal framework for public procurement (OECD, 2016[5]). The remedies system should try to delineate clear methods for different scenarios. These scenarios could include: complaints relating to tender invitation and clarification meetings, call for invitation to at least three suppliers, submission and opening of proposals and announcement of contract award, and cancellation of the tendering procedure by the contracting entity. Furthermore, it has to be clear who has the right to submit a complaint, when it must be filed, which body can consider complaints, what costs are placed on a claimant, what are the possible outcomes of the complaint and what remedies are available after the resolution of a formal complaint.

8.1.2. Process for handling non-conformities in public works

Nuevo León needs to work closely with other stakeholders and members of civil society to ensure the anonymity of public works claimants, and to prevent any conflict of interest in relation to the resolution of complaints

The legislation on public works for the state and municipalities of Nuevo León describes the procedure by which interested parties can file complaints. These parties can file complaints against acts that contravene the provisions that govern the subject matter clarifying irregularities. Claimants may do so if, in their judgment, violations of these provisions have been committed during the tendering procedure or execution of the contract – so that these violations can be corrected. The legislation implies that the interested parties may represent themselves before the internal control body of the convening entity or procuring entity when describing the reasons for their complaint. However, the legally established procedure indicates that the complaints should be presented to the state comptroller or to a corresponding municipal comptroller. Claimants can also appeal the decision of the comptroller to the Administrative Contentious Court (Tribunal de lo Contencioso Administrativo del Estado de Nuevo León). However, this court does not have jurisdiction over conflicts arising during the execution of procurement contracts (see Figure 8.2).

Figure 8.2. The process for non-conformities for public works

Source: Information provided by the State of Nuevo León

The deadline for filing a complaint about a decision during the tendering procedure, according to Nuevo León's public works legislation, is:

- 10 working days following the day on which the contested act occurred. Parties filing a complaint must inform the comptroller in writing of the acts that contravene the provisions governing the subject matter of the law. Subsequently, parties must adhere to the following deadlines:
- Parties filing a complaint have 5 business days to complete their complaint once the comptroller's office advises them of how to improve the filing (in cases where briefs do not meet requirements).
- Following the receipt of a complaint, agencies and entities have 5 business days, to provide the comptroller with the information required for its investigation.
- The comptroller's office has 45 working days from the date on which the corresponding investigations were initiated to resolve a complaint.
- The law does not establish deadlines for appealing to the Administrative Contentious Court.

During the investigation, the adjudication process may be suspended in certain circumstances. In addition, the resolution issued by the comptroller may have the following consequences:

1. nullifying the procurement procedure and establishing a new procedure that is legally sound;
2. nullifying the procurement; or
3. the declaration that the complaint is unfounded, which will produce confirmation of the validity of the contested acts.

According to information provided by the comptroller, in the few cases where complaints are filed, contracts rarely get nullified and procurement entities always comply with legal decision on remedies As stated previously, irregularities detected by bidders may also be reported to the internal control body of the convenor. Based on the principle of definiteness, the comptroller must issue the resolution corresponding to the case, so that, if the complainer does not agree with it, he can file another appeal before the Administrative Contentious Court or another competent authority. However, there are no reports of any appeals against the comptroller's resolution regarding challenges. The lodging of an appeal with the comptroller based on issues of non-conformity is likely to incur a cost for the claimant. These costs can include time and money spent within the company, as well as possible external legal fees. However, claimants are not required to pay administrative charges in order to get a claim reviewed.

Overall in the state of Nuevo León, there is limited data on public procurement, and remedies for public works are no exception. That said, during the OECD fact-finding mission, government representatives suggested that the reason no data were available was that complaints are rarely raised during the tendering process. The suppliers met during the fact-finding mission stated that they didn't raise complaints – but not because they didn't have complaints. Rather, they said nothing out of a fear of being blacklisted. The limited use of the remedies system is a cause for concern, as it suggests that there is a culture of fear of reprisal if bidders do exercise their right to complain.

There are several measures that the state of Nuevo León should take to remedy this situation. First, the state should ensure that those that complain can submit their appeals without having to disclose their identities to the requesting unit that is involved. This process should be developed by the comptroller. Second, it is important to normalise the process of filing complaints. The state of Nuevo León could do so by promoting a broad communications strategy that increases awareness of the complaint and remedies process. The state should use various channels to raise awareness and normalise these processes, including doing so by engaging with civil society.

The issue of impartiality remains with the committee for public works *comité de fallo* which provides opinions on all awarding decisions made for public works. In theory, having an internal committee of this nature would help ensure that the process is carried out according to the rules. That said, Nuevo León's committee has limited time to review all the documents, which has led to mistakes. Members of the comptroller's office also sit on this committee. While they cannot vote, they can speak out and discuss issues with the other members of committee. This is questionable. Having employees of the comptroller on the committee raises red flags, as, subsequently, appeals go to the comptroller for reviewing. This fact could be considered a conflict of interest, and might undermine the credibility of the decisions made by the comptroller.

8.2. Conflicts that arise during execution of contracts

8.2.1. Dispute resolution system

Nuevo León needs to have a clear role in relation to mediation, conciliation and arbitration, whether that is supervising, managing or actively being involved in the resolution process

According to Nuevo León's public procurement legislation, contracting parties can agree to use negotiation or mediation as a dispute settlement mechanism to resolve their distinct interpretations of the execution of contracts. Such dispute settlement mechanisms may be agreed upon in the contracts themselves, or in an independent agreement. In any case, dispute settlements must agree to the following:

1. the stage of negotiation or mediation, as well as an agreement of the time period when this negotiation will take place;
2. the parties agree to conduct bargaining or mediation procedures in good faith;
3. the applicable laws shall be those of the state;
4. negotiations or mediations must be carried out in Spanish;
5. the agreement resulting from the negotiation or mediation shall be binding to both parties.

The parties to a contract may also agree to an arbitration procedure to resolve disputes about compliance with the contract in terms of the provisions of the Law of Alternative Methods for Conflict Resolution of the State of Nuevo León. The use of negotiation, mediation or arbitration are not mutually exclusive, nor do they restrict the actions of the parties in cases of possible invalidity of acts of authority, violation of human rights or crimes. The arbitration procedure may be agreed upon in the contract itself or in an independent agreement. With the *Alternate non-adversarial method* (negotiation or mediation), one or more alternate methods service providers intervene in a dispute, without the authority to decide on the basis of the agreement that could be reached. These providers are not permitted to issue a judgment or sentence, but will facilitate communication between the participants in the conflict. The purpose of this process is that these providers take control of the case and arrive at a solution. Cases can go to a civilian court after a ruling from a provider.

In the event of a serious breach of the obligations contracted by the supplier, the contract is terminated or the guarantee of compliance. For example, according to Article 111 of Nuevo León's procurement legislation, suppliers who, for reasons other than delay in complying with the agreed dates for the delivery of goods or the provision of services, fail to comply with their obligations for any other cause established in the contract, are subject to the termination procedure of the contract, in accordance with the following procedure:

- Termination will start as soon as the supplier is notified in writing of the breach that has incurred, within a term of five working days.
- After the five working days, the Central Purchasing Body (Unidad Centralizada de Compras, UCC) will have a period of fifteen days to resolve the issue by considering the arguments and evidence that the supplier has put forward. The determination to maintain or terminate the contract must be duly substantiated, reasoned and communicated to the supplier within that period.

- When the contract is rescinded, a corresponding settlement will be made in order to record the payments that must be made by the agency or entity for the goods received or services rendered up to the moment of termination.

Even after a procedure has begun, the UCC may suspend the termination procedure. The UCC may decide not to terminate a contract when, during the procedure, it is advised that termination of the contract may cause damage or impairment to the procurement functions of the state. The UCC must prepare an opinion in which it justifies that the economic or operating impacts that would be caused by the termination of the contract would be greater than those generated by the supplier's default, and must specify how. When the decision is made not to terminate the contract, the UCC establishes another term with the supplier, which will allow it to remedy the non-compliance that caused the start of the procedure. Early termination of contracts shall not be subject to arbitration according to the public procurement regulation for goods and services, except to settle the settlement resulting from such acts.

Currently there is no data available about the frequency of cases going to mediation or arbitration relating to issues arising during the execution of public procurement contracts. The procedure has been used rarely, according government information. Hence, the effectiveness of the process is unknown, as is any impact these procedures may have had on works in progress. During the OECD fact-finding mission to Nuevo León, officials mentioned several lapses that have occurred during the execution of contracts, starting with excessive delays in orders and excessive delays in payments. These are valid issues. Unfortunately, however, officials are not going through the proper channels currently to address them.

The conciliation and the mediation process in Nuevo León has several stages. It generally starts with the two parties trying to resolve an issue among themselves. If that doesn't work, a third party is brought in, but its role and authority can vary. If the disagreement continues, the matter can be brought to arbitration.

The state of Nuevo León should clarify its role in the process, as it is not clear to what extent the state supervises or runs mediations. According to the regulations for public procurement of goods and services in Nuevo León, both procuring and supplying parties should endeavour to carry out actions that promote the total execution of the works, the delivery of the goods, the rendering of services and the complete resolution of controversies during negotiation or mediation. If both parties cannot reach an agreement on a dispute, they can, at their own expense, appoint an expert who issues his or her opinion on the disputed points. Then, a competent authority is appointed to hear the proceedings, in order to enable the parties to reconcile their interests. The costs and fees of the arbitration are supposed to be borne by the contracting parties, unless otherwise determined in the contract. In Peru, there is an institutional arbitration system managed by the Government Procurement Supervising Agency (OSCE) that specialises in dispute settlement in public procurement. It is autonomous and governed by its own regulations and by the legislative decree establishing norms for arbitration (see Box 8.3).

Box 8.3. Arbitration proceedings in Peru

The SNA-OSCE (National Arbitration System) is responsible for organising and administering institutional arbitration proceedings in Peru, with the objective of settling disputes that occur during the execution of contracts, in accordance with the regulatory framework between contractors and public entities. SNA-OSCE only organises and administers those arbitration proceedings where parties mutually agree to, as well as those that by legal mandate should be administered, in accordance with the following assumptions:

a. If the contract does not include an arbitration agreement, the clause referring to institutional arbitration will refer to SNA-OSCE as the body responsible for such an assignment.
b. If the arbitration agreement does not make reference to a determined arbitration institution, it is understood that the arbitration shall be under the responsibility of SNA-OSCE.
c. In case the arbitration agreement indicates that the organisation and administration of the arbitration shall fall to any of the functional authorities of the SNA (National Arbitration System), it will be understood that the SNA-OSCE shall be in charge of such assignment.

Additionally, there are arbitration institutions in the private sector that also administer and organise institutional arbitration.

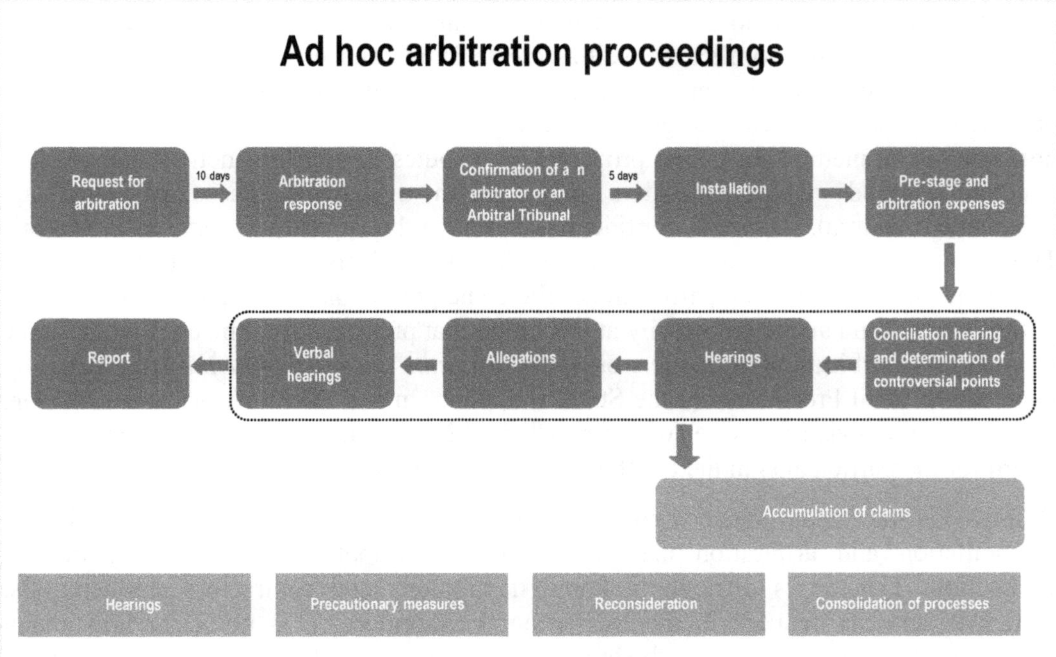

Source: (OECD, 2017[4])

8.2.2. Mediation and conciliation for the execution of public works

Nuevo León should take steps to ensure the transparency and integrity of its mediation, conciliation and arbitration processes by raising awareness and taking measure to ensure the proper registration of conflicts that arise between parties

The Public Works Act for the State and Municipalities of Nuevo León establishes that, in contracts, an arbitration clause may be agreed upon with respect to those disputes that may be jointly determined by the Secretariat of Finance and General Treasury and the comptroller's office. If this is the case, the agreement in a contract for its "execution" should be reviewed. The process of negotiation or mediation has rarely been used according to government officials in Nuevo León. There are mainly two courses of action that are applied in the state to disputes during the execution of contracts. Both actions include some kind of a conciliation clause or mediation clause – but not necessarily with a third party.

In Europe, there isn't as elaborate an arbitration system for public procurement conflicts as can be found in Latin American countries like Mexico and Peru. There is a tendency for civil courts to be used in Europe when an issue cannot be settled. In many Latin American countries, there is often a public process (i.e. with public institutions or specific courts that have a role to play once parties reach mediation or arbitration). The final phase can sometime be a civil court.

As previously mentioned, there is a law of alternative methods for the resolution of general conflicts in the state of Nuevo León. The object of the law is to promote and regulate alternative methods for preventing complaint. The law also aims, where appropriate, to resolve conflict, as well as create public and private centres that provide mediation and conciliation services to the population, and activities developed by the providers of such services. The government of Nuevo León is likely to use the alternate non-adversarial method for public procurement disputes. Under this method one or more alternate method service providers intervene in a dispute. These providers are independent, neutral, impartial, confidential and have the capacity to serve as mediators. They do not, however, have the power to make decisions. This fact facilitates communication between the parties in conflict. The goal is that these parties take control of the process, and arrive voluntarily at a solution that puts an end to the conflict in whole or in part. For arbitration in public works, the *Alternate adversarial method*, regulated by the Code of Civil Procedures of the State, is applied. In this case, one or more providers of alternate methods of service (who are called arbiters) issue a definitive and mandatory award for the participants in the conflict, in order to finalize it.

Despite the fact that Nuevo León has detailed legislation in place on mediation, reconciliation and arbitration measures, limited information is available about its application. Thus, it is difficult to know if suppliers and contractors are using the particular services detailed in the legislation. Furthermore, it is not clear how many service providers of alternate methods are in place in Nuevo León (no public or private data is available).

The state of Nuevo León should clarify its role in the mediation, reconciliation and arbitration process. The state should clarify whether it is just a supervisor or also a mediator. Information on the use of mediation and conciliation should be gathered by a unit within the government. Furthermore, the government should maintain a list of unresolved cases that have gone to court. According to government officials in Nuevo

León, no cases have ever gone to court. However, it is unlikely that no issues have been raised during execution of contracts for public works. Public works contracts tend to be more complicated, as the risks involved in infrastructure projects are significantly higher than those incurred when delivering goods and services. In addition, financial commitments are significantly higher in public works contracts.

The low number of contracts needing mediation or going into arbitration indicates that issues are being resolved outside of the proper procedures. It is also quite likely that data registration is poor, and that the state of Nuevo León could be doing a better job of accumulating information from service providers. The state needs to ensure that issues that arise are managed via the proper proceedings. Doing this will ensure transparency. Resolving issues outside of regulations is likely to increase the risk of corruption, as there is no formal process to monitor how the matter is resolved.

8.3. Proposals for action

The situation in the state of Nuevo León is quite unique. There is a rather fragmented system in place for conciliation, mediation and arbitration. This system has not been fully tested, as few complaints have been recorded. The OECD fact-finding mission to Nuevo León did establish that the current system of public procurement can be significantly improved in regards to goods, services and public works. Despite ample reasons for appealing, complaining or raising issues of non-conformities, bidders taking part in tendering processes are reluctant to complain. Currently, the dispute resolution system is not functioning as it should be – partly because the culture needs to change, and partly because of how the structure of the system is set up. Unregistered conflicts arising during the execution of contracts adds to the risk of corruption taking place. There are also concerns about conflicts of interest if cases are actually reported. In addition, suppliers do not trust that requesting units will refrain from retaliating if suppliers complain. These are serious issues that need to be looked at by the relevant authorities. To further enhance the transparency of the review and remedy system in place, and to increase the number of formal complaints being reported and registered, the state of Nuevo León could consider the actions listed below.

The functioning of the review and remedy system:

- Nuevo León needs to make its mechanism for remedies more effective for goods and services by ensuring anonymity and impartiality throughout the process.
- Nuevo León needs to work closely with other stakeholders and civil society to ensure the anonymity of public works claimants, and to prevent any conflicts of interest in relation to the resolution of complaints.

Conflicts that arise during execution of the contract

- Nuevo León needs to have a clear role in relation to mediation, conciliation and arbitration, whether that is supervising, managing or actively being involved in the resolution process.
- Nuevo León should take steps to ensure the transparency and integrity of the mediation, conciliation and arbitration process by raising awareness and adopting measures to ensure the proper registration of conflicts that arise between parties.

References

OECD (2015), *OECD Recommendation of the Council on Public Procurement*, http://www.oecd.org/gov/ethics/OECD-Recommendation-on-Public-Procurement.pdf. [2]

OECD (2016), *Towards Efficient Public Procurement in Colombia : Making the Difference*, OECD Publishing, Paris, http://dx.doi.org/10.1787/9789264252103-en. [3]

OECD (2016), "Remedies", *SIGMA Papers, Brief*, OECD, Paris, http://www.sigmaweb.org/publications/Public-Procurement-Policy-Brief-12-200117.pdf. [5]

OECD (2017), *OECD Integrity Review of Mexico: Taking a Stronger Stance Against Corruption*, OECD Publishing, Paris, http://dx.doi.org/10.1787/9789264273207-en. [1]

OECD (2017), *Public Procurement in Peru: Reinforcing Capacity and Co-ordination*, OECD Publishing, Paris, http://dx.doi.org/10.1787/9789264278905-en. [4]

Chapter 9. Ensuring results: implementing robust post-award contract management in Nuevo León

This chapter discusses the need for stronger management of the performance of public procurement suppliers in the state of Nuevo León. The chapter discusses how Nuevo León can benefit from the implementation of a broad framework for contract management based on delivery management, relationship management and contract administration. It also examines some of the key pillars of an effective performance management system for suppliers, such as information technology infrastructure and adequately trained personnel.

The proper planning and implementation of a public procurement system helps government institutions meet their goals and serve citizens more effectively and efficiently. To achieve these goals, a comprehensive public procurement system needs to accomplish a few tasks. First, it needs to acquire the tools that will allow it to provide agile answers to urgent needs. Second, it needs to be able to respond to both expected and unexpected outcomes. Third, all stakeholders in the public procurement system should abide by clearly established normative rules for good behaviour. The OECD Recommendation on Public Procurement describes these objectives, among others, in further detail (see Box 9.1).

Box 9.1. Principles of the OECD Recommendation on Public Procurement relating to performance management

The Council:

VII. RECOMMENDS that Adherents develop processes to drive efficiency throughout the public procurement cycle in satisfying the needs of the government and its citizens. To this end, Adherents should:

i) Streamline the public procurement system and its institutional frameworks. Adherents should evaluate existing processes and institutions to identify functional overlap, inefficient silos and other causes of waste. Where possible, a more service-oriented public procurement system should then be built around efficient and effective procurement processes and workflows to reduce administrative red tape and costs, for example through shared services.

ii) Implement sound technical processes to satisfy customer needs efficiently. Adherents should take steps to ensure that procurement outcomes meet the needs of customers, for instance by developing appropriate technical specifications, identifying appropriate award criteria, ensuring adequate technical expertise among proposal evaluators, and ensuring adequate resources and expertise are available for contract management following the award of a contract.

X. RECOMMENDS that Adherents drive performance improvements through evaluation of the effectiveness of the public procurement system from individual procurements to the system as a whole, at all levels of government where feasible and appropriate. To this end, Adherents should:

i) Assess periodically and consistently the results of the procurement process. Public procurement systems should collect consistent, up-to-date and reliable information and use data on prior procurements, particularly regarding price and overall costs, in structuring new needs assessments, as they provide a valuable source of insight and could guide future procurement decisions.

ii) Develop indicators to measure performance, effectiveness and savings of the public procurement system for benchmarking and to support strategic policy making on public procurement.

Source: (OECD, 2015[1])

To ensure that the purchase of goods and services is carried out according to the aforementioned principles and recommendations, it is necessary to implement mechanisms to manage contracts from beginning to end. By doing this, systems can ensure both compliance with contractual conditions and the best use of resources.

A comprehensive contract management framework should provide certainty that all contractual agreements include instruments that ensure the best results for all involved parties. This is especially important for public organisations, as they often have long-lasting contracts with very specific characteristics. To ensure that the management of contracts is carried out in a timely and efficient manner in all circumstances, it is necessary that regulations and personnel prioritise not only the fulfilment of the contracts, but also monitoring and learning from performance.

In the case of the State Government of Nuevo León (SGNL), the Secretariat of Administration (Secretaría de Administración, SA) carries out various activities to ensure an adequate selection of suppliers for the services or products required by the different central government agencies. While this work is commendable, the SA needs to expand these mechanisms to assess and obtain information on the performance of suppliers once they have been awarded contracts. The implementation of these types of mechanisms will require close collaboration between the SA and each of the agencies that use the contracted goods and services. The reason for this is that these agencies know the suppliers better than the SA, and thus they can maintain a close relationship with them.

Contract management can be understood as a process that requires three broad areas: delivery management, relationship management and contract administration.

Box 9.2. The process of contract management

Contract management activities can be broadly grouped into three areas: delivery management, relationship management and contract administration.

- Delivery management ensures that whatever is ordered is actually delivered with the required level of quality and performance, as stated in the contract. Delivery management may include checking the nature, quantity and quality of:

  1) goods supplied on delivery, and, also when appropriate, at the time of manufacture;
  2) works carried out, including conformity with designs and drawings, quality of workmanship and materials;
  3) services performed, including checking that required service levels and timescales are met.

- Relationship management seeks to keep the relationship between the economic operator and the contracting authority open and constructive. The aim of this is to resolve or ease tensions, and identify potential problems at an early stage while also identifying opportunities for improvement. Relationships should be professional, and should include a professional approach to managing issues and dispute resolution.
- Contract administration covers the formal governance of the contract and any permitted changes to documentation during the life of the contract. This area of contract management ensures that the everyday aspects of executing the contract effectively and efficiently are taken care of.

Source: (OECD, 2011[2])

By developing a comprehensive contract management framework that covers all the areas mentioned above, the SGNL could not only facilitate full compliance with its contracts, it could also obtain useful information regarding its suppliers and the quality of goods and services that they provide. Having this information could lead to a better evaluation of past purchasing procedures, as well as more strategic planning of future processes.

In addition to these planning advantages, proper contract management can have a positive impact on the quality of the immediate results of purchases. Timely monitoring of suppliers, as well as adequate management of relationships with these suppliers, improve the quality of supplier services and facilitate the fulfilment of user expectations. The following graph shows some of the possible performance contributions that can be obtained from contract management, as opposed to the costs of inefficient management.

Figure 9.1. Contract management's contribution to performance

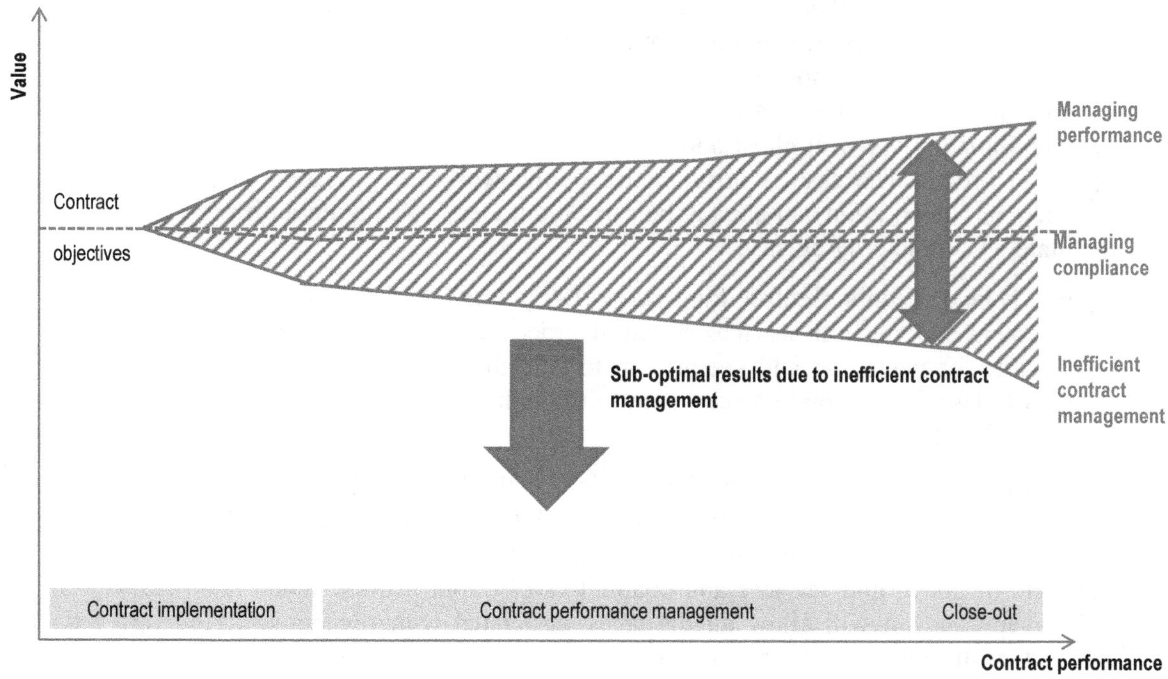

Source: (OECD, 2017[3])

To carry out adequate contract management that covers delivery management, relationship management and contract administration and favours performance monitoring, it is necessary to have sufficient information technology (IT) infrastructure and adequately trained personnel. The following sections detail some of the opportunities the SGNL has in both areas.

9.1. Monitoring the performance of suppliers

Suppliers have the potential to contribute significantly to the fulfilment of the objectives of the SGNL. By monitoring the performance of suppliers, public officials can request corrective actions when the contractual conditions are not being met. Monitoring the performance of suppliers can also provide information that will be beneficial in the future, when officials undertake the selection of suppliers. Disqualified suppliers must be registered so that contracting units do not include them in their tendering processes. This section explores the actions the SGNL needs to take to strengthen the management of suppliers' performances.

Currently, the SGNL is in the process of modernising its supplier registry. Although the current process is performed in an agile way, it still requires suppliers to deliver documents physically to the SA offices. As a part of the modernisation process, consideration should be given to what happens when the SA requests information from other states about suppliers who are unable to register in Nuevo León. In these cases, out-of-state suppliers can be at a disadvantage, as their documents have to be delivered physically to the SA offices from farther away. The same is true for the renewal of supplier registrations, which requires suppliers to complete an online renewal application and then deliver documents physically.

While Nuevo León should perhaps reconsider the requirement of physical delivery of documents for suppliers of goods and services, it should not ease registration requisites; in fact, it should strengthen them. Delivery of documents as a requirement for registration in the Register of Suppliers is not enough. There must also be a process for validating data, such as physical inspections at supplier headquarters or a requirement for proof of activity or registered turnover. Such data validation will help prevent the SA from contracting suppliers with ghost addresses or suppliers who do not have the capacity to carry out orders. The case is different for public works. Registration of public works suppliers in Nuevo León can already be carried out electronically on a different platform, the State's Contractors Registry.

Within Nuevo León's Central Purchasing Body (UCC), the General Directorate for Procurement and General Services' Head of Process and Control of Suppliers is the unit responsible for managing and keeping up to date the registry of suppliers. It is also in charge of classifying suppliers according to the industry each supplier belongs to, or the services they offer.

As mentioned in Chapter 5, with the creation of the Unique Registry of Suppliers and Contractors, the SGNL is addressing the need for the complete digitalisation of the registration process, as well as the development of a consolidated registry of both suppliers of goods and services and contractors of public works. When this platform is fully operational, it will allow all the steps associated with registration, tendering and contract awarding to be carried out via a single electronic portal. This portal already exists (with limited functionalities), and is called the Electronic System for Public Procurement (Sistema Electrónico de Compras Públicas, SECOP). Once operational, SGNL should use the SECOP to publish its calls for tender. If this is accomplished, more providers will be able to participate in tenders, and more proposals will be received. These improvements will allow for better management of the supplier registry. In addition, centralising registration, tendering and contract awarding into a single portal will simplify the process and encourage the participation of a greater number of suppliers.

9.1.1. Sources of information for supplier management: planning, collection and analysis of information

Despite the technology advances mentioned above, the SGNL should increase the scope of its IT procurement platform so that it extends to all phases of the procurement cycle. Currently, the physical records of each procurement process include information on the whole process, but they are only archived and stored with the intention of being available in the event of an audit. The content of the files, however, is not used strategically for decision-making.

To achieve the objective of generating strategic information about contracting processes, the optimal scheme does not involve the digitalisation of the files once the processes have been completed. Rather, the SGNL should generate an IT platform that will gather information about the process while it is being carried out. According to information provided by the SGNL, at present, none of the state procurement system's contract management activities are carried out electronically. Thus, the OECD recommends that Nuevo León consider extending the SECOP to include these aspects.

Table 9.1. Functions of the e-procurement system

	Is this function part of the e-procurement system? YES or NO	Which IT system is responsible for this function?
Informational platform	YES	Website
Publishing procurement plans (about forecasted government needs)	YES	Website
Supplier registry	NO	-
Publication of opportunities	YES	Website
Announcing tenders (Convocatoria)	YES	SECOP
Provision of tender documents	YES	SECOP
E-submission of bids (excluding by e-mails)	YES	SECOP
Ex-post contract management	NO	-
E-reverse auctions	YES	Website

Source: Information provided by the SGNL

As mentioned in Chapter 5 of this report, the SGNL uses different technology platforms for different parts of the procurement process. The development of a platform that covers all stages of the procurement process would be advantageous to the state. A good example of such a solution is the Korea Online E-Procurement System (KONEPS) used by the South Korean government. Among other things, this platform has facilitated access to information for all agencies involved in procurement, and has facilitated evaluation and procurement planning work.

Figure 9.2. Data connections in the Korea Online E-Procurement System (KONEPS)

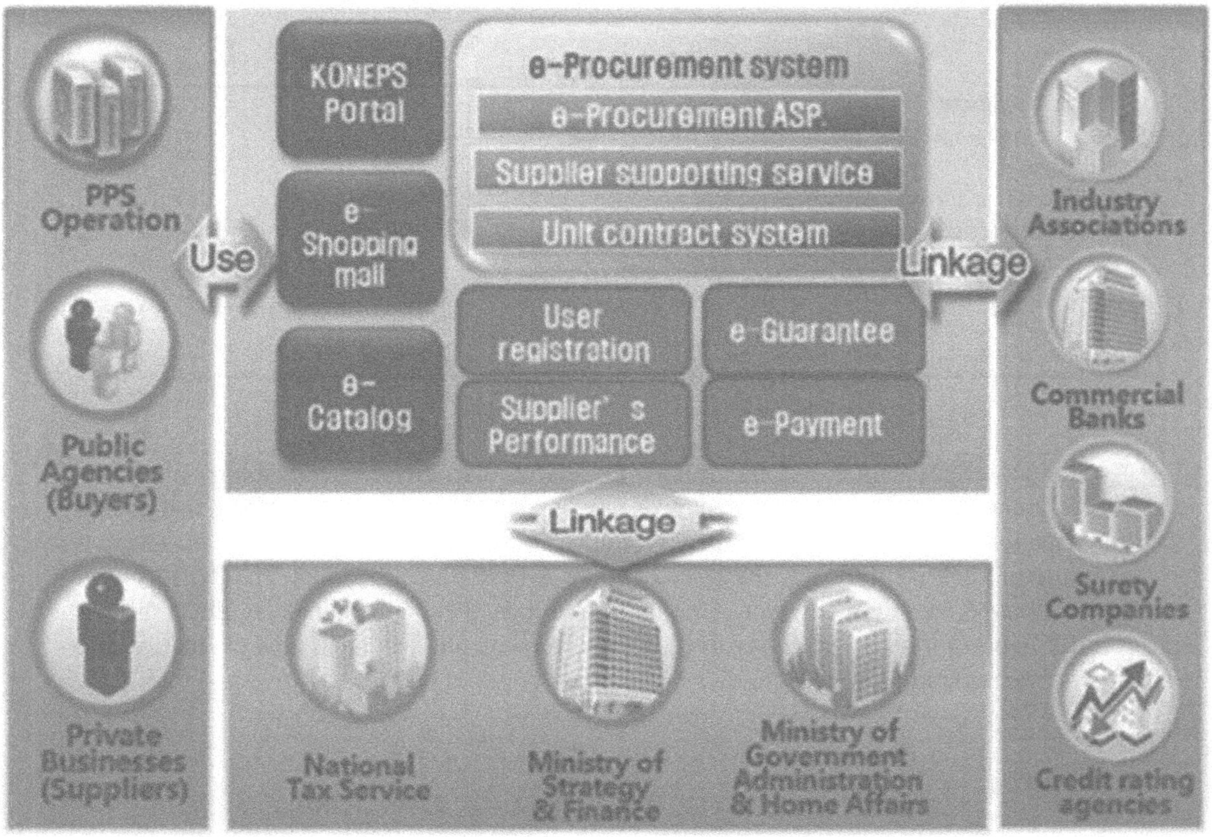

Source: (OECD, 2016[4])

9.1.2. Functions and responsibilities for supplier assessment

Different institutions of the SGNL are involved in executing and managing procurement contracts. These institutions include the SA, the requesting unit and the Secretariat of Finance and General Treasury. Each of these institutions has different responsibilities with regards to the execution and management of contracts. Based on these responsibilities, each institution should establish different relationships with suppliers. At present, none of these entities has formally established functions relating to evaluation and feedback on supplier performance. The only assessment the SGNL carries out relates to whether a breach of contract has taken place, hidden defects in products or public works have been found and whether guarantees have been fulfilled or not.

While the centralised purchasing system used by the SGNL requires that the SA manage the procurement process, other agencies have vital responsibilities. Even though the administrative process for the purchase or contracting of a service is performed by the SA, the requesting units are responsible for defining the technical specifications of the good or service to be purchased. The requesting units also approve modifications to the technical data sheets as determined by the Boards of Clarifications (Juntas de Aclaraciones). It would be beneficial to Nuevo León's procurement system if requesting units could participate to a greater degree in the management of contracts. They could do so through the evaluation of suppliers and their goods and services.

Currently, the final users of goods and services must certify that they were delivered in compliance with the requirements established in the contract. However, users do not perform any other formal evaluation of satisfaction with the performance of the supplier. In the event of an extension of the SECOP to include contract management, the OECD recommends that the SECOP include a section specifically dedicated to evaluation. A customer satisfaction survey or a formal statement could be introduced. When purchasers receive goods or services, they could fill out a survey to assess the compliance, the delivery and to what extent the product meets technical specifications. Introducing these evaluations at this stage would be more efficient than waiting till the end of the warranty period.

9.1.3. Processes, tools and key performance indicators (KPIs) to evaluate suppliers' performances

Performance indicators are one of the best tools an agency can use to verify that the goods or services it buys are helping meet the need they were intended for. Performance indicators also allow procurers to cultivate a closer relationship with suppliers. Furthermore, performance indicators can help procurers and suppliers understand more about how the performance of the contract can benefit them both.

When robust and well-designed indicators are available, monitoring and evaluation of any contract become much simpler. In addition, these indicators allow procurement staff to obtain useful, standardised and comparable information from various processes. This then allows them to perform analyses for future purchases. The OECD has developed recommendations for the design of key performance indicators (KPIs, see Box 9.3).

Box 9.3. Establishing key performance indicators

KPIs should have certain fundamental qualities that benefit the procurement organisation and suppliers alike. KPIs should be, namely:

- Relevant and linked to the key objectives of the organisation (critical outcomes or risks to be avoided) rather than to the process.
- Clear (i.e. spelled-out in the contractual document as simply as possible to ensure a common understanding between the buying organisation and the supplier).
- Measurable and objective (i.e. expressed in pre-determined measures and formulas, and based on simple data that can be gathered in a cost-effective manner without subjectivity).
- Achievable (i.e. realistic and within the control of the supplier).
- Limited (i.e. as few as required to achieve the objectives while minimising disadvantages, such as costs, efforts and risk of dispute to both entities). To the extent possible, the procurement body should use information and documentation that is already available under the contract management process, rather than collecting additional data or documentation.

Source: (OECD, 2011[2])

According to these recommendations, KPIs should not be considered to be a burden on suppliers. The correct use of these indicators helps align expectations during an acquisition process. KPIs also impose controls that make it easier to achieve the goals of the procurement. Thus, if the SGNL decides to create and use performance indicators in its procurement processes, the OECD recommends that it involve suppliers and other relevant stakeholders in their design.

The SGNL should design indicators that motivate suppliers to offer more competitive and beneficial conditions. If the indicators are not designed properly, instead of having this effect, they could discourage the participation of suppliers. Some of the main indicators used in procurement processes are illustrated in Box 9.4.

Box 9.4. Useful procurement KPIs

Procurement KPIs can be established for any of the organisation's important objectives. While a wide variety of subjects can be considered, the following subjects may be appropriate in the context of the SGNL (the list is not exhaustive):

- Timing (i.e. an indicator that includes specific timeframes for completion of procurement).
- Delivery (i.e. whether the supplier delivers on time, delivers the correct items and quantities, provides accurate documentation and information, and responds to emergency delivery requirements).
- Pricing, including competitiveness, price stability and volume or other discounts.
- Customer service, including information on the number of product shortages due to the supplier, training provided on equipment and products, warranty services, administrative efficiency (including order acknowledgement and accurate invoicing), accuracy of performance data, and reports provided by suppliers.
- Product, including information on whether the product meets specifications (percentage of rejection or defects), reliability or durability of usage, packaging, quality and availability of documents and technical manuals.

Finally, not all KPIs should be monitored with the same frequency; the majority should be assessed monthly, while some others can be assessed only quarterly or even annually.

Source: (OECD, 2013[5])

9.1.4. Information sharing and knowledge management with regards to the performance of suppliers

One of the activities that can help strengthen the procurement system of the SGNL is promoting the exchange of information between the different units involved in the procurement process. Each unit has different experiences dealing with suppliers, or different opinions about the quality of the goods or services offered (in the case of consolidated purchases, for example). Thus, the organisation as a whole can better co-ordinate its actions if it has access to the diverse information these units can provide.

The exchange of this type of information between different units can facilitate feedback on the procurement process and improve it in the future. At present, the SGNL has not implemented mechanisms to encourage the exchange of information and internal feedback on procurement processes, according to information gathered during the OECD fact-finding mission to Nuevo León. This has led to the contracting of suppliers that do not necessarily meet the needs of requesting agencies. A platform should be designed that can notify contracting authorities of suppliers that have been disqualified in other states.

To avoid such complications, the implementation of strategies for the exchange of information and joint learning is fundamental. The design of a technology platform that covers all the stages of the procurement process would undoubtedly help fulfil these objectives. However, while it is being implemented, there are other simpler mechanisms that can be put in place to encourage the continuous improvement of purchasing processes.

An example of such instruments would be the design of satisfaction surveys. These surveys could be required of shareholders and filled out at the end of contracts. In them, requesting agencies could share more information about supplier performance. Another alternative is the creation of spaces, such as debriefing meetings, in which the agencies involved in purchasing processes can share their experiences and take note of the lessons learned.

9.1.5. Incentives for performance

Ensuring the fulfilment of a procurement contract and full satisfaction with its results requires arduous work. In order to achieve these goals, officials need to monitor the contract and communicate with the user or beneficiary of the procured good or service. There are mechanisms that can be put in place to motivate suppliers to offer quality products and services that satisfy requesting units. Some of these mechanisms are:

- positive incentives associated with the good performance of suppliers in the execution of the contract;
- negative incentives associated with poor performance that does not meet the expectations of the contracting agency.

When these types of provisions are included in contracts, suppliers not only feel obligated to fulfil their obligations, they also seek to do so in the best possible way to ensure that their performance meets their client's expectations. There is a wide range of incentives that can be included in any contract for the purchase of goods or services. The Federal Government of Canada offers a good reference on the instruments available to public officials (see Box 9.5).

Box 9.5. Contract performance incentives in Canada

When required, the contract may contain various mechanisms for encouraging timely performance, such as:

- Contract financial security: Security deposits, whereby the contractor deposits securities (government guaranteed bonds, bill of exchanges or irrevocable standby letters of credit), which Public Works and Government Services Canada (PWSC) may convert to complete the contractor's obligation; or performance bonds, which are a type of surety bond used to guarantee the performance of the contract.
- Holdbacks: Whereby an amount is withheld to ensure the due performance of the contract.
- Liquidated damages clause: Whereby provision is made for Canada to recover the pre-estimated loss or rate of loss that would result from a delivery default, without being required to prove actual damages. Where the inclusion of a liquidated damages clause is appropriate, the contracting officer must incorporate such provisions by including the Standard Acquisitions Clauses and Conditions (SACC) Manual clause H1003C (Progress Payments) in the contract. Care should be taken to ensure that the rate of assessment of liquidated damages is reasonable.

The probable damages should be established by reference to the individual circumstances of the particular procurement. The contract should specify the ceilings for collection of liquidated damages. Such ceilings or maximums can be stated in either of the following two ways:

1. by specifying a fixed amount payable upon delinquency. This method should be used when it is intended that the contract will be terminated immediately when delinquency occurs and the goods or services "reprocured" elsewhere. The cost of "reprocurement" must be included in the overall fixed amount; or
2. by specifying a rate of assessment of damages. This rate per calendar day of delay must not exceed a stated percentage of the contract price. This method should be used when, upon default occurring, it is intended to serve as notice of default requiring the contractor to remedy the default within a stated period of time. The cost of "reprocurement" must be excluded in computing liquidated damages, since this item will be claimable separately if the contract is terminated and the goods or services procured elsewhere.

To ensure uniformity of application, the amount or overall ceiling should not exceed 10 % of the contract price. Ceiling prices in excess of 10% may be used when justified by the individual circumstances of the particular acquisition, subject to the approval of the contract approval authority.

Incentive payments, whereby provision is made in the pricing basis for increased value to Canada.

Such incentives (e.g., for early delivery, cost savings, enhanced performance or additional warranty, or other benefits) should be considered only in the case of major procurements with long lead times for delivery, where such payment provisions can act as an incentive to the contractor in putting forth special efforts to achieve earlier than scheduled delivery, and the client department agrees because of substantial realizable cost savings and other benefits.

Source: (Public Works and Government Services Canada, 2017[6])

As with key performance indicators, performance incentives are not meant to put unnecessary pressure on suppliers. Incentives should not encourage suppliers to commit performing in ways that are not achievable. On the contrary, these mechanisms should help suppliers take full advantage of their capabilities to meet the needs of buyers. In this sense, the OECD recommends that the SGNL establish contact with suppliers in order to get to know them better, and to ensure that performance incentives actually have beneficial impacts for all.

9.2. Implementation of a comprehensive contract management framework is necessary to ensure the maximisation of suppliers' added value

The SGNL should ensure that suppliers comply with contractual conditions. Robust contract management is important to facilitate the contribution suppliers can make to increase the value of state operations. The *2015 OECD Recommendation of the Council on Public Procurement* highlights the importance of having adequate resources and contract management expertise to advance efficiency in the post-award stage of the public procurement cycle (OECD, 2015[1]).

9.2.1. Functions and responsibilities for contract management to mitigate risks and ensure adequate execution (beyond mere compliance)

During the execution of contracts there is always the possibility of unforeseen conditions and other obstacles that threaten the achievement of planned objectives. Therefore, the management of contracts should be understood as a strategic task, rather than a purely administrative activity. Vital to this shift in perspective is also the understanding that strategic contract management should allow authorities to anticipate unforeseen situations, and respond to them.

A good start to implementing a comprehensive risk management framework is to have a sound regulatory body that anticipates and establishes consequences for the risks that may arise during the execution of a contract. These provisions are particularly useful when dealing with supplier defaults. The SGNL has a regulatory framework that provides for the inclusion of these types of provisions in each of its contracts. The framework also includes protection against any type of default on the part of the suppliers.

While these types of rigid mechanisms help ensure compliance with contracts, they do not always ensure the best results, or the best performance by suppliers. To avoid less-than optimal results, Nuevo León could use more flexible compliance mechanisms. These mechanisms would allow the state to not only react to failures when they occur, but to also follow each contract closely. In doing this, the state could prevent failures through the joint work of all the actors involved. Flexible compliance mechanisms define tasks and functions that must be followed to monitor a contract and react to problems. They also identify specific items that could fail during the execution of each contract.

The framework developed by the OECD for risk management in public procurement contains a mixture of these instruments. It is a good example of the type of framework the

SGNL could adopt to complement contractual controls with other types of tools, see Box 9.6.

Box 9.6. Understanding and managing contractual and supplier risk

Processes and plans

- Contractual and supplier risk management is in place with clear responsibilities and processes, and procurers identify who is best placed to manage risks, as well as supplier involvement, where appropriate
- Risks are formally identified and monitored regularly, with mitigating actions developed and implemented where possible, and "obsolete" risks removed from consideration where appropriate.
- Escalation and reporting routes are in place for risk governance.
- Contingency plans are developed to handle supplier failure (temporary or long-term failure or default), exit strategies are developed and updated through the life of the contract.

Contractual terms

- Contractual terms around termination are understood and monitored by the contract manager. Contractual terms around warranties, indemnities and insurance are understood and monitored by the contract manager.
- Contractual terms around security and confidentiality are understood and monitored by the contract manager, particularly issues relating to the security and confidentiality of personal data.
- Dispute resolution processes are in place, including agreed-upon award procedures, mediation and arbitration.

Ongoing supplier risk management

- The contract manager monitors the supplier's financial health and business performance.
- The contract manager monitors supplier compliance.

Source: (OECD, 2011[2])

9.2.2. Monitoring tools (including IT-based tools) and reports on contract execution that provide standardised information and allow for decision-making

The proper management of the risks associated with a contract involves the timely follow-up of contracts to identify and solve problems when they occur. This prevents the occurrence of situations in which failures are identified once products or services have been delivered or completed definitively.

At present, the SGNL does not have systems or monitoring tools in place that allow the state to obtain information beyond the administrative steps established in its contracts. Put simply, the state is only able to obtain information on the delivery and reception of goods and services. As a result, it is difficult for officials in Nuevo León to have accurate information on the risks that can occur during the execution of a contract.

It is imperative that the SGNL consider designing tools that can help it identify potential risks and report these risks or poor practices when they materialise. Some of these risks are described in Box 9.7.

Box 9.7. Risk and risk management

Many of the risks involved in contract management relate to the economic operator being unable to deliver, or suppliers delivering goods and services with a dissatisfactory level of quality. The risk of these issues arising increase when the following failures occur:

- Lack of capacity.
- The economic operator's key staff is re-deployed elsewhere, which erodes the quality of the works delivered or the service provided.
- The economic operator's business focus moves to other areas after the award of the contract, reducing the added value for the contracting authority in the arrangement, or impacting the timeliness for delivery of goods or works.
- The economic operator's financial standing deteriorates after the award of the contract, eventually endangering its ability to maintain agreed-upon quality requirements for goods purchased or levels of service.
- Demand for goods or services is much greater than expected, and the economic operator is unable to cope
- Demand for a service is too low, meaning economies of scale are lost and operational costs are disproportionately high.
- Staff at the contracting authority with knowledge of the contract get transferred or move on, weakening the relationship between the contracting authority and supplier.
- Factors beyond the economic operator's control disrupt delivery of goods or services. For example, premises cannot be accessed because of a natural disaster
- The contracting authority is unable to meet its obligations under the contract.

Source: (OECD, 2011[2])

The SGNL could adopt different indicators based on previously mentioned categories to enable it to more appropriately monitor the risks associated with its contracts. Examples of these indicators are those developed by the government of Queensland, Australia, for its public procurement guide (see Box 9.8).

Box 9.8. What to monitor and measure?

Some examples of factors the SGNL may want to address during contract monitoring include the following:

- ensuring that the contractor meets minimum service standards
- tallying the number of customer complaints
- reporting against key criteria as required by the contract
- benchmarking of performance with other suppliers and other comparative performance activities
- quality of regular stakeholder meetings
- financial management aspects
- information technology aspects
- other performance measures specifically applicable to procurement.

Source: (Queensland Government, 2017[7])

9.2.3. Delivery processes, assessment of results, and inspections

Without proper supervision, the contract execution stage can result in corruption. When this happens, involved parties often render fictitious work, inflate work volume, change orders, use lower quality materials than specified in the contract, supply goods of a lower price and quality than quoted and render contracted services in an improper way (Chartered Institute of Purchasing & Supply, 2007[8]).

To avoid the development of any of these situations, the SGNL could benefit from strengthening the mechanisms of control and inspection that it currently carries out in relation to procurement. These types of instruments allow parties to report incidents as they occur, and describe them appropriately. Such actions allow the state to gain useful information for decision-making (see Box 9.9).

Box 9.9. Spot checks and inspections

Spot checks and inspections may be necessary to ensure that the goods or services delivered by a supplier conform to the contract standard. Spot checks of supplier performance can either be announced or unannounced. Spot checks and inspections are a powerful tool for monitoring supplier performance, but agencies should take great care not to overuse them. Over-reliance on unannounced spot checks is likely to damage relationships between agencies and suppliers, and to make it difficult to build business relationships that are based on trust and mutual commitment to excellence through continuous improvement. In addition, spot checks and inspections must be included in the conditions of contract all parties enter into.

Contract reports

In some contracts, it is appropriate to require that the contractor provide written reports. It is critical that the contract manager receives such reports in a timely manner, otherwise the performance management opportunity may be lost.

Non-conformance reports from the field

Sometimes, officials do not address non-conformance with specifications promptly. Reporting of non-conformance from the field allows rapid responses to real or potential problems. Information on non-conformance from the field allows strategic and risk managers in an organisation to adjust plans. When managers have information regarding non-conformance, they are able to advise the supply chain to ensure strategies can be put in place to minimise and manage potential exposure to time or cost overruns. These actions can also mitigate any potential impact on the organisation's own core activities and clients.

Source: (Queensland Government, 2017[7])

9.2.4. Contract modifications and controls to justify them – handling changes during the execution of a contract

Maintaining strict control over contracts is necessary to facilitate proper execution. If the rules under which the contracted services are to be carried out are not well defined, poor results are likely to be obtained. That is why having a strong regulatory framework that delineates the conditions under which modifications and adjustments to contracts can be made is of paramount importance for any institution.

Regulations in the state of Nuevo León establish that contracts should contain provisions regarding cases in which extensions may be granted for the fulfilment of contractual obligations. However, it is not clear what other types of modifications can be made to procurement contracts in the state. In addition, as mentioned prior, in Nuevo León, civil servants often put compliance first, even though some regulations are excessive in some cases.

A good framework for the modification of contracts should contain rigid controls like the ones mentioned above, but it should also be flexible enough to leave room for unforeseen events. These types of situations can jeopardise the execution of a contract. By imposing a flexible framework, officials can solve unforeseen issues by making modifications to the contract. These modifications need to be in line with the budget allocation of the work, as well as technical specifications. Furthermore, they should not be considered an extension of the contract. Again, for the implementation of this type of mechanism, the SGNL should work with suppliers to ensure that the decisions taken are beneficial to all parties.

Box 9.10. Effective handling of changes to contracts

Whenever processes are carried out to change a contract, orderly procedures should be followed to provide certainty to all the parties involved, and to enhance the transparency of the process. The following are examples of different processes that should be followed:

Change processes

- Officials should regularly review contracts (with a view to updating where necessary) to ensure they meet evolving business needs.
- Processes should be in place that clearly lay out the governance of contractual change – who needs to approve what and how it will happen – with a focus on effective and prompt change implementation.
- The state should have clear processes for the management of minor changes and contract variations, with a focus on the cost or effort being proportionate to the importance and value of the change.
- The state should have more rigorous processes to handle major contractual changes, including clear approval mechanisms and accountability measures, and controls to demonstrate that changes offer value for money.
- Where appropriate, officials should test existing services for the value for money they provide through benchmarking or other processes.
- The state should have processes to cover the introduction of new services under contracts, including market testing where necessary.
- The state should have processes to handle disputes in place to manage disputes arising from change-related issues.

Processes for different types of change:

- Both parties should have a clear understanding of the arrangements for any extension of the contract (both in terms of scope and time), as well as related issues.
- The state should have processes in place to handle commercial (financial) changes to contracts in a fair and structured manner.
- Officials should manage price changes fairly and effectively with the use of mechanisms such as benchmarking, competitive tendering (e.g. for major additional works), and other techniques like open book pricing as appropriate, to test value for money.
- Officials should consider the rationalisation of specifications and demand management as options to achieve better value for money.

Source: (OECD, 2011[2])

Because the current approach SGNL officials take prioritises compliance with the terms of the contract, any modification is complicated. Even in critical situations, officials may prefer to obtain poor results than to make contractual changes because of their fear of violating a regulation. Currently, a violation of a regulation triggers an Administrative Responsibility Procedure (Procedimiento de Responsabilidad Administrativa) or a

Compilation of Remarks (Pliego de Observaciones) due to the diversion of resources allocated to a specific programme.

This situation prevents the government from seeking value for money in the face of contingencies that come up during the execution of contracts. When these situations occur, the SGNL does not have the tools to react strategically and make informed decisions. Therefore, the SGNL should revise its current control scheme to allow for streamlined contract modifications in exceptional circumstances, which should be anticipated. The control plan should be proportional to the risks incurred, with instructions stating the institutional and normative reasons for the modification of a contract in normal and exceptional situations.

9.2.5. Management of finances – invoices and payment issues

A comprehensive system of contract management should allow an agile closing of all agreements, facilitating timely and efficient payment to suppliers. Having a well-coordinated payment processing scheme can help increase the competitiveness of public procurement processes, making them more attractive to businesses, particularly small and medium enterprises (SMEs), which cannot stand long and uncertain payment periods. Nuevo León's legal framework allows for advanced payments to take place in tenders where SMEs are participating in order to allow them to deliver their goods in a timely manner.

If a system is efficiently integrated, certain actions should work almost automatically. For example, once goods or services have been received and accepted by the requesting unit, the step towards the issuance of a request for payment, the corresponding comparison with the administrative area and the subsequent transfer of funds should occur quickly and without difficultly. However, in Nuevo León, different obstacles impede the process. This results in inefficient and unclear steps that delay payment to suppliers.

According to the information provided by the SGNL, the state's Financial Management Department establishes the terms under which payments must be completed for each procurement contract. To date, a payment term of 45 working days after the delivery of services is usually established in contracts. In practice, however, this term extends for periods that are much longer – double or triple the time.

These delays result in significant disruptions to suppliers. According to information provided by suppliers interviewed by the OECD, delayed payment is one of the most significant reasons new companies do not participate in public bidding processes. Small and medium-sized enterprises do not always have the economic capacity to withstand these terms, which reduces the number of potential suppliers to the SGNL, hindering the potential for competition and lower prices.

Managing payments to suppliers requires the intervention of different divisions and subdivisions of the SGNL (see Table 9.2).

Table 9.2. Stakeholders and responsibilities in payment procedures

Stakeholder	Responsibilities
User	It is responsible for receiving the goods and services and issuing the corresponding satisfaction note (*devengo*).
General Directorate for Procurement and General Services	It is responsible for authorising the processing of orders and authorisations of payment.
Director for Procurement	For goods purchases, it is responsible for determining if a penalty is applied to suppliers for breach of delivery times agreed in contracts.
Director for Maintenance and General Services	For services contracts, it is responsible for determining if a penalty is applied to suppliers for breach of delivery times agreed in contracts.
Head of Operations Control	It is responsible for the authorisation of orders and authorisations of payment, according to the delegation of functions by the General Directorate for Procurement and General Services.
Administrative Assistant of the Head of Operations Control	It is responsible for the preparation and review of the documents related to payment orders and authorisations.
Budget and Budgetary Control	It is responsible for the authorization of the current expenditure orders and payment authorisations in the State Investment System, for the preparation of the corresponding check or transfer.
Filing within Operations Control	It is responsible for the custody of orders and authorisations of payment delivered to the supplier, as well as copies of invoices processed

Source: Information provided by the SGNL

Nuevo León offers delineates the procedures and tasks each actor involved in the procurement process should follow. However, the state has not established response times for these actions. In practice, timing for the delivery of work depends on the workload that each agency has or the pressure exerted by suppliers. Officials also attribute delays to budget constraints, and issues with authorisation and approval of the delivery of products and services.

The above complications increase because the different entities involved in the procurement process do not communicate in a fast and precise manner, and because the different steps they perform are not carried out on a standardised platform. While some steps are carried out via the Electronic Integrated Government Resources System (Sistema Integrador de Recursos Electrónicos Gubernamentables, SIREGOB), others are performed via the SECOP. In addition, some steps are handled through paper files. To resolve these complications, it is of the utmost importance that the SGNL implements IT platforms that cover the entire procurement process.

In addition, one of the most important causes of late payments is the lack of co-ordination between the Secretariat of Finance and General Treasury, the Secretariat of Administration and user agencies in Nuevo León. This lack of communication can result in outdated procurement plans and budgets, which generate incomplete information for all parties. Therefore, as mentioned in an earlier chapter of this report, the SGNL needs to implement a better system for linking procurement planning and budgeting.

9.3. Performance assessment frameworks need to be proportional to the complexity of suppliers and contractor deliverables

A contract management system must be able to complete complex and prolonged tasks requiring robust internal and external communication. Hence, it is necessary to develop a balanced and sustainable framework for Nuevo León's contract management system. In developing this framework, state officials should consider including supplier segmentation. By incorporating supplier segmentation into its framework, Nuevo León can strategically allocate resources for contract management based on their potential impacts. In Nuevo León priority is generally given to immediate needs and to the list of providers with immediate responsiveness.

9.3.1. Supplier segmentation

At present, the SGNL does not have instruments that allow it to carry out appropriate supplier segmentation. The information available to government agencies only states the industry to which each provider belongs, or the services that they offer. The SGNL does not compile accurate or up-to-date information regarding the degree of added value each supplier contributes, or how these suppliers can help the state achieve its objectives.

Using effective segmentation tools would allow the SGNL to have better knowledge of the market and of suppliers. It would help officials gain better negotiation skills and mechanisms to make more strategic selections of suppliers, according to their utility.

Suppliers can be classified into one of four categories, according to the good or service they provide (see Tables 9.3 and 9.4) (Chartered Institute of Procurement & Supply, 2017[9]).

Table 9.3. Supplier segmentation framework

Supplier segmentation according to the products or services that they provide	
Commodity	Strategic
Standard	Key

Table 9.4. Advanced supplier segmentation

Advanced categories for supplier segmentation	
Money spent	Product complexity
Breadth of supply base	Volume of supplied goods and/or services

Source: (Chartered Institute of Procurement & Supply, 2017[9])

Considering that an updating of the supplier register is currently taking place, the SGNL would benefit from using these categories to classify each of its suppliers.

9.3.2. Management of relationships, negotiations, and meetings with suppliers – a framework for supplier relationship management

Proper management of the relationship between the SGNL and its suppliers is key to maximising the usefulness of contracts. When relationships are handled well, they can foster collaborative alliances that work to achieve the best possible outcomes for all parties. While the relationship between two parties should be close and flexible to the extent that it allows for better joint work, the relationship should also be subject to proportional controls in order to avoid agreements that contravene contracts – or open opportunities for collusion.

Currently, the SGNL has little space to manage its relationships with suppliers. This is because, according to the information provided during the OECD's fact-finding mission, once a contract has been started, in most cases there are only two opportunities for exchanges between suppliers and the government. The Law for Acquisitions, Leasing and Services of the Public Sector establishes the first moment of contact between users and suppliers during the issuance of the award and the emission of the corresponding purchase orders. Additionally, the Government Accounting Act establishes that the second moment of contact occurs when the process of delivery and receipt of goods and services is performed. This contact includes the emission of a satisfaction note (*devengo*).

Because the state has few opportunities to manage its relationships with suppliers, the OECD recommends that the SGNL strengthen its framework for establishing relationships with suppliers. It can do so by including other spaces for exchange and appropriate follow-up of contracts. In general, it is in the contracting authority's own interest to make these relationships work. Doing so allows procurers to avoid the costs of late termination and the consequences of poor performance and unplanned supplier changes. The three factors for success in managing these relationships are mutual trust and understanding, openness and excellence of communication, and a joint approach to managing delivery.

In building a collaborative relationship, it is helpful to have working meetings in which all parties can express their expectations, problems and thoughts on the specifics of the contract. Some of the main objectives that can be pursued at these meetings are described in Box 9.11, as well as the way in which they should be conducted to achieve positive results.

Box 9.11. Content and structure of initial and contract monitoring meetings

This is an illustrative, but non-exhaustive list. Some processes may not be necessary for all contracts, while others, though important in some situations, may not be covered here, as what is relevant depends on the nature of the contract being managed.

The inaugural or initial meeting: For any major contract, it is a good practice to have a formal inaugural or initial meeting soon after the contract is officially awarded. At this meeting, representatives from both the economic operator and the contracting authority meet for the first time within the context of the contract. These individuals might have met before, but any prior meetings would have taken place while the parties were going through the procurement process. At the inaugural meeting, it is critical that both sides move from a competitive to a co-operative viewpoint. The reason for this is they will be working together for the life of the contract, and they both want a successful outcome. The objectives of the meeting include:

1) understanding the roles and responsibilities of everyone present;
2) discussing the project plan and its implementation;
3) discussing issues that impact the operation of the contract;
4) discussing control mechanisms.

Although this meeting is important for managing the relationship between the supplier and contracting authority, it should not be used as an opportunity to make changes to the specifications, requirements or conditions of the contract. Where necessary, such changes can be dealt with according to previously agreed upon procedures (that are delineated in the contract precisely for this purpose).

Review meetings: Review meetings between contract parties are another practical means of managing a contract, particularly when the contract is complex or has a duration of several years. The frequency and coverage of the review meetings, if any, will depend on the nature of the contract. Review meetings are a useful means of communication between parties during a contract's execution. Not having them can have negative consequences. These meetings must be well prepared, focused and not too time consuming. Review meetings are intended to be a forum for the parties that are subject to the contract – not for other beneficiaries or stakeholders. In some cases, such as major infrastructure projects, other beneficiaries or stakeholders may need to be consulted or informed about the ongoing delivery of the project. This process is a separate one from the review meetings.

Source: (OECD, 2011[2])

9.4. Proposals for action

The SGNL would benefit from the implementation of a broad framework for contract management based on: delivery management, relationship management and contract administration. Such a comprehensive scheme should address the following:

Delivery

- The SGNL would benefit from developing a series of KPIs that would allow it to obtain and compare useful information about the performance of its suppliers.

- To ensure optimal results for each contract, the SGNL should review its monitoring and control mechanisms. This will allow for more timely decision-making when modifications are required.
- The SGNL must generate a comprehensive contractual incentives system that does not only focus on punishing non-compliance, but also rewards and recognises suppliers who exceed their expectations.
- The SGNL should allow requesting units and the departments responsible for procurement processes to have a closer relationship. This will allow both parties to develop deeper knowledge of the performance of concluded contracts. To achieve this, end users should report on the quality and timeliness of the goods or services received, as well as the relationship they had with each supplier.
- The SGNL should invest in information materials and training for public officials in charge of procurement. These trainings should include a strategic vision of performance-based purchasing processes.

Relationship management

- The SGNL should build better collaborative relationships with its suppliers. For this reason, it is important to formalise spaces for exchanges. During these exchanges, contracting authorities and suppliers should discuss their expectations, the progress they have made and their experiences. These meetings can take place via contract kick-off meetings, follow-up meetings and debriefings or evaluations.
- To foster a better understanding of suppliers and the market in which they participate, the SGNL should make use of better segmentation tools. These tools should adequately indicate the capacity of each of the providers, as well as how critical the goods or services they provide are.

Contract administration

- The SGNL must take advantage of IT tools that would allow it to manage contracts more efficiently. The OECD recommends that the SGNL develop an IT platform that covers all the stages of the procurement cycle, including contract management.
- The SGNL should implement a more detailed framework for handling contract modifications. This would allow the state to react to unforeseen circumstances without compromising contract results.

References

Chartered Institute of Procurement & Supply (2017), *Supplier Segmentation*, https://www.cips.org/en/knowledge/procurement-topics-and-skills/srm-and-sc-management/supplier-positioning1/supplier-segmentation/ (accessed on 25 June 2017). [9]

Chartered Institute of Purchasing & Supply (2007), *Contract Management Guide*, The Chartered Institute of Purchasing & Supply, https://www.cips.org/documents/CIPS_KI_Contract%20Management%20Guidev2.pdf. [8]

OECD (2011), "Contract Management", *Sigma Policy Briefs*, No. Brief 22, http://www.oecd-ilibrary.org/governance/contract-management_5js4vmns819v-en. [2]

OECD (2013), *Public Procurement Review of the Mexican Institute of Social Security: Enhancing Efficiency and Integrity for Better Health Care*, OECD Publishing, Paris, http://dx.doi.org/10.1787/9789264197480-en. [5]

OECD (2015), *OECD Recommendation of the Council on Public Procurement*, http://www.oecd.org/gov/ethics/OECD-Recommendation-on-Public-Procurement.pdf. [1]

OECD (2016), *The Korean Public Procurement Service: Innovating for Effectiveness.*, OECD Publishing, Paris, http://dx.doi.org/10.1787/9789264249431-en. [4]

OECD (2017), *Public Procurement Review of Mexico's PEMEX: Adapting to Change in the Oil Industry*, OECD Publishing, Paris, http://dx.doi.org/10.1787/9789264268555-en. [3]

Public Works and Government Services Canada (2017), *Contract Performance Incentives*, https://buyandsell.gc.ca/policy-and-guidelines/supply-manual/section/4/70/25 (accessed on 20 June 2017). [6]

Queensland Government (2017), *Procurement guidance: Managing and monitoring suppliers' performance*, Office of the Chief Advisor – Procurement, http://www.hpw.qld.gov.au/SiteCollectionDocuments/ProcurementGuideSuppliersPerformance.pdf. [7]

ORGANISATION FOR ECONOMIC CO-OPERATION AND DEVELOPMENT

The OECD is a unique forum where governments work together to address the economic, social and environmental challenges of globalisation. The OECD is also at the forefront of efforts to understand and to help governments respond to new developments and concerns, such as corporate governance, the information economy and the challenges of an ageing population. The Organisation provides a setting where governments can compare policy experiences, seek answers to common problems, identify good practice and work to co-ordinate domestic and international policies.

The OECD member countries are: Australia, Austria, Belgium, Canada, Chile, the Czech Republic, Denmark, Estonia, Finland, France, Germany, Greece, Hungary, Iceland, Ireland, Israel, Italy, Japan, Korea, Latvia, Luxembourg, Mexico, the Netherlands, New Zealand, Norway, Poland, Portugal, the Slovak Republic, Slovenia, Spain, Sweden, Switzerland, Turkey, the United Kingdom and the United States. The European Union takes part in the work of the OECD.

OECD Publishing disseminates widely the results of the Organisation's statistics gathering and research on economic, social and environmental issues, as well as the conventions, guidelines and standards agreed by its members.

OECD PUBLISHING, 2, rue André-Pascal, 75775 PARIS CEDEX 16
(04 2017 16 1 P) ISBN 978-92-64-23543-4 – 2018

www.ingramcontent.com/pod-product-compliance
Lightning Source LLC
Chambersburg PA
CBHW080536250926
51846CB00016B/1104
* 9 7 8 9 2 6 4 2 3 5 4 3 4 *